The Data Storytelling Workbook

From tracking down information to symbolising human experiences, this book is your guide to telling more effective, empathetic and evidence-based data stories.

Drawing on cross-disciplinary research and first-hand accounts of projects ranging from public health to housing justice, *The Data Storytelling Workbook* introduces key concepts, challenges and problem-solving strategies in the emerging field of data storytelling. Filled with practical exercises and activities, the workbook offers interactive training materials that can be used for teaching and professional development. By approaching both 'data' and 'storytelling' in a broad sense, the book combines theory and practice around real-world data storytelling scenarios, offering critical reflection alongside practical and creative solutions to challenges in the data storytelling process, from tracking down hard to find information, to the ethics of visualising difficult subjects like death and human rights.

Anna Feigenbaum is a Principal Academic in Digital Storytelling at Bournemouth University where she runs the Civic Media Hub, a knowledge exchange enterprise that specialises in data storytelling for human rights, social equity, and health and wellbeing. Anna regularly publishes in media outlets and academic journals. She is a co-author of *Protest Camps* (2013) and author of *Tear Gas* (2017).

Aria Alamalhodaei is an independent writer and researcher. She received her Master of Arts in Art History from the Courtauld Institute of Art. She has written extensively about science, technology, and art for academic and popular publications.

The Data Storytelling Workbook

Anna Feigenbaum +
Aria Alamalhodaei

Routledge
Taylor & Francis Group

LONDON AND NEW YORK

Design and typesetting:
Minute Works

Comics illustrations:
Alexandra Alberda

Bournemouth University
Civic Media Hub website:
www.civicmedia.io

First published 2020
by Routledge
2 Park Square, Milton Park, Abingdon, Oxon OX14 4RN

and by Routledge
52 Vanderbilt Avenue, New York, NY 10017

Routledge is an imprint of the Taylor & Francis Group, an informa business

British Library Cataloguing-in-Publication Data
A catalogue record for this book is available from the British Library

Library of Congress Cataloging-in-Publication Data
A catalog record has been requested for this book

ISBN: 978-1-138-05210-9 (hbk)
ISBN: 978-1-138-05211-6 (pbk)
ISBN: 978-1-315-16801-2 (ebk)

Typeset in Neue Haas Unica and IBM Plex Mono

Publisher's Note: This book has been prepared from camera-ready copy provided by the authors.

For all those becoming data storytellers

Acknowledgments

The Civic Media Hub came to life through internal funding from Bournemouth University for initiatives that sought to bring together academics, students and practitioners to co-create knowledge and resources. That first grant funded our 'BU Datalabs' training project in 2015 leading to many more small pockets of funding, partnerships, and creative enterprises. Together these enabled us to grow from an initial idea into an internationally recognised Civic Media Hub.

Thanks to the early dreamers who helped envision the Civic Media Hub: Einar Thorsen, Phillipa Gillingham, Duncan Golicher, Edward Apeh and Dan Jackson. Alongside them, our wonderful research assistants provided the enthusiasm and open-mindedness to bring our most bizarre ideas to life. Over the past five years we have watched them grow from RAs to esteemed collaborators and project leaders: Daniel Weissmann, Ozlem Demirkol and Alexandra Alberda, you're the heart and soul of these projects.

In more recent years, Isabella Rega, Brad Gyori, Phil Wilkinson, Mike Sunderland and Andy White joined, stretching the possibilities of what we could do with data storytelling. Thanks also to Karen Fowler-Watt, Shelley Thompson and Julian McDougall for their unwavering support through all we've tried to manifest, including this workbook.

Tom Sanderson from the Centre for Investigative Journalism has offered invaluable insight, energy and access to an amazing network of passionate practitioners, many of whom are featured here. Omega Research Foundation and Public Health Dorset, we are so grateful for our adventures in data storytelling that now fill these pages.

Thanks are also due to Routledge, and particularly Niall Kennedy, who invited us to dream up a textbook unlike other textbooks. Before leaving Routledge Niall made it possible for us to co-create this workbook with our hugely talented and incredibly collaborative graphic design studio Minute Works. Partnering with Jimmy Edmondson and Dom Latham has not only led to five years of beautiful data storytelling artefacts, but also to seeing research as inseparable from how we visually communicate it to empower audiences.

A huge thank you goes to everyone around the world who hosted us, partnered with us, let us do weird things at your events, encouraged our experiments and reminded us time and again that it is ok to break the moulds, challenge the canons, and refuse the silos of academia.

Finally, this workbook would not be possible without our students. Teachers are only able to be as imaginative as their pupils and institutions allow. It is a blessing to work at a university, where when you walk into a room with an emoji shit pillow and a bag of Sharpies, everyone dives right in.

Contents

Introduction   001

How We Came to Write this Workbook   002
The BU Civic Media Hub   003
Why Storytelling?   003
Becoming a Data Storyteller   004
Challenges to Data Storytelling Education   005
A Guide to Using this Workbook   006
Workbook Design   011
Works Cited and Further Reading   012
Spotlights   013

A Narrative Approach to Data Storytelling   017

A Holistic Approach to Data   018
Understanding Your Audience   020
Different Audiences, Different Data Stories   022
Audience Listening   026
What's Narrative Got to Do with It?   027
Narrative in Data Storytelling   028
Types of Narrative   031
Data as Characters   034
All Data Has a Backstory   035
What is Conflict in Data Storytelling?   037
Details, Details   040
Works Cited and Further Reading   043
Spotlights   045
Activities   061

Navigating Data's Unequal Terrain   067

The Growing Data Divide   068
How Open is Open Data?   071
Defining Big Data   074
Big Data Past and Futures   076
Counting the Uncounted   077
Data and Bias   080
Standpoints Matter   082
Data Discrimination   084
Works Cited and Further Reading   085
Spotlights   087
Activities   109

Visual Data Storytelling

Feminist Data Visualisation 117
Challenges for Data Visualisation 120
A Quick Guide to Structuring Your Data 122
Semiotics for Data Storytelling 124
Four Pillars for Data Storytelling 126
Chartjunk 141
Storytelling with Andy Kirk's CHRT(S) 143
The Power of Trees 149
Narrative Networks 151
Tinkering with Timelines 154
Visualising Absence 159
Learning from Comics 160
Graphic Medicine 163
Graphic Social Science 165
Multisensory Data Storytelling 166
Works Cited and Further Reading 170
Spotlights 173
Activities 193

Data Storytelling with Maps

Making Maps that Matter 202
Storytelling with Maps 203
The Cartographic Gaze 204
The Problem with Maps as Representations 205
Participatory Maps 208
Counter-Mapping 209
Story Mapping 210
Seeing Cartographically 212
No Symbol is Neutral 213
Contested Coordinates 214
No Platform is Neutral 215
Mapping without Maps 218
Works Cited and Further Reading 221
Spotlights 223

Future-Proof Principles

The Four Cs 240
Act like the Data Storyteller You Want to Be 243
Works Cited and Further Reading 244

Index 245

Visual Data Storytelling 115
Data Storytelling with Maps 201
Future-Proof Principles 239

Introduction

How We Came to Write this Workbook

The move in recent years toward open and big data brings with it opportunities for information re-use, increased transparency, and new forms of civic participation in data analysis and communication. Alongside this, digital transformations in communications have led to the increasing popularity of infographics, data visualisations, and the use of maps for representing data and communicating its significance. But while datasets and digital archives grow bigger and more open, information remains difficult to collect, complex to analyse, and challenging to communicate. As we've seen over the past two decades of this proliferation, more data does not necessarily lead to better data stories.

Responding to these recent changes, a wide range of industries and organisations, from academia to journalism, from health care to city councils, find themselves increasingly wanting to communicate more effectively—and more empathetically—with data. This has led to the demand for more professionals trained to engage with data in innovative ways. Likewise, an increased emphasis on visual communication techniques needed to create engaging infographics and maps has brought greater attention to the importance of visual storytelling for impacting audiences.

Perhaps the earliest adopters of this contemporary wave of data storytelling were journalists. When *The Guardian*'s data blog launched in 2009, it paved the way for data-driven storytelling on an international scale. As these early adopters have argued, while spreadsheets and data visualisation tools allow us to discover stories, they "do little to aid narrative communication of these findings to others" (Segel and Heer, 2010, p. 1139). In other words, a better-looking bar chart is not enough to effectively bring information to audiences. Storytelling with data involves combining visual and narrative forms of communication.

Beyond journalism, this data storytelling approach is increasingly being used in health communications. Research has found that storytelling is particularly important when visual presentation is used as part of a medical decision-making process. Here the "succinct presentation of important facts is crucial" (Kosara and Mackinlay, 2013, p. 50). As medical information is often dense and complicated, data storytelling is proving to be an excellent way to connect with patients, break down communication barriers, and give people more ability to navigate and discuss their health and wellbeing.

At the Bournemouth University Civic Media Hub our approach is to begin from the basics. As we teach our students, colleagues, industry clients, and community partners, it is important to develop basic understandings of storytelling in order to communicate more effectively—and empathetically—with data. At the same time, we believe that to tell better data stories one must also take a reflective approach as to what data is, where it comes from, and why this matters for evidence-based storytelling.

The BU Civic Media Hub

Established in January 2015 by Dr. Anna Feigenbaum, with the support of Bournemouth University, our Civic Media Hub was designed to bring together a multidisciplinary, cross-faculty team of researchers and students from Communications, Geography, Health Sciences, and Data Science to work in collaboration with journalists, NGOs, and digital designers to co-create effective ways of engaging with sensitive social issues through data analysis and communications. Through workshops and public events, we take a participatory approach to data storytelling that combines principles of design, narrative theory, scaffolded technology learning, and hacklab-style collaborations.

Over the past five years we have put on over 50 local, national, and international events; given dozens of talks around the world; and created infographics, interactive websites, data comics, policy reports, media tool kits, beer mats, and even a board game! Pushing the boundaries of traditional data visualisation, our approach to data storytelling embraces all kinds of creative forms. Our aim is not to make a prettier pie chart or more advanced network analysis visualisation. Rather, our goal is to get people talking, feeling, and thinking critically about data through the use of evidence-based storytelling.

Why Storytelling?

Stories are thought to be one of the oldest forms of human communication. They have been defined as:

"intentional communicative artefacts"
↳ Gregory Currie (2012)

dramatization of meaning "in an interesting, evocative, informative way"
↳ Theodore Cheney (2001)

Our approach combines these understandings of storytelling. For those who like a definition, this is our vision of data storytelling:

Data stories are intentional communicative artefacts that present data in an interesting, evocative, and informative way.

As Professor Jennifer L. Aaker (2013) says, "When data and stories are used together, they resonate with audiences on both an intellectual and emotional level."

Before we raise too many eyebrows, it is important to state clearly that our goal in introducing storytelling and narrative technique to data communication is not about dramatising or embellishing for the sake of a more engaging story. We are not after the best spin or selling points. Rather, our aim is to focus on the human elements of what is in a dataset in order to be able to more clearly pinpoint what is at stake, and to communicate it effectively and empathetically to our audiences. It is also important to keep in mind that every dataset contains many possible stories. Our aim in this workbook is not to teach you how to create one true story, or even how to develop the best story. Rather, the aim of this workbook is to cultivate the mind-sets needed for you to become a better data storyteller.

Becoming a Data Storyteller

When researchers write an academic article they often provide an account of the steps they took to conduct their project. The structure of the paper takes the reader through their process, showing how a conclusion was reached. This writing style is often compared to a recipe or roadmap. Clear signposting, as we say to our students, helps others follow along. Similarly, when writing a policy or report, the aim is often to present information in a persuasive way, taking the reader through the reasons for a set of proposals or guidelines. In both of these cases people are frequently writing with or about data. But rarely do we consider this kind of writing as storytelling. Why is that?

Most often it is because the conventions of producing academic and policy documents shun writing that seems overly descriptive, evocative, or dramatic. Yet these are the essential ingredients of good storytelling. In *Writing Creative Nonfiction* Theodore Cheney says that "creative nonfiction doesn't just report facts, it delivers facts in ways that move the reader toward a deeper understanding of a topic" (2001, p. 1).

People sometimes presume that 'moving people' must mean 'making stuff up' or being 'too emotional.' Reporting on research or policy is supposed to be stripped down, serious stuff. Just the facts. Evidence only. But the problem is, as Cheney puts it, "nonfiction that doesn't let us hear the human interaction tends to lose readers" (2001, p. 15). Most people want narratives, not just numbers.

In other words, many of us want data humanism. As Giorgia Lupi (2017) put it, "We are ready to question the impersonality of a merely technical approach to data, and to begin designing ways to connect numbers to what they really stand for: knowledge, behaviors, people."

Among other practices, she advocates for visually communicating the complexity of data, sketching with data as part of the design process, capturing broader contexts and remembering that data—like people—is flawed. In the following sections of this book we will delve into each of these areas, sharing our own vision of a more holistic approach to data storytelling. From the hundreds of queries we receive, it is clear that many people are hungry for new methods. Yet, many barriers remain to establishing more robust data storytelling education programmes in schools, universities, and professional workplaces.

Challenges to Data Storytelling Education

→ See Spotlight: Centre for Investigative Journalism.

A range of provisions for data storytelling development currently exist to teach students and professionals about data storyteling. There are online resources (Google tutorials, web scrapers, Stack Exchange); introductory classes (*Guardian* Masterclasses, CIJ Summer School); and software training (Excel, Tableau). However, our own experience of training, alongside research evidence, suggests that these provisions alone are not enough for creating a culture of data storytellers (Demirkol et al., forthcoming; Feigenbaum et al., 2016; Stoneman, 2017).

Even when people are able to attend training classes online and offline, skill development and retention is difficult without regular engagement. Like learning a language, without the ability to practise everyday conversation, skills get lost. Trainers find that the same people are attending their introductory classes each year (Stoneman, 2017) and people report that the daily demands of their jobs, limited support structures, and a lack of confidence inhibit their ability to advance their data skills (Demirkol et al., forthcoming).

At the heart of developing data storytelling education is the task of balancing truth, accuracy, and transparency with engaging narratives. At the same time, it is crucial that we educate ourselves and the next generation not just to tell data stories, but to tell them responsibly. Hewett (2016) argues that higher education institutions have been slow to incorporate digital training and the rise of data journalism into their curriculum. Similarly, in public and third sector organisations, there is often little—if any—resources or time available for professional development in data storytelling. Where budget lines exist, one-off workshops are usually the go-to, resulting in a lack of skills retention or workplace capacity building in data storytelling. While industry publications continue to call for these skills to be developed, as outlined in reports from Nieman Lab, journalism.co.uk, and PBS MediaShift, the formal adoption of data storytelling education remains limited (Hewitt, 2016). This workbook is our contribution to the development of a more robust data storytelling education for everyone.

A Guide to Using this Workbook

In this workbook we will introduce you to basic concepts in visual and narrative storytelling and explore how they might help transform the ways you communicate with data. Likewise, we will cover some of the foundational terminology and concepts in working with data, data visualisation, and mapping, highlighting our storytelling approach throughout. By drawing together practitioner perspectives across a range of different sectors, from rural cartography to human rights campaigning, this workbook explores the different practices and techniques that contemporary data storytellers use. Focused around the importance of reflective and sustainable collaborations, we try to offer language lessons that can help foster communication between people involved in telling data stories, from computer scientists to social theorists to social media marketers. Rather than focus on specific software or tools, this workbook focuses on the resources, skills, and mind-sets needed to turn ideas into communicative artefacts.

Underpinned by cross-disciplinary research, as well as projects that inspire us, the bulk of this workbook comes from our experiences working together at the BU Civic Media Hub. Many of the examples we draw on and showcase come from work produced by and with our collaborators. Examples span the fields of health, environmentalism, human rights, and community advocacy. While there are thousands of other examples from around the world we could have chosen to illustrate our points, we decided to spotlight those that are closer to our hearts, enabling us to share not just the shiny outcomes of data storytelling projects, but the challenging, exciting, occasionally sad and sometimes comical, collaborative processes that led to their creation. This first-hand approach gives us a unique perspective, inviting you on a behind the scenes tour into our world of making data stories together.

Practically, the workbook features three main types of content: key concepts, spotlights, and activities. These are illustrated on the next pages.

Key Concepts – These short write-ups define key concepts, techniques and challenges in data storytelling.

Some of the key concepts sections in this workbook will cover terms you have heard a hundred times before, like 'big data,' while others are meant to explore issues that don't always get talked about explicitly when putting together data stories. Our concept entries such as 'Standpoints Matter' and 'No Platform is Neutral' discuss the difficulties of trying to humanise data, including how we represent multiple perspectives when giving narratives to numbers. Other key concepts like 'Graphic Medicine' and 'Multisensory Data Viz' are intended to introduce you to emergent areas that we think have a lot to offer our data storytelling practices.

→ Like interdisciplinary, transdisciplinary refers to work that crosses more than one discipline or branch of knowledge. As these different knowledges come together, a new, more holistic knowledge base emerges.

Data storytelling is a transdisciplinary field, informed by hundreds of years of practice and theoretical reflection. The key concepts we've chosen to highlight come from English, Geography, Data Science, Media Studies, Art History, and Medical Humanities—to name only a few. Selecting what to include often led to keyboard paralysis—hours of staring at the contents spreadsheet hitting 'delete row,' 'insert row.' In the end, what made it into the workbook were those terms and ideas that we kept coming back to in our research, teaching, and practice.

This does not mean that the concepts we have chosen are the most important, or even the things that we think that everyone should know. Rather, they are our sticking points, our foundations, our North Star that guides the way we think about the intersections of data and story. We also did not want to cover what has already been done many times before. As we argue throughout this workbook, standpoints matter. The 50 key concepts presented here are heavily shaped by our backgrounds and biographies. However, we did our best to point you in the direction of different approaches, in addition to those that inspire our own. You will find at the end of each key concepts section, a list of works cited and further reading that will point you to deeper insights and debates, as well as to more technical information for working with data.

When you are done reading this workbook, we'd love to hear what would be in your top 50 and why.

Spotlights – The spotlight sections feature inspiring people and projects that capture our ethos of data storytelling.

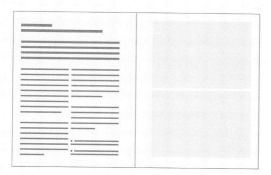

When we began this project we imagined 100 concepts and a handful of spotlights. But as we began to pull together the ideas, images, people, and projects that would make up the contents of this workbook, we discovered something very important about our project. It was less about what we know and more about who we have met along the way. Our work at the BU Civic Media Hub is driven by collaboration, by the kind of magic that can only happen when different perspectives, skills, and mind-sets get into a room together. So rather than pick a few 'best of' or award-winning projects to feature, we opted to include a wide range of amateur and professional projects.

Each spotlight has its own story of how it made its way into this book. Many feature people and organisations that we have worked with before. Others are artists we admire, activists who energise us, and colleagues whose creativity never ceases to amaze us. Some spotlights highlight the work of folks we saw present at a conference or community forums. And a few of the projects featured here found us. What ties all the spotlights together is their ethos. They embody key principles in this book from embracing data humanism to challenging data biases, from celebrating messiness to transparently documenting the difficulties of data collection.

When you are done reading this workbook, we'd love to hear who you would spotlight and why.

Activities – Activities pages feature innovative exercises that can help foster effective and empathetic data storytelling practices.

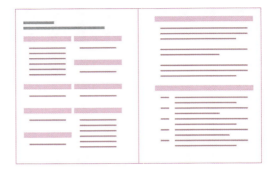

In addition to key concepts and spotlights, this workbook features activities that you can use in classrooms, professional development trainings, or even on your own with friends and colleagues. All of the featured activities have been tried and tested in our BU Civic Media Hub workshops, with our students, or by partner organisations. We created an easy-to-navigate template for these data storytelling activities in order to help you tailor them to your available time and resources.

If you have an activity that you think could help others become data storytellers, you can submit them to share on our project website.

Additional Materials – In addition to these sections this workbook features:

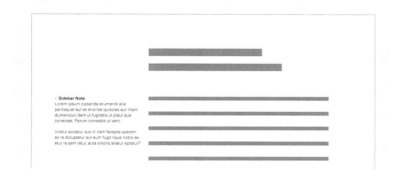

→ **Case Studies** to help explain how we put our concepts and principles into practice.

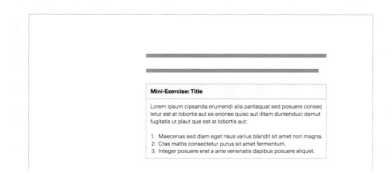

→ **Pop-out sidebars** to provide definitions, further insights and suggestions for resources you can explore.

→ **Mini-Exercises** and reflective questions to help you become a data storyteller.

Workbook Design

This workbook itself is a collaboratively created data storytelling arte-fact. It is designed by Minute Works, a creative studio dedicated to sustainability that prioritises social justice projects. They have worked with Greenpeace, Toxic Remnants of War, and the United Nations, among other NGOs, universities, and social enterprises. In 2015, after a chance encounter at the book launch of Mel Evans' *Artwash: Big Oil and the Arts*, the BU Civic Media Hub and Minute Works began to collaborate. Since then Minute Works and the Civic Media Hub have co-produced dozens of data storytelling resources, hosted hands-on workshops, co-present-ed talks in three countries, eaten loads of vegetarian curry, and even hit the gym together.

While pull-ups and poppadums may not be essential for successful data storytelling, an on-going commitment to collaboration is. For us, this means committing to curiosity-driven work, clarity in mutual expecta-tions, coordination of working practices, and care for how we treat each other. We will discuss these Four Cs in more detail in the final chapter of this workbook. For now, it is time to dive into our world of data storytelling.

 Collaboration Curry

Works Cited and Further Reading

→ Aaker, J. (2013, September 14). *Persuasion and the power of Story: Jennifer Aaker (Future of StoryTelling 2013)* [Video file]. Retrieved from https://www.youtube.com/watch?v=AL-PAzrpqUQ.

→ Cheney, T.A.R. (2001). *Writing Creative Nonfiction: Fiction Techniques for Crafting Great Nonfiction*. Berkeley, CA: Ten Speed Press.

→ Currie, G. (2012). *Narratives and Narrators: A Philosophy of Stories*. New York, NY: Oxford University Press.

→ Demirkol, O. Feigenbaum, A. & Sanderson, T. (forthcoming) Open Data for Whom? Exploring the Barriers to Data Skills Acquisition for Investigative Research.

→ Evans, M. (2015). *Artwash: Big Oil and the Arts*. London, UK: Pluto Press.

→ Feigenbaum, A., Thorsen, E., Weissmann, D., & Demirkol, O. (2016). Visualising data stories together: Reflections on data journalism education from the Bournemouth University Datalabs Project. *Journalism Education*, 5(2), 59-74.

→ Hewett, J. (2016). Learning to teach data journalism: Innovation, influence and constraints. *Journalism*, 17(1), 119-137.

→ Kosara, R., & Mackinlay, J.D. (2013). Storytelling: The next step for visualization. *IEEE Computer*, 46(5), 44-50.

→ Lupi, G. (2017, January 30). Data humanism: The revolutionary future of data visualization. Retrieved from https://www.printmag.com/information-design/data-humanism-future-of-data-visualization/.

→ Rothman, L. (2012, October 8). Margaret Atwood on serial fiction and the future of the book. *TIME*. Retrieved from http://entertainment.time.com/2012/10/08/margaret-atwood-on-serial-fiction-and-the-future-of-the-book/.

→ Segel, E., & Heer, J. (2010). Narrative visualization: Telling stories with data. *IEEE Transactions on Visualization and Computer Graphics*, 16(6), 1139-1148.

→ Stoneman, J. (2017). Training data journalists of the future. Unpublished chapter.

Spotlight:
Crafting Canada Revenue Agency Stories

Knowledge exchange within any organization, especially large organizations that are highly compartmentalized and structured by a variety of disciplines, involve specific communicative challenges. The Canadian Revenue Agency (CRA), Canada's national tax organization, is no exception.

As a result, a team of professionals at the CRA have begun developing a data storytelling workshop, created because of expressed need within the organization to enhance its data-driven culture. Taking inspiration from the work of geomorphologist John Phillips, we would like to explore the specific forms that narratives/plotlines take in CRA's Small and Medium Enterprises Directorate's (SMED) Business Intelligence (BI) unit, and how they can be applied to the CRA context. In his article "Storytelling in Earth Sciences: The Eight Basic Plots" (2012), Phillips identifies the plot/storylines that characterize the work of his discipline. He does so in order to highlight how disciplinary preferences for different plot narratives in Earth Sciences may result in different interpretations and conclusions for similar events (evidence), and thus enhance critical thinking within geomorphology.

Data storytelling is not a method/methodology that the quantitative researchers within the unit are familiar with or have expressively used. But they have acknowledged that they might benefit from a different approach than the communicative conventions within their own disciplines. In addition to introducing the workshop audience to a variety of more conventionally used data storytelling formats/structures, we are attempting something slightly more innovative and hopefully self/organizationally reflective.

Our aim is to better understand how BI researchers can more effectively communicate their findings using data stories that are common to their disciplines in a way that also recognizes the types of stories that CRA decision makers (from backgrounds in accounting and administration etc.) have been using to communicate what is important to them. It is precisely the intersection of these two sets of "story/plotlines" that

may inform the kinds of communicative strategies that will be most effective in addressing any ongoing data communication needs within the agency.

The first workshop, for BI researchers, elicits the plot/storylines used within the BI research unit; while another workshop, for managers and auditors (etc.), explores the kinds of stories and narratives that capture the attention of decision makers within the organization. Each group will participate in exercises that will encourage reflection upon their work and "tease" out the major story themes and plotlines that captivate and influence them. The results of the intersection of these two sets of stories, "CRA story/plotlines," is what will help build the larger workshop material, as a potential data storytelling structure, and ultimately benefit the data-driven culture within the agency as a whole.

Ruth Bankey (B.Arch, MA, Ph.D) is currently a Geographic Projects Team Lead with the Canada Revenue Agency, located in Ottawa, Ontario since September 2018.

Christian Nicol (MA) is currently a Project Leader with the Canada Revenue Agency since November 2004. Prior to his position with the Agency, Christian was an economist with Statistics Canada where he started his career in June 1990.

By Ruth Bankey and Christian Nicol

→   Phillips, J. 2012. Storytelling in Earth sciences: The eight basic plots, *Earth-Science Reviews,* 115, 153-162.

EXERCISE #1

CRA STORY COMPONENTS - STORY ELEMENTS & STORY STRUCTURES

1) *What are the different story ELEMENTS of a typical data story in your experience? What about the following list (for discussion):*

- *Study Design*
- *Definitions*
- *Variables & Metrics*
- *Analyses*
- *Results*
- *Tables & Charts*
- *Graphs & Figures*

How do these help to organize a narrative structure of your research, which then can be transformed into story? Do these story elements correspond to more traditional storytelling elements such as characters, settings, point of view, tone, style, etc...? Can you think of other ELEMENTS that should be considered?

2) *Plotlines are examples of story STRUCTURE in data storytelling, which is a type of story element. They act as a device to organize/frame those elements in order to generate different ways of understanding, sharing and communicating the data (sense and meaning making).*

Should Plotlines be thought of as Research Questions/Hypotheses - specific to a particular question, issue, or problem OR should Plotlines be structured into various plot themes? What might those themes look like? Which Plot types do you use most often in your work? Can you think of specific projects or types of work they relate to? What about the following examples:

- **Differential Plot** – *These are stories that are concerned to describe or summarize features of a collection of a data set(s).*
- **Comparison Plot** – *These are stories concerned with comparative patterns, clusters, outliers, etc...*
- **Distribution Time Series Plot** – *These are stories concerned with distributive patterns, outcomes or findings, etc...*
- **Prediction Plot** – *These are Stories concerned with the prediction of outcomes.*
- **"Goodness of Fit" Plot** – *These are Stories concerned with evaluation of one's method and process.*

↳ An excerpt from the *Data Storytelling Workbook*, Canada Revenue Agency. Courtesy of the authors.

Spotlight:
Data Storytelling for Everyone

Uprated is a digital agency delivering insight-driven analysis, information architecture, development, and design. The agency works to connect data with decisions, strategy with technology, and goals with measurable results. Co-founder and technical director Andy White offered his team professional development that was outside of anyone's existing skill set. Here he shares its unexpected outcome.

Our story begins back in July 2017. Bournemouth University ran their Festival of Learning event which I always try to make an effort to attend. Day-to-day my colleagues and I navigate a veritable ocean of data, and it is impossible to avoid being told that 'stories' are like manna from heaven in the digital industry. So, I attended the aptly named 'Data Storytelling for Beginners' workshop. Over the course of the next 3 hours Dr. Anna Feigenbaum delivered top-drawer insight into the considerations and practices surrounding factually accurate, yet evocatively informative, written communication.

The concepts covered seemed to be far-reaching and I felt they could be applied across everything we and our peers do in the digital industry. So, like Charlie with his golden ticket, I rushed back to the office to share my newfound understanding with the team. With a reassuringly positive reception to the idea, I set about the task of bringing everyone up to speed. This began with a couple emails and meetings with Anna. We (mostly her) developed an agenda and before long we were all set for our very own custom Uprated data storytelling workshop.

The content ran as follows:
→ Mini Masterclass – Data Storytelling
→ Activity 1 – Focusing on Narrative Structure
→ Activity 2 – Narrative Structure in Uprated's Case Studies
→ Activity 3 – Stats as Stories

After Anna initially furnished us with an underlying understanding of adding dramatic structure to our content, it was time to bring in the Superheroes. She introduced the morally ambiguous Deadpool to the room and asked us to hone our new skills by dissecting this complex character's story. This really set the tone for the session: understanding how to employ the long-established dramatic arc to bring about a more engaging journey through what can sometimes be dry-read content.

The unexpected side effect of the morning was a fascinating insight into our team's diversity, both in how we interpret popular stories, and in our own internal communications. Importantly, I think everyone gained a newfound appreciation for how different we are to one another. In the time since, we have all developed a more considered approach to some of our visual and textual communication both for ourselves and our clients. The points touched upon in the workshop have begun to come up in planning meetings, and our Game of Thrones conversations are now far more learned!

Andy White is the co-founder and technical director at Uprated. From the beginning of his 15-year digital career, he has been hands on with the business-end of systems and development projects all the way from inception to delivery.

By Andy White

Client Report

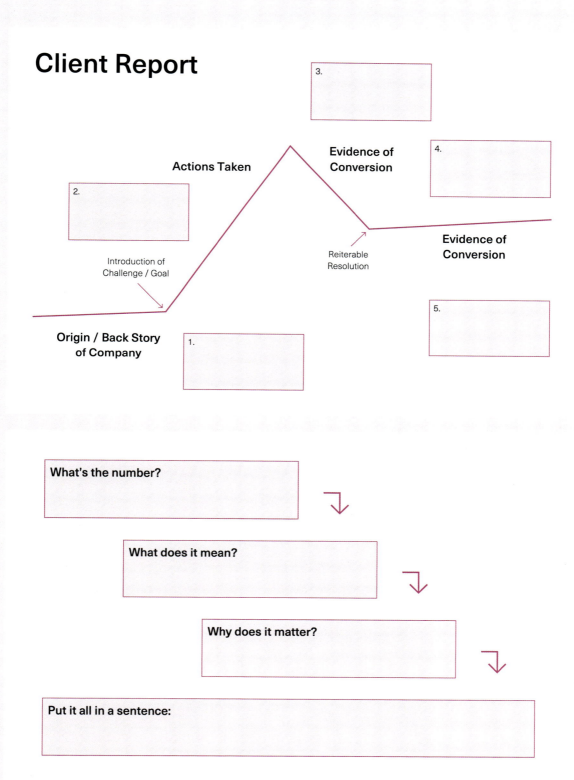

3.

Actions Taken

Evidence of Conversion

4.

2.

Introduction of
Challenge / Goal

Reiterable
Resolution

Evidence of Conversion

Origin / Back Story
of Company

1.

5.

What's the number?

What does it mean?

Why does it matter?

Put it all in a sentence:

↳ Excerpts from Dr. Feigenbaum's *Data Storytelling for Beginners* workshop.

A Narrative Approach to Data Storytelling

A Holistic Approach to Data

What is data? Is it information? Facts? Evidence? There are many different ways to define data. The definitions given by statisticians look different from those given by computer scientists. Likewise, what data means to a cartographer is different from the meaning of data for an ethnographer. Even among these groups of people who produce and work with data, definitions will vary. This variation can be seen in these two definitions from prominent online sources:

> "Data are pieces of information about individuals organized into variables."
> ↳ University of Florida, Biostatistics Open Learning Textbook
>   https://bolt.mph.ufl.edu/6050-6052/preliminaries/what-is-data/

> "[Data is a] value or set of values representing a specific concept or concepts. Data become 'information' when analyzed and possibly combined with other data in order to extract meaning and to provide context. The meaning of data can vary depending on its context."
> ↳ Data.Gov
>   https://www.data.gov/glossary

In the first example data is seen as pieces of information, whereas in the second example data is seen as something that comes *before* information. This distinction between data and information is common in definitions that see data as raw material. Like feelings before we give them names, or food before it is cooked, data is said to be raw before it is processed. Data, in this way of thinking, is what comes before our analyses or insights. This understanding of data is perhaps best illustrated in the DIKW pyramid.

→ **The DIKW Pyramid.**

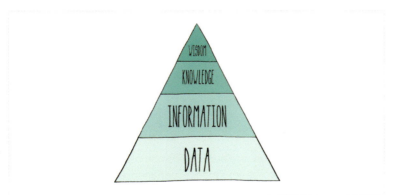

Using a visual model, popular in data storytelling trainings, the pyramid shows data at the bottom, unprocessed. The next layer, information, refers to the process that makes data meaningful, giving it a purpose or context. The third layer, knowledge, is produced when information is combined with understanding and expertise. And wisdom, at the top of the pyramid, occurs when this knowledge is put to good use.

While this DIKW model is popular, critical data scholars contest the idea that data can ever exist in a raw, pure form, as these models imply. Lisa Gitelman and Virginia Jackson write in the introduction to their edited collection *"Raw Data" is an Oxymoron* (2013), "Indeed, the seemingly indispensable misperception that data are ever raw seems to be one way in which data are forever contextualized—that is, framed—according to a mythology of their own supposed decontextualization" (p. 5-6).

In other words, we come to believe in this myth that data is untouched and pure. We act as if data can exist in a realm apart from humans. But, as Gitelman and Jackson (2013) argue, just as a photograph is not an objective representation of reality, neither is data. A photo, they remind us, is shaped and framed by the photographer. Likewise, data require human participation. Just like photography, it "needs to be understood as framed and framing" (2013, p. 5).

Informed by Gitelman and Jackson, we take a more holistic approach to data in this workbook. We ask not 'what is data,' but how do we effectively and empathetically tell stories using data? Books including David Herzog's (2015) *Data Literacy* and Andy Field's (2016) *An Adventure in Statistics* offer accessible introductions on what data is and how you can work with it. While their approaches are different from ours, we use these resources in our research, teaching, and training. Below are a few definitions of terms that will be important in this workbook.

→ Andy Field's website Discovering Statistics offers a range of tutorials from Cluster Analysis to Presenting Data at www.discoveringstatistics.com.

Structured data refers to data that is highly organised and formatted in ways that make it easy to input, search, and manipulate. When we teach people about structured data for data storytelling in our trainings, we start by using a basic spreadsheet, with its neat rows and columns. Each column in the spreadsheet represents a category of information, each row a unique entry, and each cell a discrete data point. Whether you are working with numeric data like monetary values or temperatures, or text data like a first name or descriptive word, a spreadsheet provides a systematic structure for how your data is recorded.

In contrast, unstructured data refers to data that is not organised in a pre-defined way. This can include documents, photographs, social media feeds, or audio files.

Quantitative data are numerical expressions of values or quantities.

Qualitative data is non-numeric. It is commonly used to gain a deeper understanding of a phenomenon, experience, or other aspect of the social world. Qualitative data is often collected via interviews, focus groups, observation, or action research.

While quantitative data is more often associated with structured data, working with codes, themes, and other labelling systems can turn qualitative data into structured data, making it ripe for visual storytelling using charts and graphs.

Like Gitelman and Jackson (2013), Nathan Yau (2013) also uses the metaphor of photography to explain data in his book *Data Points: Visualization that Means Something*. Data, Yau says, "is a snapshot of the world in the same way that a photograph captures a small moment in time" (p. 2) Yau uses this analogy of the photograph—and the pixels that comprise its image—to offer us a more holistic way of imagining data. Yau writes, "A single data point can have a who, what, when, where and why attached to it" (p. 3) . However, "extracting information from a data point isn't as easy as looking at a photo ... You need to look at everything around, find context, and see what your dataset looks like as a whole. When you see the full picture, it's much easier to make better judgements about individual points" (p. 3).

Yau uses the example of photos from his wedding to illustrate this approach. He explains that if we look at pictures of his wedding over time, trends begin to emerge. We can see differences, for example, in colour. When all guests are present the colours are more varied than when only the wedding party is there. We can also see differences in the volume of photos taken at different points in time. The ceremony is heavily photographed, whereas later at the reception less formal photographs are taken.

Zooming out farther, we can see that questions about context cannot be answered through these wedding photographs alone. For example, the photos cannot tell us that the pastor is his wife's uncle and that the flowers came from a local shop. These contextual and personalising anecdotes Yau offers remind us that small slices of information often need stories to make sense. Motivation, emotion, and meaning are rarely discernible from a photograph's pixels alone. Rather, data points form part of a broader data storytelling process that brings us from pixels and pictures to the story of a wedding.

The more we zoom in on a data point, the more we see its complexity, while the more we zoom out, the more we see its context. When presenting data, the goal is to zoom in enough to realistically relate complexity, while zooming out enough to give the context the audience needs to understand its potential meanings and significance. This is even more pertinent when the aim of telling your data story is to create an intervention or a call to action. In these instances it is also often crucial to reach your audience emotionally. But in order to provoke your audience to think, to feel, or to do, first you must understand them.

Understanding your Audience

What makes us compelled to tell a story? It may be a deep desire to share a new discovery, an expertise, or an insight. Perhaps it is to highlight an injustice or make harm visible. Some of us want to tell stories to change minds, to secure funding, or to implement new programmes or treatment plans. Or maybe you tell data stories simply because it is what you are paid to do. Regardless of why you tell stories with data, for them to be effective, they need an audience. As author J.K. Rowling once said, "No story lives unless someone wants to listen" (Treneman, 2003). Imagining who that eager listener might be can help shape your data stories and motivate you to keep working on a project. John Steinbeck famously advised aspiring authors to pick one person, real or imagined, and write to them.

Before starting any data storytelling project, we always think first about audience. Recently we have started to use a simple activity to link story to audience. The task is called 'Think, Feel, Do' and is adapted from Susan O'Halloran's (2014) communications training for the non-profit sector. O'Halloran writes that stories are told for specific reasons. "When you think of your communication objective, you're really asking two questions:

1. What do we want our audience to think, feel, or do?

2. And then, thinking backwards from this objective: what key messages does our audience need to receive, understand and believe in order to perform these actions?" (p. 37).

'Think, Feel, Do' is a powerful exercise as it allows us to tease apart gained knowledge (think) from responsive emotion (feel) in order to capture how those two things together can influence or inform behaviour (do). While many projects have objectives and mission statements that guide them, without a clear understanding of what you want to evoke in your audience, objectives and mission statements can only describe what we want to happen. In storytelling terms, they can provide the moral of the fable, but not the story that makes that moral stick. According to Chip and Dan Heath (2007), authors of *Made to Stick: Why Some Ideas Survive and Others Die*, stories can get people to act, can tell people how to act, and can give people energy to act.

→ **Think, Feel, Do**
We use a simple worksheet with clients for the Think, Feel, Do exercise. This one was designed by Daniel Weissmann and Alexandra Alberda for our BU Civic Media Hub collaboration with Public Health Dorset.

Primary Audiences for All Together Better
Think, Feel, Do exercise

Who are your three primary audiences? (*write them below*)

What do you want them to..

	1.	2.	3.
Think			
Feel			
Do			

Different Audiences,
Different Data Stories

Of course, when telling a story there is usually not just one person in the audience you are trying to reach. At the same time, specificity is key for effective—and efficient—data storytelling. Editors I've worked with often complain that too many proposals and pitches state that an author's target audience is 'the general public.' "There is no such thing as a general public," these editors say. Instead, editors want their prospective authors to be more specific about the different kinds of audiences they imagine themselves writing for. It is only when we are specific about our audience segments that we can begin to tell stories more effectively.

→ Audience segmentation is a process of dividing audiences into subgroups based on their behaviours and demographics.

Understanding your audience segments involves asking questions about who you are writing for: How much detail is too much? When is it better to use technical terms versus translating your findings into everyday language? What elements of your data's backstory should you include?

→ See the upcoming section All Data Has a Backstory for more.

In addition to who you are writing for, where you will publish and share your data story matters. If you are presenting your work on national radio you would not use the same narratives or terminology as if you are presenting your work at an industry conference. Likewise, if you are delivering a presentation to funders in a boardroom, your key messages should look different than if you are pitching a policy change in a press release. When we take a step back from our own work, the fact that we need to alter our storytelling by audience segmentation can seem obvious. Yet, so often people fail to consider their audience when communicating with data. Either they assume that everyone is an expert in their field, or, at the other end of the spectrum, they treat people as if they are too dumb to understand any kind of complexity.

A good data storyteller needs to know their audience and adjust accordingly. Understanding what each audience segment wants in terms of data complexity and narrative delivery can help you pitch your stories more effectively and efficiently. It might be that you need to present the same finding in five different ways. As long as you are clear on the key messages, this kind of tailoring becomes easier to do over time.

We use the task Five Levels of Data Literacy to help clients focus on the different kinds of audiences for their data stories. It is adapted from communication strategist Jim Stikeleather's (2013) *How to Tell a Story with Data*.

Five Levels of Data Literacy	
Level of Data Literacy	**What They Want**
Novice	Layman's terms; data that is immediately accessible (e.g. simple ratios); relevant to what they're doing (or to them); links to more information; short
Generalist	Concise; *their* language; relevant to what they're doing;
Colleague	Use of shorthand / acronyms; references; (too many) assumptions; methodology; caveats; awareness of context; range of understanding
Expert	How rather than what (detail); anticipate questions; past work; more precise / specialist language;
Trustee/Funder	Clarity / simplicity / brevity; challenges with answers / decision-making options; how to make them look good; emotion; message vs political

Case Study: explaining expired tear gas by audience segment

Here is an example of how we segmented one of our data stories for three different identified audiences using the 'Think, Feel, Do' exercise. This example is from our project RiotID that uses civic media techniques to help people monitor, identify, and record the use of less lethal weapons against civilians. This project involves speaking to policy-makers, journalists and protesters, among others.

This example takes up the issue of the use of 'expired tear gas.' The dangers of tear gas are primarily determined using clinical data. Animal or human subjects are exposed to quantities of the gas in laboratory settings, usually in military research facilities, and the amount that is safe to use on people is determined by how the subjects respond. Similar to how household products are tested, the stability of tear gas canisters is tested through trials. Data is collected on the conditions that lead tear gas canisters to explode, go off unexpectedly, or cause other kind of faults. Because the chemicals in tear gas change over time, as with many products, they come with an expiration date. It is through these kinds of data collection that expiry dates are created and assigned to products, including tear gas.

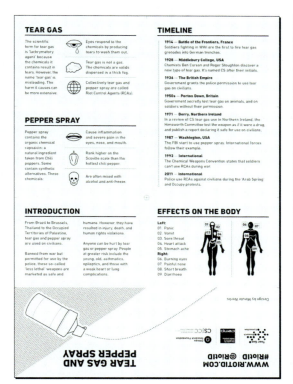

After tear gas expires it is supposed to be destroyed according to protocols for disposing of toxic waste. Yet sometimes during the policing of protests expired canisters of tear gas are used. While many people worry that expired tear gas is more potent, the larger danger is that it is more volatile.

↳ **RiotID Tear Gas and Pepper Spray**
Design by Minute Works. Available to download at www.riotid.com.

Audience	Think	Feel	Do
Policy-makers	The use of expired gas is a public health problem and must be addressed	Determined	Include a ban on expired gas in policy guidelines
Journalists	Expired gas has particular effects on civilians that it is in the public interest to report	Dutiful	Report on the problems of expired gas when it is used
Protesters	Expired tear gas is volatile. It can be more likely to cause fires and should be disposed of by professionals	Informed	Understand the dangers of expired gas in order to make safer decisions

While some people presumed expired tear gas was more potent, most people had never really considered the issue before. It is very unlikely that a member of the public—or even a seasoned protester—would have ever encountered clinical trial data or product testing data on tear gas.

On the one hand, this lack of knowledge means that we have a long way to go in making the data stick regarding the dangers of tear gas use. However, on the other hand, we are not competing against strongly held pre-existing opinions or beliefs. This means that while there is a large gap in existing knowledge, there are fewer barriers to closing that gap. In other cases, communicating data to audiences requires challenging pre-existing ideas that are deeply ingrained or emotionally loaded.

Worksheet: Think, Feel, Do

You can give it a go using this blank worksheet.

Audience	Think	Feel	Do
1.			
2.			
3.			

Audience Listening

In order to close the gap between what you would like your audience to think, feel, or do, and what they currently think, feel, or do, you need to understand them. In some instances, you may already have data or insights on what your audience subgroups think, feel, and do. These insights might be based on previous research or experience. However, in many cases you will need to figure out what your audience is thinking, feeling, and doing. In audience research this is normally done through interviews, focus groups, or surveys. More recently it is also done through social media listening—gathering insights from conversations across social media about an issue. This form of listening can be cost and resource effective, using data that is already available online. Whatever strategy for gathering insights on audiences you employ, it is important to identify gaps between current mind-sets and the mind-set your work aims to achieve.

To address the issue of information gaps we use a simple exercise called 'Mind the Gap.' Here we ask our clients to identify the current thoughts and feelings of each audience segment and compare these to what they want each audience subgroup to 'Think, Feel, and Do.'

→ Social media listening can be thought of as a smaller-scale practice of data mining. In relation to big data, data mining involves the process of using computational techniques to look for patterns that can yield insights. Social media listening does not require large-scale datasets or computational techniques, although these are often employed. Social media listening is the process of monitoring social media channels for mentions of your topic of interest (whether it's a person, company, product, or service, etc.).

If you would like to practise social media listening, see our workbook activity called Listening For.

Worksheet: Mind The Gap

You can create a simple table template to track the gaps between what your audiences currently Think, Feel, and Do versus what you are aiming for them to Think, Feel, and Do.

Audience Segment	Currently Think	Want them to Think	Mind the Gap	Currently Think	Want them to Think	Mind the Gap	Currently Think	Want them to Think	Mind the Gap
1.									
2.									
3.									

When creating a data story you need to meet your audience half-way. As the data storyteller your job is to provide a structure for your audience to follow and embed the messages for what you want them to think, feel, and do. Data visualisation researchers Segel and Heer (2010) talk about this as finding a balance between author-driven and reader-driven approaches. Where the goal is for your audience to do something quite directed (i.e. stop using plastic packaging; vote for a particular political candidate), an author-driven approach is more common. If the desired

→ We will explore these two approaches further in the Four Pillars section of the chapter Visual Data Storytelling.

'do' is more open-ended or exploratory, a reader-driven approach may fit better (i.e. explore data on plastic pollution; compare candidates' positions on different issues).

From Segel and Heer (2010), Properties of Author-Driven and Reader-Driven Stories.	
Most visualisations lie along a spectrum between these two extremes.	
Author-Driven	**Reader-Driven**
Linear ordering of scenes	No prescribed ordering
Heavy messaging	No messaging
No interactivity	Free interactivity

When finding the balance and 'minding the gap,' the goal is to get your messages across, while leaving the audience with enough room to explore and reflect for themselves. These techniques for understanding and connecting with audiences are important whether you are producing a report or an interactive website. Whatever approach you choose, narrative is key to telling better data stories.

What's Narrative Got to Do with It?

The most fundamental structure of a data story is its narrative. The narrative is what you construct to deliver your message. It's how you embed what you want your audience to know, how you inspire them to feel, and the way you incite them to act. A basic definition of narrative is "a spoken or written account of connected events." How these events unfold over time forms the narrative structure of a story.

While there can be an infinite amount of stories we tell, research has shown that there are certain narrative structures that commonly recur. Many of these can be visualised in relation to Freytag's Pyramid. Gustav Freytag was a German writer that argued for a model of narrative based on Aristotle's theory of tragedy. Today this model is called Freytag's Pyramid, illustrated by a graphic that lays out the five stages of this narrative arc in a peaked shape of rising and falling action:

Exposition – Setting up the scene of the story, background, and characters

Rising Action – The conflicts and events that build the story

Climax – The turning point or most intense moment in the story

Falling Action – The actions that happen as a result of the climax

Denouement – End of action

A seven-step version of the pyramid includes two further turning points:

Inciting Incident – Something that happens to begin the action

Resolution – Conflicts in the narrative are tied together or solved

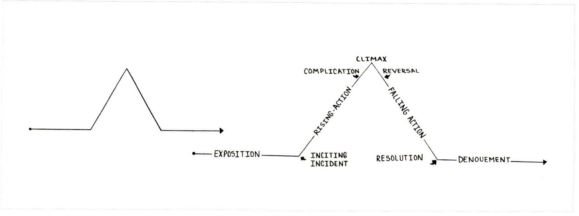

↳ Freytag's Pyramid

Narrative in Data Storytelling

While it might be obvious how this basic narrative structure works in fiction, it can be harder to see how it might apply to a set of research findings or policy recommendations. Addressing this, data storyteller Brent Dykes adapted Freytag's pyramid:

Exposition – Set-up/Background

Inciting Incident – Deviation from the expected

Rising Action – Supporting facts

Climax – Main insight

Resolution – Recommendation and next steps

Dykes argues that while it can be tempting to structure a data story around your process of data analysis, by starting with your research question or hypothesis, instead a data storyteller should be focused on key insights. The exposition and inciting incident should backup the 'climax' of the main insight, rather than explain how you got to your research question or hypothesis—as would be common in more traditional styles of writing up findings.

Here again you must think like a storyteller. Looking at an example can help illustrate this difference and show how Freytag's model can be used to give narrative structure to data insights.

Case Study: Belonging at BU

A few years ago Anna Feigenbaum was part of a team tasked to better understand how incoming students talked about my university on social media. If we were writing a narrative based on the research question or brief, then the exposition would be about our process of gathering tweets, coding them, and looking for patterns. While this could be dramatised into a story, it is far less interesting to an audience of stakeholders than narrating our main insight: that BU is a friendly campus.

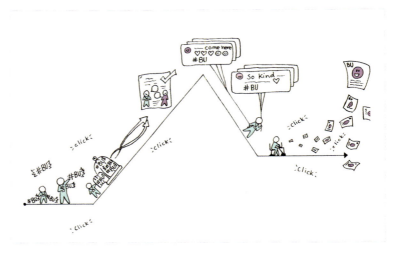

→ EX 1: The Data Analyst's Narrative Arc

Exposition – The researchers gathered a sample of tweets from BU students during their first days of university.

Inciting Incident – The tweets were entered into coding software.

Rising Action – Content analysis showed positive student sentiments toward BU when discussing interactions with other people around the university.

Climax – BU was frequently talked about as a friendly place.

Resolution – BU Marketing can expand images and stories of friendliness in its promotional materials in order to help recruit and retain students.

→ EX 2: The Key Insight's Narrative Arc

Exposition – Going to university is an exciting step in young people's lives, but can also be a time of anxiety and loneliness as one leaves friends and family behind.

Inciting Incident – Meeting fellow students and staff in the first few days of being on campus makes a huge impact on how students adjust to university life.

Rising Action – Friendly interactions and kind words can create a welcoming environment.

Climax – In fact, friendliness is what makes BU a place students say they want to be.

Resolution – Drawing on this quality, BU Marketing can expand images and stories of friendliness in its promotional materials in order to help recruit and retain students.

In example 1, the character of the data story is the researcher and the narrative arc of the story is about research methodology. This might make sense if the target audience is other researchers. However, because the story is told from the data analyst's point of view, students are only in the story as data points.

In example 2, the characters in the story are students. The narrative is about students' journeys, not the data analyst's journey. Instead of taking centre stage, the data analyst fades into the background, and the data points become humanised. The narrative represents the emotional journey of going to university, rather than the research journey of studying students going to university. Example 2, told from the perspective of students as data points, follows a familiar narrative arc of leaving home. It moves from anticipation, through a process of self-discovery, before finding a new sense of belonging.

Types of Narrative

In addition to Freytag's Pyramid, data storytellers can also model their projects using what Christopher Booker (2004) famously termed *The Seven Basic Plots*. Reviewing vast amounts of literature, films, and even operas, Booker argued that the stories we tell fall into seven basic types. These plots can be found not only in art, but in politics and organisational practice.

→ Cognitive is an award-winning creative studio that uses great script writing, intriguing visuals and eye-catching animations to create informative, engaging and unforgettable animations and illustrations. They pioneered the whiteboard animation technique when building the RSA Animates series on YouTube, which now has over 100,000,000 views. Find out more about how Cognitive supercharges stories at www.wearecognitive.com

Christopher Booker's Seven Basic Plots	
Plot Type	**The Protagonist...**
Overcoming the Monster	Protects and struggles against an antagonist
Rags to Riches	Acquires and loses something valuable as a learning process
The Quest	Journeys to acquire an object or goal, facing obstacles along the way
Voyage and Return	Journeys to a new place, facing obstacles and experiencing growth before returning home
Comedy	Triumphs over adversity through confusing or complicated circumstances
Tragedy	Faces adversity that leads to their undoing
Rebirth	Is forced to change, leading to a new life and sense of self

It is important to note that stories can contain more than one of these plots and that the events that unfold may look very different from story to story.

→ **Tuesday Tip**
Cognitive used visual thinking and narrative techniques to condense the original 736 page book into a short tweet, making a huge amount of information more accessible to more people.

Inspired by author Kurt Vonnegut, Andrew Reagan and colleagues (2016) from the Computational Story Lab at the University of Vermont brought a 'big data' approach to this question of story structure. The research team worked with a sample of 1,327 digitised stories housed by Project Gutenberg, an online repository of over 60,000 free to access, digitised books. Analysing this sample, the team argued that there are six core emotional arcs in fiction. They used three independent tools to analyse the emotional trajectories in these works of fiction, drawing from Vonnegut's model of an emotional arc that runs across two axes: beginning to end, and ill fortune to great fortune.

→ For more on big data see Phil Wilkinson's concept post in the next chapter.

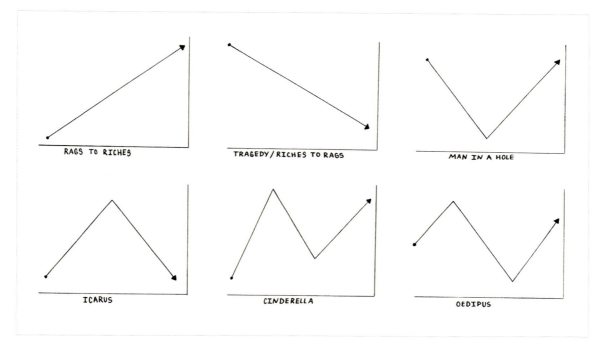

These action timelines, plot types, and emotional arcs can be used as templates to help you construct a data story. While the basic plot types can help to imagine overall stories, emotional arcs can assist in how a story is structured for emotional engagement with the audience. Take the example of Cinderella. This is a classic Rags to Riches story. Through the course of the narrative Cinderella goes from being locked up in her stepmother's house as a servant to marrying a handsome prince with the help of her fairy godmother. The emotional arc of Cinderella, however, is not just from poor and sad to rich and happy. Rather, Cinderella goes from isolated (stuck in the house) to elated (at the ball), from distraught (locked in the house) to happily ever after (or at least married to the prince).

↳ Illustrations of the six emotional arcs identified by Andrew Reagan et al (2016).

While most data stories will lack the drama of Cinderella, understanding emotional story arcs can help strengthen your storytelling. If we take the earlier example of the 'BU is friendly, data story, the emotional arc could resemble this Cinderella structure. A new student may go from 'anxious to leave home,' to 'excited to get to university,' to 'overwhelmed by all the changes,' to 'feeling a sense of belonging and settling in.'

Case Study: The Hero's Journey

During one of our workshops for Bournemouth University's Festival of Learning, we used the Hero's Journey to explore narrative structures for data storytelling. Teaming up with our clients at Public Health Dorset, the aim of the workshop was to create data stories that captured the health benefits of battling unhealthy eating, alcoholism, and smoking.

The Hero's Journey arises from the work of Joseph Campbell. Like Booker, Campbell looked across stories to identify common narrative structures. Working with mythology in particular, Campbell came up with 17 stages that a hero goes through, organised into three acts: departure (from the ordinary world), initiation (tasks and trials of the special world), and return (transformation and growth upon returning to the ordinary world).

Since the publication of Campbell's work in 1949, others have proposed adapted structures with 8 or 12 stages. Whether showcasing the original 17 or a revised 8, the stages of the Hero's Journey are usually visualised as a circle, charting the hero's voyage from the ordinary world to the special world. Examples of this story structure are rife in literature that's been adapted into blockbuster films. For example, *Lord of The Rings*, *Star Wars*, *Hunger Games* and the recent *Black Panther* film all share this popular narrative structure. The Hero's Journey also bears similarity to the Voyage and Return plot identified by Booker.

> "A hero ventures forth from the world of common day into a region of supernatural wonder: fabulous forces are there encountered and a decisive victory is won: the hero comes back from this mysterious adventure with the power to bestow boons on his fellow man."
> ↳ Joseph Campbell, *The Hero with a Thousand Faces*

→ **A Hero's Journey**
This Hero's Journey worksheet was designed by Anna Feigenbaum with Daniel Weissmann and Alexandra Alberda for the BU Festival of Learning.

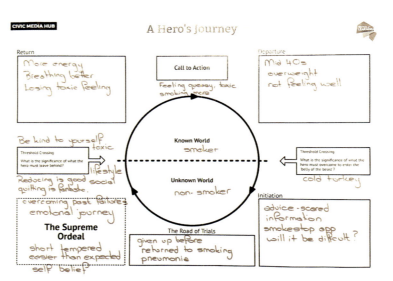

For our data storytelling Hero's Journey exercise we worked in small groups. Every group was given a set of research findings based on data about the health benefits of eating healthier food, drinking less, or quitting smoking. In addition, each group was provided with a few testimonials from people who had made successful interventions in their lives around these behaviours. We asked each group to plot these testimonials onto a Hero's Journey template, incorporating findings from the data into each stage.

Data as Characters

with Brad Gyori

Of course, there can be no Hero's Journey without the Hero. Stories need characters and data stories are no different. A character can be any person, animal, or object in a narrative. Places and events can also be characters. For example, in Netflix's hit show *Stranger Things* there are a number of human characters, as well as superhuman characters like Eleven who have special powers. Then there is the character of 'the Upside Down,' a living underworld that largely drives the TV show's plot.

The same kind of variety of characters can be found in nonfiction writing. News stories are often a good place to look out for this and to begin to think about how you might use character to help tell stories with data. Using news stories based on data about the Olympics as an example, you can see how journalists use different types of characters to create narrative:

1. **Event as Character** – 2020 Olympics: Climbing faces challenge for acceptance (BBC 22 September 2017 https://www.bbc.co.uk/sport/olympics/41348585)

2. **Person as Character** – Dina Asher-Smith: Why British sprinter could win Olympic gold at Tokyo 2020 (BBC 12 Aug 2018 https://www.bbc.co.uk/sport/athletics/45163546)

3. **Place as Character** – Tokyo 2020 Olympics: Japan debates daylight saving to avoid heat (BBC 6 Aug 2018 https://www.bbc.co.uk/news/world-asia-45080980)

Example 1 relies on data about the history of Olympic sports and people's responses to them, and the sport of 'climbing' is the main character. Example 2 utilises data on past medal winners and features a person as character, Dina Asher-Smith. Drawing on weather data, example 3 uses a place as the main character with its personification of 'Japan'.

Looking in more detail at an example from the news, consider news stories about the 'Best Places to Live.' In news articles about such rankings, the towns or cities in the top list are presented as the characters. These characters are the 'main points,' or protagonists, in the datasets. Their 'character traits' are assessed—from health stats to crime stats to average weekly incomes. In the rainy United Kingdom, weather data on the 'amount of sunlight' are taken into account for the rankings, as well as quality of infrastructure indicators like broadband access and the number of pubs and fitness centres. These traits together comprise what survey makers Halifax see as the key metrics for quality of life, allowing rural towns to be assessed and win top ranks. But just as these places-as-characters can rise, they can also fall. As a 2017 *Daily Echo* article headline read, "Winchester loses title of 'best place to live in UK,'" dropping from first place in 2016 to fifth.

Composite characters are also common in storytelling. A composite character is a character based on more than one individual person (or nonhuman). Composite characters in fiction are similar to those that arise from data. For example, case studies in psychological profiles, target audiences in marketing demographics, or guides to a specific breed of dog all use the technique of creating composite characters. Composite characters help reduce complexity for audiences and can provide a more diverse range of traits. At the same time, composite characters carry the danger of collapsing differences and making the composite too unbelievable.

Mini-Exercise: Data Characters

Try to find your own example of a data story in the news that uses data in each of the following ways:

1. Event as character
2. People/person as character
3. Place as character
4. Composite character

All Data Has a Backstory

In order to empathise with a character, the audience needs to connect to that character. Rather than a caricature or symbol, a character should be well rounded, revealing rather than hiding their flaws. In narratives, characters are given backstories in order to create these connections. In fiction, a backstory refers to key events that shaped a character's current condition. Backstories are perhaps most explicit in superhero narratives and fairy tales. Cinderella's fate as the family servant is tied to the death of her father, while Batman's crime-fighting is directly linked to witnessing his parents' murder as a young child. A backstory is shared with the audience to help build connection and empathy with the situations a character is navigating. The lack of a good backstory often leads to critiques of 'oversimplified' or 'unbelievable' characters.

Taking this idea and applying it to data, we can ask important questions about what kinds of contextual information is needed to make a data set come alive. In the same way that we say a character is too simple, we might also think that a statistic seems too simple. Often we want more than just a numeric figure. At first it may seem far-fetched to think of data as having a backstory in the same way as Cinderella or Batman. But if we again follow Nathan Yau and think of data as 'having stories to tell,' then the idea of a data backstory becomes easier to imagine.

The first point to consider is that all data comes from somewhere. For example, survey data comes from people filling out surveys. Survey designers made those surveys. Those survey designers were influenced by previous studies and experiences. The more you know about the backstory of the data in front of you, the more able you are to tell effective data stories with it.

Mini-Exercise: All Data has a Backstory…

Every data story starts before a dataset is completed. This is the data's backstory. To begin to investigate a dataset's backstory, select a completed dataset and ask these three questions:

1. How was the data gathered and refined? By who?
2. What analyses were run and why?
3. What are the patterns and anomalies so far? How might they link or connect to aspects in the data's backstory?

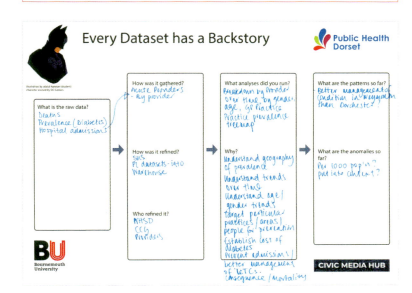

→ **Every Dataset has a Backstory**
This worksheet was created by Anna Feigenbaum and Alexandra Alberda for one of our BU Civic Media Hub workshops with Public Health Dorset. It was designed to help participants ask questions about their data's backstory.

Data backstories are important whether your story involves huge datasets or small collections of testimonies. Many data journalists and data visualisers have taken up the practice of keeping a data diary that records where they got their figures and what they did to collect, store, further investigate, or statistically analyse them. This practice encourages transparency, shares skills, celebrates collaboration, and demonstrates the idea that no data is truly 'raw'—and no data storyteller works entirely alone.

What is Conflict in Data Storytelling?

Conflict is a major aspect of narrative storytelling. In fact, some say that without conflict, there can be no story. The need to build a story around conflict can be challenging when working in nonfiction genres. When working with data, the idea of generating a conflict where one is not obviously already present can feel uncomfortable. 'Making up a conflict' can feel like it will transport you out of the realm of the evidence-based and propel you too far into a world of fiction. However, if you expand how you think about conflict, the potential for conflict as a narrative tool in data storytelling becomes clearer.

There are a number of different types of conflict that generally form the backbone of a story. The seven listed below are commonly cited.

Seven Types of Conflict in Stories

↳ Person vs. Self

↳ Person vs. Person

↳ Person vs. Nature

↳ Person vs. Society

↳ Person vs. Machine/Tech

↳ Person vs. Fate/God(s)

↳ Person vs. Supernatural

These seven types of conflict are formulated around human characters. However, as discussed in an earlier section, people are not the only kinds of characters in a story. Stories can also be about conflicts between machines, societies, or animals, among other permutations. The same is true for a data story.

For example, Andrew Brooks and Katelyn Toth-Fejel's (2015) collaboration *The Journey of Jeans*, explores the "very complex global systems of garments' lives through the lens of one type of clothing: the pair of jeans." In this infographic data story, jeans are the central character. Here we see data presented around an object that serves as composite characters—a universal pair of jeans that stands in for jeans in general. The life of this garment type is revealed to us through the jeans' point of view, as it journeys from production to redistribution. Utilising techniques from sequential art, the reader learns about the political economy of this everyday fashion item by scrolling through a series of hand-drawn infographics panels. The conflict that drives the story is subtle, but we can see it set-up in the very beginning:

> Is it possible to relate to statistics about millions of dollars and billions of kilos? Probably not. But by having a browse we hope you get enough sense of the truly global reach of these ubiquitous objects in your wardrobe to see them in a new way.

While there is not a traditional conflict of one side vs another, Andrew Brooks' research on clothing poverty hints toward a familiar conflict between consumerism and exploitation. The key data insights relate to wage disparity, agricultural impacts, and the effects of globalisation. For example, part of the final panel reads, "Many Kenyan clothing factories have closed after being undercut by cheap imports" and, "In some African countries used clothes are known as *the clothes of the dead whites*." A subtext of colonialism reinforces the background context and gives emotion to the data story told here.

When writing nonfiction, conflict needs to be understood loosely with a focus on sparking curiosity, connecting with core values, or igniting compassion from your audience. Consider the following data stories and how they immediately set up a conflict to frame their data and draw the audience in:

Worksheet: Conflict in Data Storytelling

Data Story	Conflict in Data Story	Conflict Type
Spies in the Sky Peter Aldhous and Charles Seife 6 April 2016 — Buzzfeed See maps Showing Where FBI Planes Are Watching From Above America is being watched from above. Government surveillance planes routinely circle over most major cities — but usually take the weekends off. https://www.buzzfeednews.com/article/peteraldhous/spies-in-the-skies	American People vs. US Government + Their Spy Planes	Person vs. Society + Technology
Infographic: Renault Sport Formula One Team by numbers The Renault Sport Formula One Team comprises 1,000 engineers, designers and IT staff, based in the UK and France. The team's 2017 schedule will see it compete against nine constructors at 20 race locations around the world, with all-new cars reflecting the radical changes to regulations. The cars produce big power and big data. Explore the graphics below to uncover the complexity behind motorsport's greatest spectacle. https://www.wired.co.uk/partnerships/infographic-renault-sport-formula-one-team-by-numbers	Renault Sport Formula One Team + Cars + Big Data vs. limits of our technological imagination	Person + Machine/Technology vs. Fate/Gods

In both of these quite different examples of data stories, the reader is pulled in through the set up of tension. In the *BuzzFeed* interactive story "Spies in the Sky," text and maps are used together to show the operation of FBI surveillance planes. By creating an opening scene of US civilians being watched from above, the authors are able to quickly establish narrative tension. The reader is interpellated into an already existing set of ideas or ideologies around government surveillance. Similar to *The Journey of Jeans*, this kind of narrative tension between familiar entities can help the reader navigate a story and provide background context beyond the content of the data story itself. Because of the pre-existing power imbalance between the two (or more) sides, this approach is particularly useful when creating data stories that involve civil rights, corporations, governments, or other large institutions in contrast to smaller organisations or individuals.

The second example works with a very different sense of conflict. This graphic draws on a sense of human wonder. The limits of innovation are set in productive tension with what humans can currently create with technology. Rather than mobilising conflict in a negative sense, this kind of narrative tension is created through the collision of human-technological advancement with the contemporary limits of invention. This kind of productive tension sparks curiosity and taps into audience's creative imagination. It can be very effective when telling data stories about new discoveries, products, models, or programmes.

Details, Details

While conflict propels a story along, it is detail that gives it lasting memory. Nonfiction author and former *New York Times* editor Francis Flaherty (2009) writes, "All stories are divided into two parts, the action and the commentary" (p. 75). Flaherty uses the metaphor of a boat to show the two duties of a writer: to keep the boat moving and, at the same time, to explain the passing scenery to passengers. The boat driver must balance her focus on driving the boat, while at the same time conveying enough information about the surrounding landscape to keep passengers interested. Flaherty uses this metaphor to explain that if a writer gets too caught up in the details of description, the reader can quickly get bored and put down their story altogether. The challenge is getting the right balance between movement and detail.

If you are working with data that you gathered yourself or that is on a subject you are already very familiar with, chances are your understanding is full of details. Your mind is cluttered with tiny bits of niche information. There are caveats for your caveats, footnotes that could go on for pages, anecdotes that illustrate everything from the most mundane finding to the greatest anomaly you ever encountered. Over the course of a career all these details may have a part to play. But in any single story, too much detail can lose your audience and muddle your main insights. In contrast, perhaps you are new to your dataset. It may have been given to you as part of an assignment or brief for a client. Without having a lot of background contextual information, teasing out what details to include and what to leave out is likewise challenging, from a different angle. Whatever your situation is in relation to your data, the trick is finding what details to include and when to give description the axe.

Writing teacher Stephen Koch (2003) argues in the *Modern Library Writer's Workshop*:

> Every story—like every human situation—swims in a vast shoreless sea of possible information and detail. Almost all that information is totally uninteresting. Some small—very small—part of it is revelatory (p. 76).

So how do you decide what details to include and what details to leave out? Marcy Kennedy (2016) offers this advice in her *Description: A Busy Writer's Guide*:

> In order to justify its existence, every passage of description should do two or more of the following things:
> → Ground the reader in the setting
> → Symbolize or foreshadow something important to the story
> → Enhance the theme
> → Add subtext
> → Show something about the viewpoint character's personality
> → Add conflict or complications
> → Hint at backstory

Translating this advice into a data storytelling context, we've created a 'Details Tick List Test' that can be used for thinking about what detail to include in a data story. While you don't need to include all of these elements, like a two-drink minimum, it is useful to follow a two-ticks minimum principle:

❑ Provide background information on context
❑ Add further evidence to the main data insight
❑ Add depth to the broader context
❑ Show something unique about the data
❑ Add conflict or complicate the data
❑ Provide data backstory

An example can help illustrate how this 'Details Tick List Test' works. In 2014 the *New York Times* ran a graphic called 'Mapping the Spread of the Military's Surplus Gear.' This editorial graphic told the story of how a US Defense Department program created in the early 1990s allowed for state and local police departments to obtain surplus military-style equipment. The graphic shows a map of the United States using orange fill with white boundary lines to show counties that obtained surplus equipment. A light shaded grey is used to fill the space where there is no data or no equipment. Six icons representing aircraft, armoured vehicles, body armour, grenade launchers, night vision, and assault rifles are used as filters that the viewer can click on to see what counties received which set of goods.

There are no details of the methodology used for data collection aside from the introductory note that says detailed data was obtained from the Pentagon. It is noted that the data starts in 2006. There is also a bracketed comment in the introductory paragraph that tells the reader "(most of [the gear] is paid for by the departments or through federal grants)."

How do these details fare under the Two Tick Minimum test?

Filter By Icons
- ❑ Provide background information on context
- ❑ Add further evidence to the main data insight
- ❑ Add depth to the broader context
- ❑ Show something unique about the data
- ❑ Add conflict or complicate the data
- ❑ Provide data backstory

Gear from Federal Grants
- ❑ Provide background information on context
- ❑ Add further evidence to the main data insight
- ❑ Add depth to the broader context
- ❑ Show something unique about the data
- ❑ Add conflict or complicate the data
- ❑ Provide data backstory

Data since 2006
- ❑ Provide background information on context
- ❑ Add further evidence to the main data insight
- ❑ Add depth to the broader context
- ❑ Show something unique about the data
- ❑ Add conflict or complicate the data
- ❑ Provide data backstory

Each included detail fulfils at least two of the tick boxes. The viewer is given enough details to become familiar with the idea of surplus military gear. Designed for a novice or generalist audience, this data story avoids jargon, introduces terms where necessary, and tries to make the data relevant to readers by allowing them to drill down and explore information by county. We'll discuss this element further later on in the workbook.

For those seeking more detail on this data story, later in the week the *New York Times* put out a follow-up story "What Military Gear Your Local Police Department Bought" that provided readers with a GitHub link to the original dataset obtained through a Freedom of Information request sent to the Pentagon. This article embeds the original data story in it, going into further detail on the background of the equipment transfer program, as well as providing greater description of the dataset. For those who choose to explore further and go onto GitHub, there is another layer of detail presented, as well as a link out to a larger project on military surplus equipment transfers conducted by MuckRock, an organisation specialising in Freedom of Information Act requests, that obtained a list of every law enforcement agency that took part in the programme, allowing them to breakdown data in more detailed ways than just by country (as the *New York Times* project had done). These issues in data gathering will be looked at again in the next chapter.

Works Cited and Further Reading

→ Aldhous, P., & Seife, C. (2016, April 6). Spies in the sky: See maps showing where FBI planes are watching from above. *Buzzfeed News*. Retrieved from https://www.buzzfeednews.com/article/peteraldhous/spies-in-the-skies.

→ Apuzzo, M. (2014, August 19). What military gear your local police department bought. *The New York Times*. Retrieved from https://www.nytimes.com/2014/08/20/upshot/data-on-transfer-of-military-gear-to-police-departments.html.

→ Booker, C. (2004). *The Seven Basic Plots: Why we Tell Stories*. London, UK: Continuum.

→ Brooks, A. & Toth-Fejel, K. (2015). The Journey of Jeans [Infographic]. Retrieved from http://www.clothingpoverty.com/jeans.

→ Campbell, J. (1968). *The Hero with a Thousand Faces*. Princeton, NJ: Princeton University Press.

→ Field, A. (2016). *An Adventure in Statistics: The Reality Enigma.* Thousand Oaks, CA: SAGE Publications.

→ Flaherty, F. (2009). *The Elements of Story: Field Notes on Nonfiction Writing*. New York, NY: HarperCollins.

→ Giratikanon, T., Parlapiano, A., & White, J. (2014, August 15). Mapping the spread of the military's surplus gear. *The New York Times*. Retrieved from https://www.nytimes.com/interactive/2014/08/15/us/surplus-military-equipment-map.html.

→ Gitelman, L., & Jackson, V. (2013). Introduction. In L. Gitelman (Ed.), *"Raw Data" is an Oxymoron* (pp. 1-14). Cambridge, MA: The MIT Press.

→ Heath, C., & Heath, D. (2007). *Made to Stick: Why Some Ideas Survive and Others Die*. New York, NY: Random House.

→ Herzog, D. (2015). *Data Literacy: A User's Guide.* Thousand Oaks, CA: SAGE Publications.

→ Infographic: Renault sport Formula One team by numbers. *Wired UK*. Retrieved from https://www.wired.co.uk/partnerships/infographic-renault-sport-formula-one-team-by-numbers.

→ Kennedy, M. (2016). *Description (A Busy Writer's Guide)*. Ontario, Canada: Tongue Untied Communications.

→ Koch, S. (2003). *The Modern Library Writer's Workshop: A Guide to the Craft of Fiction*. New York, NY: Random House.

→ O'Halloran, S. (2014) *Compelling Stories, Compelling Causes: Nonprofit Marketing Success*. Self published. ISBN: 1502314746

→ Reagan, A., Mitchell, L., Kiley, D., Danforth, C., & Dodds, P. (2016). The emotional arcs of stories are dominated by six basic shapes. *EPJ Data Science*, 5(31). Retrieved from https://epjdatascience.springeropen.com/articles/10.1140/epjds/s13688-016-0093-1.

→ Segel, E., & Heer, J. (2010). Narrative visualization: Telling stories with data. *IEEE Transactions on Visualization and Computer Graphics*, 16(6), 1139-1148.

→ Stikeleather, J. (2013, April 24). How to tell a story with data. *Harvard Business Review*. Retrieved from https://hbr.org/2013/04/how-to-tell-a-story-with-data.

→ Treneman, A. (2003, June 20). J.K. Rowling: The Interview. *The Times*. Retrieved from https://www.thetimes.co.uk/article/j-k-rowling-the-interview-dshhr7c5fjf.

→ Vogler, C. (2007). *The Writer's Journey: Mythic Structure for Writers*. Studio City, CA: Michael Wiese Productions.

→ Yau, N. (2013). *Data Points: Visualization that Means Something*. Indianapolis, IN: John Wiley & Sons.

Spotlight:
Visualizing Impact

Visualizing Impact (VI) is a non-profit collective that creates data-driven, visual stories for social justice. Since 2012, VI has worked independently and with partners to communicate on topics such as Palestinian human rights, refugee rights, economic empowerment, collective action, and freedom of expression. All VI stories are published under Creative Commons licensing to serve human rights advocates and educators, and we have tracked use cases of our visuals in 65 countries since 2015.

Data-Driven Stories for Social Justice

Visualizing Impact's communications have two requirements: first, they must facilitate a deeper understanding of a topic through accurate and truthful analysis of data and information. Second, they must serve as a tool for taking action for social justice.

Data-driven storytelling is a set of practices that help us bridge these two requirements. By merging data and story, we are able to navigate the strengths and limitations of each as a tool for social justice engagement.

Both data and stories produced within dominant power structures often, intentionally or unintentionally, reinforce inequality and render groups of people less visible, while claiming the mantle of scientific reason or journalistic objectivity. VI's first and largest project, *Visualizing Palestine,* is an example of how communities facing injustice are not only extracting insight from credible data to build movements and bolster calls to action, but are also contributing to conversations that problematize how data is produced, interpreted, presented, and used.

Visualizing Palestine launched in 2012 with *Hunger Strikes*, an infographic that places protests by Palestinian political prisoners into a broader context, capturing how hunger striking is a form of nonviolent resistance often used as a last resort by oppressed people to challenge systems of power. The story is told through the lens of medical research and historical events associated with various social movement influencers. Since its initial publication, several activists have adapted *Hunger Strikes* to draw attention to emerging cases, such as the hunger strike undertaken by Iranian human rights activist and political prisoner Arash Sadeghi in 2017.

In eight years of collaboration, the VI team has released more than 100 data-led visuals that serve as a regularly-tapped pool of resources for advocates and educators. We choose what stories to work on by monitoring current events, reviewing emerging data and studies, speaking with partners and constituents, and brainstorming around themes we've identified as strategically important, eye-opening, and emotionally and intellectually compelling. We monitor the use and impact of our visuals primarily through online analytical tools and feedback obtained from people who download our visuals.

A collaborative process

Visualizing Impact has published several tools documenting the skills and steps required to create a mature data story, in our experience. The process wheel was born out of the trial and error of VI's early work. A 2012 article by Andy Kirk refers to "the seven hats of data visualization design", another model we find helpful for explaining the multidisciplinary, collaborative, and iterative nature of data storytelling.

Steps two through four on the process wheel capture a critical phase of development in any data story: moving

The following text appears within the process wheel image:

RECEPTION

CONCEPTION

PRODUCTION

INCREASING SHIFT IN PERCEPTION

FROM INFOGRAPHIC TO NEW PERCEPTION

INCREASING EMOTIONAL APPEAL

FROM DATA TO STORY

INCREASING SHIFT IN VISUAL EXPRESSION

FROM STORY TO VISUAL EXPRESSION

Identify new directions and ideas

Get the raw data and validate sources

Make it into a compelling story

Translate it into a brief

Bring in designers to express it visually

Review the work to ensure quality

Publish the work online

Track its impact and virality

1 IDENTIFY
2 RESEARCH
3 STORY
4 BRIEF
5 DESIGN
6 REVIEW
7 PUBLISH
8 MEASURE

↳ Visualizing Impact created this process wheel to capture steps that allowed for successful collaboration on infographics and data visualizations. Courtesy of Visualizing Impact.

from broad subject-matter research and raw data to a coherent story. In the early days of VI, researchers were handing over large volumes of data and information to designers, who were then finding themselves stuck on identifying the story. Observing this issue, we made two changes to our process. First, we developed a 'brief' format that helps everyone involved in a project align on communication objectives, audience, potential stories, and information hierarchy (step four). This is a living document that evolves as the project progresses. Second, we allocated more time to exploratory analysis, where researchers and designers work together to identify potential stories and visual concepts, sharing the analytical and creative load.

The role of *challenger* is integral in our process. A challenger is a person (or several people) who comes in at various points in the development of a data story to offer a fresh and experienced eye, capturing red flags, gaps, or missed opportunities. For example, a challenger with an academic background in the topic we're working on might draw our attention to important data or information during the research stage, or verify that we are using accurate and nuanced terminology in our copywriting. At the story stage, challengers can act as a brainstorming partner if we feel stuck, or a test audience to judge whether a story is valid, clear, and compelling. At the design stage, a challenger may be an information designer who spots subtle refinements that make a difference in the overall clarity or emotional impact of a design. Creating space for challengers in our process allows us to access the wealth of experience and inspiration that might be at the disposal of a significantly larger team. The ability to draw on challengers depends on building and nurturing a trusted network over time.

By the time we reach the review stage (step 6), our focus is on final fact checking and verification of sources. Every visual we publish contains sources in the footer. It is critical to reference our sources directly on the visual to maintain credibility and trust.

Visualizing Impact produces content in two languages, English and Arabic. Beyond shifting between the left-to-right orientation of English and the right-to-left orientation of Arabic, this involves deepening our understanding of the nuances of certain words and visuals and their associations for different communities. The challenge of producing content bilingually invites us to think more deeply about design inclusivity and the degree to which our work is responsive to the needs of different groups of people.

Our team is currently distributed across six countries from West Asia to North America, so we are constantly looking for ways to tap into the strengths of remote collaboration, as well as minimize or overcome its challenges. For example, we established a pipeline of production that helps us track and schedule work as it advances from idea to brief to visual development. Regular weekly rhythms like team challenge sessions every Monday or weekly feedback deadlines keep us focused and aligned.

Visualizing Impact's ongoing vision includes experimenting with data-driven storytelling in mediums and spaces that are new to us, such as art institutions. One recent example of this is *A National Monument,* a limited-edition series of 21 wooden topographic reliefs created by Visualizing Palestine and artist Marwan Rechmaoui. The works recreate a three-dimensional snapshot of the major Palestinian cities and towns circa 1947, based on detailed British surveys from that period combined with digital elevation data from NASA.

View more Visualizing Impact visuals and follow our work at www.visualizingpalestine.org and www.visualizingimpact.org.

By Visualizing Impact

HUNGER STRIKES

 DAY 1 HUNGER PANGS & STOMACH CRAMPS DISAPPEAR AFTER THE 2ND - 3RD DAY

DAY 7 NELSON MANDELA PRISONERS STRIKE ENDS

DAY 14 "CATABOLYSIS" THE BODY STARTS TO BREAK DOWN MUSCLE TISSUE FOR SURVIVAL

 **DAY 15** LOSS OF THE SENSATION OF THIRST

 "LIGHTHEADEDNESS" OR INVERSELY "MENTAL SLUGGISHNESS"

 SENSATION OF COLD

STANDING UP MAY BECOME DIFFICULT TO IMPOSSIBLE **DAY 18**

DAY 21 MAHATMA GANDHI ENDS HIS LONGEST STRIKE

 DAY 22 LAILA SOUEIF ENDS HER STRIKE FOR HER SON ALAA

 **DAY 26** 200+ GUANTANAMO DETAINEES 2005 COERCED TO END STRIKE

 DAY 27 33 SOUTH AFRICAN DETAINEES END THEIR STRIKE 1989

DAY 28 18% WEIGHT LOSS

DAY 35 EXTREMELY UNPLEASANT SENSATIONS OF VERTIGO INCOERCIBLE VOMITING

 FAST, UNCONTROLLABLE MOVEMENTS OF THE EYES

 DOUBLE VISION "DIPLOPIA"

DAY 42  INDIFFERENCE TO SURROUNDINGS, INCOHERENCE, CONCENTRATION BECOMES DIFFICULT OR IMPOSSIBLE

 LOSS OF HEARING

 POSSIBLE BLINDNESS

DAY 45 DEATH CAN OCCUR AT ANY TIME DUE TO HEART FAILURE "CARDIOVASCULAR COLLAPSE"

DAY 66

 BOBBY SANDS DIES IN PRISON

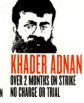 KHADER ADNAN OVER 2 MONTHS ON STRIKE NO CHARGE OR TRIAL

DAY 70

"WE ARE NOT IN SEARCH OF DEATH, WE ARE LOOKING FOR REAL LIFE."

June 1989, Tiananmen square hunger strike declaration

Sources:
The information presented is based on a range of medical sources. Symptoms may vary from person to person.

Altun, G et al., 2004 Deaths due to hunger strike: post-mortem findings. Forensic Science International 146(1), pp.35-38

Crosby, S et al., 2007 Hunger Strikes, Force-feeding, and Physicians' Responsibilities. The Journal of the American Medical Association 298(5), pp.563-566.

Peel, M., 1997 Hunger strikes. Understanding the underlying physiology will help doctors provide proper advice. British Medical Journal 315, pp.829-830.

VISUALIZING**PALESTINE**

DESIGN BY NA**EL MIR** FOR VISUALIZING**PALESTINE**.ORG
@visualizingpal · fb.com/visualizingpalestine
SHARE AND DISTRIBUTE FREELY. CREATIVE COMMONS BY-NC-ND 3.0 LICENSE. FEB 2012.

↳ Visualizing Palestine, the first and largest project of Visualizing Impact, published *Hunger Strikes* as its debut data story in 2012. Courtesy of Visualizing Impact.

Spotlight:
Dying Homeless

In her October 18, 2018 article, "'Utterly Shocking' – How UK-Wide Collaboration Revealed Number of Homeless Deaths," Maeve McClenaghan from The Bureau of Investigative Journalism details how she worked with collaborators to find out how many homeless people were dying in the UK. She knew the number of people living homeless had risen, but on investigation, it turned out that no one was counting or recording how many died. Here she explains how she went about gathering the data that led to the national headlines declaring that 449 people had died homeless in the last year.

How we did it

The project, titled "Dying Homeless," started back in February after a series of homeless deaths made headlines when icy storms hit the UK. Those stories got me thinking—I knew that there had been a huge increase in homelessness, with the number of rough sleepers in England and Wales rising by 169% since 2010, but I wondered how often were people dying homeless?

What I thought was a simple question turned into weeks of calls and enquiries to coroners' offices and councils, hospitals or police—it turned out no one kept a comprehensive record of these deaths.

So the Bureau set out to do so. I searched out information on how and when people were dying. I sat quietly in funerals, talked to family members, collected coroners' reports, travelled to doctors' surgeries, shadowed homeless outreach teams, contacted soup kitchens and hostels, and compiled scores of Freedom of Information requests.

But we couldn't do it alone. The Bureau Local was set up with the belief that regional journalism is a crucial part of a healthy society and that collective reporting produces broader and deeper investigations than would be possible by any individual newsroom. This project was the perfect example.

"These figures are nothing short of a national scandal"

We knew that many of these deaths never made it onto the national radar, but many were reported at a local level. Indeed about a quarter of all the 449 deaths we logged, and the human stories behind the numbers, came from local news reports that we found, proving what a valuable role local papers have to play.

We also worked directly with our amazing network of journalists and collaborators across the UK, who got stuck in to exploring and reporting on deaths in their area.

Rory Winters, from *The Detail* in Northern Ireland, worked with us to reveal that 148 people had died homeless while waiting to be housed by the Northern Irish Housing Executive. One local politician called the figures "brutally shocking."

In Scotland, Karin Goodwin, who reports for *The Ferret*, spoke to charities and experts across the country and found that at least 94 people had died in the last year. Michael Yong from the *Bristol Post* did equally impressive work and managed to log the names of 50 people that had died homeless in the last five years in his city.

We asked them to submit all their findings through an online form, which we worked to cross-check and

verify. The reporting also formed the basis for many powerful features in regional papers, telling the stories of those who died and investigating the particular issues in their local area.

Homeless charities and outreach teams were also vitally helpful. In London, Housing Justice, Streets Kitchen, and St Mungo's helped us put names together, while doctors from Edinburgh and Brighton also gave us insights into deaths in their cities. House of Bread in Stafford let us in to see their work, while the *Big Issue* helped us link up with those that knew vendors that had died.

Together we put together a tragic jigsaw, and tried to tell the stories of those that lost their lives in the past year.

It has been a long road but it is not over yet. The Bureau will keep recording names of people that pass away throughout the winter and will keep working with our network so we can continue to #MakeThemCount. If you want to join us, get in touch via the Bureau's website.

To read the full article and find out more about the Bureau for Investigative Journalism visit: https://www.thebureauinvestigates.com/blog/2018-10-18/utterly-shocking-a-uk-wide-collaboration-reveals-the-scale-of-homeless-deaths.

You can find every single local story that was published by visiting: https://www.thebureauinvestigates.com/projects/homelessness/local-stories.

By the Bureau of Investigative Journalism

Spotlight:
Arthur Frank's Three Narrative Structures

Arthur W. Frank's *The Wounded Storyteller: Body, Illness, and Ethics* describes three prominent narrative structures that exist in illness literature: the restitution narrative, the quest narrative, and the chaos narrative. Each type has distinctive themes and features that help frame the storyteller's narrative.

Arthur Frank's concept of narrative structures is a generative example of the different ways that storytellers make sense of their experiences. The first narrative structure, restitution narratives, harkens back to models that seek to return someone to a previous normal. These narratives focus on restorable health like recovering from a common cold, a light injury, or something else that is considered easily overcome. These narratives appear most frequently in advertisements for medicine and in social myths for overcoming illness. A message such as, "This [pill/salve/stretch/herb] will get you back to work in no time," is an example of a restitution narrative. Stories aimed at children often feature restitutionary outcomes, whereby heath is restored after intervention.

The second narrative structure, and arguably the most extensively published and consumed, is the quest narrative (or the 'hero's journey' as it is known in fiction). In this structure, the protagonist starts from a previous 'normal' (which may happen off-scene) and falls from this pre-established foundation either by devastating illness or other tragedy. In the hero's journey the protagonist encounters complications in improving their health, they interact with a series of key supporting characters (mentors, allies, counsellors, etc.), and they learn from their illness to achieve a new enlightened 'normal.' Protagonists of a quest narrative are never assumed to regain their previous sense of 'normal' as in the restitution narrative; rather, it is understood that the individual is fundamentally transformed by the skills and experiences they gained in their journey. In the public health sector, quest narratives appear in campaigns that encourage the sick person to 'become a better version of yourself.'

Finally, there is the chaos narrative. It is the anti-narrative, temporally disjointed and without a definite resolution. Frank writes that "chaos is the opposite of restitution: its plot imagines life never getting better" (97). Chaos narratives reject progress, provoke anxiety, and are utterly unmediated. In a recent interview, Frank said that the closest anyone has come to publishing a chaos narrative is Allie Brosh's memoir *Hyperbole and a Half: Unfortunate Situations, Flawed Coping Mechanisms, Mayhem, and Other Things That Happened*.

Scholars have questioned the validity of the restitution narrative. Can we ever return to a pre-sickness normal after being ill? Is there even a 'normal' to which we can return? Others critique the valorisation of quest narratives, such as those found in breast cancer campaigns, as the most restorative or useful kind of life writing. Despite these critiques, Frank's narrative structures continue to be helpful in thinking about how narratives can adequately capture the complexity of lived experience.

By Alexandra Alberda

→ Frank, Arthur W. (1995). *The Wounded Storyteller: Body, Illness, and Ethics*. Chicago, IL: University of Chicago Press.

→ Williams, I. (Producer). (2015, July 10). *Arthur Frank: When Bodies need Stories in Pictures* [Audio podcast]. Retrieved from https://www.graphicmedicine.org/arthur-frank-when-bodies-need-stories-in-pictures/.

THE RESTITUTION NARRATIVE

THE CHAOS NARRATIVE

THE QUEST NARRATIVE

↳ Arthur Frank's illness narratives illustrated by Alexandra Alberda.

Spotlight:
Data Worlds

Dr. Jonathan Gray is Lecturer in Critical Infrastructure Studies at the Department of Digital Humanities, King's College London, where he is currently writing a book on data worlds. He is also co-founder of the Public Data Lab, and Research Associate at the Digital Methods Initiative (University of Amsterdam) and the médialab (Sciences Po, Paris). More about his work can be found at www.jonathangray.org.

In an influential 2006 TED talk, the late Hans Rosling sought to "debunk myths about the so-called 'developing world'" in a presentation with global statistical data and visualisations from the Gapminder tool. Later remembered as one who "made data dance" and "statistics sing," Hans's presentation may be considered an example of *telling stories with data*, using interactive graphics to engage those beyond researchers, policy-makers and other professional users of global statistics.

Later in the talk he says that projects like Gapminder are only possible if "publicly funded data" is made freely available to use. In a slide he depicts such projects as flowers, growing from the soil of data, with the sun of the public. In this account, institutions should therefore work to remove "prices" and "stupid passwords" from their data, to "liberate" it for all to use. This may be considered an example of *telling stories about data*. We may find such stories about data in many places – in policy documents, political speeches, magazine features, science fiction films, social media posts, technical mailing lists, and advocacy materials. Such stories not only tell us about the role and reception of data in society, they may also serve to institutionally stabilise certain imaginaries and visions of the future (Jasanoff, 2015) and to guide how data practitioners use and make sense of data (Dourish & Gómez Cruz, 2018). Thus we may read of data as, for example, "oil", "soil", "ecosystem", "infrastructure", "resource", "right" and "control".

Stories about data can also concern what kinds of *stories with data* are possible. Aside from notions of data as a resource which can be liberated or protected (Gray, 2016), stories about data can tell us about the ways of knowing the world which are inscribed into information systems and their associated creators, users, projects, frictions and trajectories. We might tell stories about what is included and what is left out of data, how phenomena are performed, as well as when, where, why and for whom. As Donna Haraway puts it, "it matters what we use to think other matters with; it matters what stories we tell to tell other stories with" (2016).

I have proposed the term "data worlds" to consider the worlds and world-making capacities of data (Gray, 2018). In the case of the global statistical data used by Gapminder, we might consider the forms of understanding which are made possible by statistical data infrastructures, the historically contingent interests and concerns which inform how phenomena are categorised and transformed into data fields – whether populations, ethnicity, education, economic growth, birth rates, natural resources or otherwise. Following such specific styles of sensemaking may lead us to stories of collectives or "social worlds" (eg. statisticians, activists, accountants) for whom these data fields came to matter in various ways. Such collectives may also be involved in various forms of political world-making, whether through international organisations or the management of the "world economy" (Slobodian, 2018).

What kinds of stories can be told about data and data worlds? As Gapminder illustrates, the internet and digital technologies change who can make and make sense of public data – and thus who can participate in the composition of data worlds. What counts as public data is being challenged by big technology companies, who, in what has been called the "double logic" of platformisation (Helmond, 2015), encourage the widespread use of data from their platforms arising from the activities of users at the same time as centralising and monetising these data flows. But data is not only created and used by institutions, experts and companies but also by other kinds of data practitioners and "data publics" (Ruppert, 2015).

How can we tell such stories about data? As with any story, how to tell well is not something that be exhaustively codified in advance, but must be undertaken as an open-ended, collective task of telling and retelling. One starting point is attending to and learning from how other stories about data are told, and how they might be told differently. For example, researchers in science and technology studies have sought to challenge stories about innovation which were focused on the role of a handful of great figures in unfolding progress, and to also look towards paths not taken; background infrastructures and labour; the role of women and people of colour; the role of non-human actors, instruments and publication processes; and the social, cultural, economic, political dimensions of inquiry, from funding and policy to colonialism and biopolitics. Taking inspiration from such retellings, we might "follow the actors", changes and controversies around data projects (Latour, 2007) and "stay with the trouble" that we find (Haraway, 2016), rather than smoothing this into more familiar narratives and tropes.

In telling stories about data we must consider who we are telling with and for, and what stories may hope to perform and produce in the world. Stories about data can come to matter not just for researchers, but also as a way to facilitate participation, intervention and resistance by activists, communities, journalists and others.

By Jonathan Gray

→ Dourish, P., & Gómez Cruz, E. (2018). Datafication and data fiction: Narrating data and narrating with data. *Big Data & Society*, 5, 2053951718784083.

→ Gray, J. (forthcoming). *Data Worlds*.

→ Gray, J. (2016). Datafication and democracy: Recalibrating digital information systems to address societal interests. *Juncture*, 23, 197–201.

→ Gray, J. (2018). Three aspects of data worlds. *Krisis: Journal for Contemporary Philosophy*. Retrieved from http://krisis.eu/three-aspects-of-data-worlds/

→ Gray, J., & Bounegru, L. (Eds.). (forthcoming). *The Data Journalism Handbook: Towards a Critical Data Practice*. Amsterdam: Amsterdam University Press.

→ Gray, J., Gerlitz, C., & Bounegru, L. (2018). Data infrastructure literacy. *Big Data & Society*, 5, 1–13.

→ Gray, J., Lämmerhirt, D., & Bounegru, L. (2016). *Changing What Counts: How Can Citizen-Generated and Civil Society Data Be Used as an Advocacy Tool to Change Official Data Collection?* CIVICUS and Open Knowledge International.

→ Haraway, D. J. (2016). *Staying with the Trouble: Making Kin in the Chthulucene*. Durham, NC: Duke University Press Books.

→ Helmond, A. (2015). The platformization of the web: Making web data platform ready. *Social Media + Society*, 1, 2056305115603080.

→ Jasanoff, S. (2015). Future imperfect: Science, technology, and the imaginations of modernity. In S. Jasanoff & S.-H. Kim (Eds.), *Dreamscapes of Modernity: Sociotechnical Imaginaries and the Fabrication of Power*. Chicago, IL: University of Chicago Press.

→ Latour, B. (2007). *Reassembling the Social: An Introduction to Actor-Network-Theory*. Oxford: Oxford University Press.

→ Ruppert, E. (2015). Doing the transparent state: Open government data as performance indicators. In R. Rottenburg, S. E. Merry, S.-J. Park, & J. Mugler (Eds.), *A World of Indicators: The Making of Governmental Knowledge Through Quantification* (pp. 127–150). Cambridge, UK: Cambridge University Press.

→ Slobodian, Q. (2018). *Globalists: The End of eEmpire and the Birth of Neoliberalism*. Cambridge, MA: Harvard University Press.

Spotlight:
Seeing Data Project

Seeing Data is a group of research projects which aim to understand the place of data visualisations in society. Interactive learning material is available on the Seeing Data website at www.seeingdata.org.

How do people engage with data visualisations?
Seeing Data explored how people engage with the data visualisations that they encounter in their everyday lives, often in the media. It focused on the factors that affect engagement and what this means for how we think about what makes a visualisation effective. On *Seeing Data* we used focus groups and interviews to explore these questions, to enable us to get at the attitudes, feelings and beliefs that underlie people's engagements with dataviz. 46 people participated in the research, including a mix of participants who might be assumed to be interested in data, the visual, or migration (which was the subject of a number of the visualisations that we showed them) and so 'already engaged' in one of the issues at the heart of our project and participants about whom we could not make these assumptions.

In the focus groups, we asked participants to evaluate eight visualisations, which we chose (after much discussion) because they represented a diversity of subject matters, chart types, original media sources, formats and aimed either to explain or to invite exploration. After the focus groups, seven participants kept diaries for a month, to provide us with further information about encounters with visualisations 'in the wild' and not chosen by us.

Factors which affect dataviz engagement
Subject matter – Visualisations don't exist in isolation from the subject matter that they represent. When subject matter spoke to participants' interest, they were engaged – for example with Civil Society professionals who were interested in issues relating to migration and therefore in migration visualisations. In contrast, one participant (who was male, 38, white British, an agricultural worker) was not interested in any of the visualisations we showed him in the focus

group or confident to spend time looking. However, his lack of interest and confidence and his mistrust of the media (he said he felt they try 'to confuse you') did not stop him from looking at visualisations completely: he told us that when he came across visualisations in *The Farmer's Guide*, a publication he read regularly because it speaks to his interests, he would take the time to look at them.

Source or media location – The source of visualisations is important: it has implications for whether users trust them. Concerns about the media setting out to confuse were shared by many participants and led some to view visualisations encountered within certain media as suspect. In contrast, some participants trusted migration visualisations which carried the logo of the University of Oxford, because they felt that the 'brand' of this university invokes quality and authority.

Beliefs and opinions – Participants trusted the newspapers they regularly read and therefore trusted the visualisations in these newspapers, because both the newspapers and the visualisations often fitted with their views of the world. This points to the importance of beliefs and opinions in influencing how and whether people take time to engage with particular visualisations. Some participants said they liked visualisations that confirmed their beliefs and opinions. But it is not just when visualisations confirm existing beliefs that beliefs matter. One participant (male, 34, white British, IT worker) was surprised by the migration data in an ONS visualisation in Figure X. He said that he had not realised how many people in the UK were born in Ireland. This data questioned what he believed and he enjoyed that experience. Some people like, or are interested in, data in visualisations that call into question existing beliefs, because they provoke and challenge horizons. So beliefs and opinions matter in this way too.

Time – Engaging with visualisations is seen as work by people for whom doing so does not come easily. Having time available is crucial in determining whether people are willing to do this 'work'. Most participants who said they lacked time to look at visualisations were women, and they put their lack of time down to work, family and home commitments. One working mother talked about how her combined paid and domestic labour were so tiring that when she finished her day, she didn't want to look at news, and that included looking at visualisations. Such activities felt like 'work' to her, and she was too tired to undertake them at the end of her busy day. An agricultural worker told us in an email that his working hours were very long and this impacted on his ability to keep his month-long diary of engagements with visualisations after the focus group research.

Confidence and skills – Audiences need to feel that they have the necessary skills to decode visualisations, and many participants indicated a lack of confidence in this regard. A part-time careers advisor said of one visualisation: 'It was all these circles and colours and I thought, that looks like a bit of hard work; don't know if I understand'. Many of our participants expressed concern about their lack of skills, or they demonstrated that they did not have the required skills, whether these were visual literacy skills, language skills, mathematical and statistical skills (like knowing how to read particular chart types), or critical thinking skills.

Emotions – Although last in our list, a major finding from our research was the important role that emotions play in people's engagements with data visualisations. A broad range of emotions emerged in relation to engagements with dataviz, including pleasure, anger, sadness, guilt, shame, relief, worry, love, empathy, excitement, offence. Participants reported emotional responses to: visualisations in general; represented data; visual style; the subject matter of data visualisations; the source or original location of visualisations; their own skill levels for making sense of visualisations.

What this means for making effective visualisations
What makes a visualisation effective is fluid – no single definition applies across all dataviz. Visualisations have various objectives: to communicate new data; to inform a general audience; to influence decision-making; to enable exploration and analysis of data; to surprise and affect behaviour. The factors that affect engagement which we identified in our research should be seen as *dimensions* of effectiveness, which carry different weight in relation to different visualisations, contexts and purposes. Many of these factors lie outside of the control of data visualisers, as they relate to consuming, not producing, visualisations. In other words, whether a visualisation is effective depends in large part on how, by whom, when and where it is accessed. Sadly, our research doesn't suggest a simple checklist which guarantees the production of universally effective visualisations. However, if we want accessible and effective data visualisations, it's important that people producing data visualisation engage with these findings.

By Helen Kennedy, Rosemary Lucy Hill, William Allen, Andy Kirk

---

→ Kennedy, H., Hill, R., Allen, W., & Kirk, A. (2016). Engaging with (big) data visualisations: Factors that affect engagement and resulting new definitions of effectiveness. *First Monday*, 21(11). doi:https://doi.org/10.5210/fm.v21i11.6389

→ Kennedy, H., & Hill, R. L. (2017). The feeling of numbers: emotions in everyday engagements with data and their visualisation. *Sociology*, 52(4), 830–848. doi: 10.1177/0038038516674675

Spotlight:
The Tactical Technology Collective

The Tactical Technology Collective is a Berlin-based non-profit organisation working at the intersection of technology, human rights, and civil liberties. Since 2003 they have provided training, conducted research, and created cultural interventions, remaining dedicated to driving practical solutions for an international audience of civil society actors and engaged citizens.

In October 2013 The Tactical Technology Collective released *Visualising Information for Advocacy*, a workbook based on their experience as researchers and trainers. The workbook was designed to help people implement practical strategies into their campaigning projects. One of the resources documented in their workbook is *10 Techniques to Help People 'Get the Idea'*. This set of techniques is particularly useful for constructing stories that can close information gaps—as feelings gaps—in hopes to ignite action.

We created the chart on page 58 to summarise their 10 techniques and adapt them for data storytelling. An individual data story may use one of these techniques or a combination of a few. The overview below is meant as a quick reference. We recommend you check out their entire book, published in English, Arabic, and Spanish.

For more information on Tactical Tech, visit their website www.tacticaltech.org. For more information on the workbook, go to www.visualisingadvocacy.org.

10 Techniques to Help People 'Get the Idea'

Technique	How it Works	What it Does
Juxtapose	Make striking comparison but putting two things unexpectedly together	Shows similarities and resonances, understand a problem that is difficult to grasp
Subvert	Play with dominant meaning	Challenge audience expectations
Invert	Swap out the dominant meaning	Shifts audience attention
Materialise	Gives representation to the abstract or hidden	Make invisible visible
Compare	Look at in relation to each other	Consider data relationally and ask questions
Contrast	Make differences stand out	Change audience point of view or perception
Illuminate	Highlight significance	Put a spotlight on a bit of data
Provoke	Contextualised irony or humour	Engage an audience to bring them into a story
Parody	Humour that plays on stereotypes or dominant culture	Draw people into an issue to make them question it
Intrigue	Grab attention with arresting images	Challenge audience assumptions

↳ The Glass Room by Tactical Tech and Mozilla, London, October 2017, photo by David Mirzoeff.

Spotlight:
Kate Evans

Kate Evans is a British comics artist, graphic novelist, and zinester. Her award-winning work explores issues ranging from breastfeeding to the migrant crisis. Her most recent graphic novel, *Threads*, was published by Verso in 2017.

In books such as *Threads* (2017), *Red Rosa* (2015), and *Bump: How to Make, Grow, and Birth a Baby* (2014), cartoonist Kate Evans combines numerical data with creative visual imagery to produce work that challenges status quo assumptions. "I definitely want to educate people," said Evans (video interview, January 26, 2018). Many of her projects are guides or explainers that break down complex information into an easy-to-understand format.

Evans' zine *Funny Weather We're Having at the Moment: Everything you Didn't Want to Know About Climate Change but Probably Should Find Out* (2006), uses statistical data to tell a funny, engaging story about climate change. The zine features two main characters: a little boy, who acts as the foil for the audience, and a 'fat cat' banker in a suit, whose refusal to acknowledge global warming is as comedic as it is tragic. Their dialogue, while often hyperbolic, clearly lays out the data-driven arguments for why climate change is not only real, but should be taken seriously as an imminent threat.

Accessibility is a paramount concern in Evans' work. While paywalled science articles or specialised climate reports generate data, they are often unavailable to the average person outside of academia. In this sense, *Funny Weather* is a work of translation, bringing specialised knowledge to a lay audience. But the work is not merely accessible; it's funny, too. Although humour may seem out-of-place in a book about climate change, Evans views it as a powerful way to connect with her reader. "Humor is probably the simplest and most effective way to make anything accessible and meaningful to people," she said (2018). The result is a highly entertaining narrative that bridges the gap between objective data reporting and subjective narration.

Evans' work pushes back against claims to objectivity that rely on a non-locatable standpoint. In her most recent work, *Threads* (2017), Evans' graphic novel about her experience volunteering in a migrant camp in Calais, France, she made the editorial decision to only depict what she saw firsthand. In doing so, she made a conscious decision to insert herself into the narrative and to frame the narrative from her point of view. This decision echoes calls by feminist philosophers for researchers to situate themselves within their projects, not as disembodied observers but as living beings with histories, perspectives, and social circumstances.

Evans is highly sceptical that complete objectivity is possible in any work of art. She recognizes the importance of the author's political and social identities in the process of creation. According to her, "In your so-called objectivity, you're missing out a layer of political information that people need to make sense of the world. I don't attempt to be objective in the representations I make. What I do is, I make a representation of events that's consistent with the facts, but I make it as emotionally engaging as possible to the reader" (2018). In this sense, much of her work significantly parallels that of graphic medicine artists Ellen Forney, Ken Dahl, and MK Czerwiec. Like Evans, their projects transform facts (or data) into affective narratives, often using a first-hand perspective.

IN 1896, SWEDISH SCIENTIST SVANTE ARRHENIUS WORKED OUT HOW PUMPING **EXTRA CARBON DIOXIDE** INTO THE AIR, WITH THE LARGE-SCALE BURNING OF FOSSIL FUELS, IS **ADDING** TO THE NATURAL INSULATING PROPERTY OF THE ATMOSPHERE...

...IT'S NOW 2006 AND NO-ONE SEEMS TO HAVE LISTENED VERY MUCH. HUMANS ARE DUMPING **7 BILLION TONNES** OF CARBON DIOXIDE INTO THE ATMOSPHERE EACH YEAR. WE HAVE ARTIFICIALLY INCREASED THE AMOUNT OF CO₂ IN THE AIR BY A **THIRD.** ①

AT THE SAME TIME AS CO₂ (FROM FOSSIL FUEL BURNING) IS HOTTING THINGS UP, **SO₂**, THAT'S **SULPHUR DIOXIDE** (ALSO FROM FOSSIL FUEL BURNING) FORMS SULPHATE PARTICLES WHICH **COOL THE PLANET DOWN** BY REFLECTING INCOMING LIGHT BACK INTO SPACE. THESE TWO PROCESSES HAVE TO BE CONSIDERED TOGETHER TO GET AN ACCURATE PICTURE OF GLOBAL TEMPERATURE, BUT WHEN THEY ARE, IT'S CLEAR THAT **THINGS ARE GETTING WARMER.**

OTHER GASES CONTRIBUTE TO THE GREEN-HOUSE EFFECT. **METHANE** LEVELS HAVE RISEN 150%, **NITROUS OXIDE** HAS RISEN BY 15% AND MANMADE CHEMICALS **SULPHUR HEXAFLUORIDE** AND **CFC**s HAVE BEEN FOUND TO HAVE A POWERFUL WARMING ACTION ON THE PLANET. ②

THE GREENHOUSE EFFECT ISN'T THE ONLY FACTOR THAT DETERMINES GLOBAL CLIMATE. **VOLCANIC ACTIVITY** AND **SUNSPOT CYCLES** ALSO PLAY A PART, BUT THESE NATURAL PHENOMENA **SHOULD** HAVE ACTED TO COOL THE PLANET DOWN OVER THE PAST 100 YEARS. NOT HEAT IT UP...

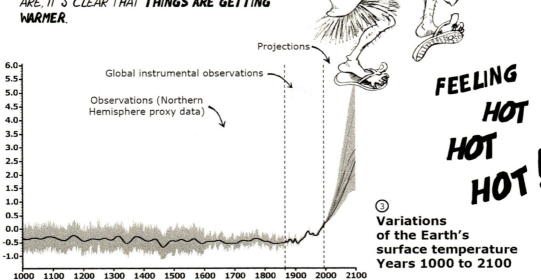

Projections

Global instrumental observations

Observations (Northern Hemisphere proxy data)

FEELING HOT HOT HOT!

③ **Variations of the Earth's surface temperature Years 1000 to 2100**

ASK YOURSELF, WILL _YOUR_ GREENHOUSE BE AFFECTED? THE ANSWER IS ALMOST CERTAINLY YES!

11

↳ An excerpt from *Funny Weather*, (2006). Courtesy of the artist.

Activity:
Colon Surgery!

 Author

Name
Anna Feigenbaum

Affiliation
Bournemouth University

Biography
Dr. Anna Feigenbaum is the founder of BU Civic Media Hub

Twitter
@drfigtree

 Materials

→ Pens
→ Pencils or digital tool for text editing
→ Dice

 Space Needed

Anywhere!

 Aim

This task is designed to learn how to make titles and headlines punchier and more audience-friendly. It is based on advice from Helen Sword's book *Stylish Academic Writing*.

 Go Digital / Go Analogue

You can use pen and paper, a tablet and digital pen, or track changes tools to conduct this activity.

 Group Size

This activity was designed as a 'pop-up' that people came by to participate in.

 Duration

15 minutes per 'treatment'.

 Top Tips or Additional Notes?

Bring in colour to spice up this game. We used a colour dotted dice and bright editing pens to make the interaction more visually vibrant.

As an incentive, we had book voucher prizes from publishers for the top surgeons.

Task

This activity is based on advice from Helen Sword's book *Stylish Academic Writing*. Activity participants become editors of report headlines or article titles. Give each participant (i) a report title and executive summary or (ii) an academic title and abstract and a handout explaining the task:

Diagnosis
Many papers suffer from the excessive use of colons. While less severe, the double-barrelling of question and exclamation marks is also prevalent amongst this population.

Treatment
The colon can be removed through a simple surgical procedure. For the title to regain proper function without a colon, there are six certified treatment option plans detailed below. To determine your treatment plan, roll a dice. Now remove the colon from your patient and put your treatment plan into place!

Treatment options
1. Ask a question – ex: Will the media ever be the same after Brexit?
2. Set a scene – ex: Media reform in Brexitland
3. Make a challenging statement – ex: Why Brexit was good for the news business
4. Invoke a metaphor – ex: The Lord Voldemorts of Brexit and their media spells
5. Create an Unexpected Juxtaposition – ex: The international relations of Marmite
6. Make a grand claim – ex: Brexit is the best thing that's happened to media studies

 Sample Activity Plan

This activity can be scaled for all different sized groups. People can do one edit or try their hand at all six. We ran this activity from a table in the publishers' area at a conference so people could just pop by and play.

2 min:	Explain the task
5–10 min:	Edit the Title
2 min:	Feedback

Activity:
Listening For

 Author

Name
Anna Feigenbaum

Affiliation
Bournemouth University

Biography
Dr. Anna Feigenbaum is the founder of BU Civic Media Hub.

Twitter
@drfigtree

 Materials

→ Printouts
→ Highlighters in four colours
→ Pens

 Space Needed

Tables for small group work.

 Aim

The aim of this exercise is to enhance understanding around what target audiences are concerned about and how they are currently discussing an issue or event.

 Go Digital / Go Analogue

Go Digital – Create a file folder with pdfs of the documents you want to 'listen to'. You can cut and paste text from the pdfs or use a pdf markup tool to do this as a paperless activity.

 Group Size

This activity can be scaled, we recommend people work in pairs or small groups.

 Top Tips or Additional Notes?

Select your social media examples from the platforms that your target audience is most likely to be using.

 Duration

2 hours.

☰ Task

For this activity you will need to gather examples from social media where the issue or event you are working on has been discussed by members of your target audience. This can be Twitter posts, Facebook pages with comments, Instagram post comments, articles with comments underneath, YouTube video comments, or discussions from online forums, etc. The more directly related to your data story project that the examples are, the better this activity will work. For example, if you are working with data on post Brexit immigration to the UK, locate social media talk that is directly on this issue rather than migration or Brexit more broadly.

Give every group a printed out copy of the examples and a set of four different coloured highlighters, as well as a pen to annotate the handouts.

Read your set of documents and highlight in four different colours:
→ concerns or fears
→ frustrations, known obstacles
→ misconceptions
→ desires, wishes, dreams, visions

Every time you make a highlight, annotate who is talking (i.e. For the above example it might be MPs, British-born citizens, EU-born people, etc). Ideally the people talking should be members of your target audience segments. NB: You may highlight the same statement in more than one colour

Summarise and transcribe – Pull together your highlighted text across documents and organise them by who is talking. Pay attention to any patterns, noting down what thoughts and feelings were most dominant, marginalised, questioned, etc.

Feedback to the whole group.

▤ Sample Activity Plan

15 min:	Introduction to task
30 min:	Reading and annotating printouts
30 min:	Gathering together the findings in your group
30 min:	Feedback from groups
15 min:	Key takeaways to carry into data storytelling planning

Activity:
Five W Questions for Data Storytelling

 Author

Name
Anna Feigenbaum

Affiliation
Bournemouth University

Biography
Dr. Anna Feigenbaum is the founder of BU Civic Media Hub.

Twitter
@drfigtree

 Materials

→ Pencil or pen
→ Paper

 Space Needed

Any space!

 Aim

This activity aims to tie together the different elements of character, backstory and audience for data storytelling.

 Go Digital / Go Analogue

Go Digital – Use a virtual learning space or collaborative document editing to digitally archive your answers.

 Group Size

This activity can be scaled, we recommend people work in pairs or small groups.

 Top Tips or Additional Notes?

Pair this activity with Think, Feel, Do or Listening For... to create a longer lesson plan.

 Duration

30–60 minutes.

Task

Working in pairs or small groups with a specific dataset, write down answers to the following Five W questions:

1. Who is this information about? Think through the people, objects, animals, etc. that the numbers represent. Can you describe what a few of them might be like and how they've come to be part of this dataset.
2. What does this information tell us about these people, objects, animals, etc.?
3. Where does this information matter? Write down both the geographical location the data may refer to, as well as the other key places implicated.
4. When does this information refer to? If it is predictive, what period does it cover? What other changes or major events might be relevant during this time?
5. Why should your target audience care? This should capture what you want your audience to do with the information you are giving them.

Sample Activity Plan

10 min:	Introduce the task and dataset or information pack you will be using
20 min:	Work in pairs or small groups to answer the 5 W questions
20 min:	Debrief and report back on your answers
10 min:	Wrap-up and note down key takeaways

Navigating Data's Unequal Terrain

The Growing Data Divide

with Tom Sanderson

Over the past few years we have seen increases in the number of software tools, handbooks, and online resources available for data storytelling. Equipped with narrative strategies and storytelling techniques, datasets can be turned into powerful and persuasive evidence. Yet, to become a data storyteller dedicated to transparency and accountability, one must be equipped to ask difficult questions about where data comes from, who can access it, and who can engage with the tools and skills needed to analyse and visualise it.

As both a practice and a growing cultural industry, data storytelling has taken shape within the uneven terrain of digital media where power remains concentrated amongst corporate firms, dominant in the West, and unequally distributed along racial and gender lines. Together these imbalances in power, resources, and access are leading to a data divide.

The data divide is growing for a number of reasons. First, accessing, analysing, and visualising data requires time and resources. While larger organisations may be able to fund full-time data workers, small organisations face limited budgets, resources, and time. According to the National Civil Society Almanac (2017), over 80% of civil society organisations in the UK are working with less than a £100,000 annual income (NCSA, https://data.ncvo.org.uk/a/almanac17/civil-society-data/). Allocating such limited resources to either employ a data professional or train up a team in the necessary data skills is frequently deemed impossible.

This means that few people in these non-corporate workplaces are able to scrutinise data or create persuasive arguments with data as part of their job role. This disadvantage also manifests itself in the lack of resources afforded to certain technologies or to creating institutional best practices. Data visualisation designers thus tend to work in the corporate sector, often being "snatched up" and employed under non-disclosure agreements (Wilson, 2011). As civil society organisations are essential to the advocacy and protection of people's well-being, on everything ranging from health care to the environment to economic rights, the fact that they are being left behind in terms of both data literacy development and data capacity building in an increasingly dataified world is cause for concern.

→ The term dataified world or sometimes 'dataified society' refers to the ways that data analytics has impacted institutions and practices across all sectors of life.

In efforts to close this gap, there is an uptake of 'coding for good' initiatives that apply data analytics to problem-solve social welfare issues. There is also an increase in partnerships between data analytics companies and the non-profit sector. However, watchdogs note that these initiatives often support big name charities and NGOs, leaving the 80% of smaller organisations still lagging behind. In addition, they are often social enterprises linked to for-profit data analytics companies; thus, the knowledge and skills offered remain retained by the corporate sector.

Second, while the rise of digital tools and techniques certainly diversifies the kinds of narratives we can tell with numbers, not all data stories are easy to capture. Sensitive subjects (such as information on refugees, prisoners, children, detainees, and those living in conflict zones) often have no straightforward data source, or documents are scattered across agencies and organisations. This makes some issues easier to gather data on—and therefore to tell stories about—than others. In this sense there is also a data divide between data that is easy to access, analyse, and share (for example: weather patterns, traffic, sports statistics, baby names) versus data that is difficult to capture, yet very important for understanding the world (for example: climate change-based migration, deaths of refugees, rates of rape and sexual assault).

Thirdly, there is what media scholar Mark Andrejevic (2014) calls the big data divide, describing the asymmetry of data power. Andrejevic uses the phrase to describe "asymmetric relationship between those who collect, store and mine large quantities of data and those whom data collection targets" (p. 1673). Businesses and governments collect information about everything from our shopping habits to our search histories, from our driving routes to our average daily steps. Yet, while the majority of people are targets of data collection, only a minority are in roles that benefit directly from the collection and analysis of this data. This is a particular cause for concern when the data being gathered on people is used either to create profit for the few, or to create profiling systems, as we will discuss in more detail in the sections on data and bias and data discrimination.

Below is a table we developed to help capture and explain these three key aspects of the growing data divide. The causes and effects mapped out in this table are ilustrations of these dynamics, rather than an exhaustive list.

The Growing Data Divide

Type of Data Divide	Data Literacy and Capacity	Availability of Data	Aysemmetry of Data Power
Causes	limited time and resources usually due to organisational budgets	data difficult to obtain because of sensitive nature, lack of record, security concerns	power imbalances between people collecting, storing, and analysing data and the people that data collection targets
Effects	civil society organisations are not equipped to deal with data power to make persuasive arguments with data only available to minority	majority of data stories told rely on the most easily accessible data, not necessarily the most significant difficult to create evidence-based arguments when no data is recorded	data profiteering or shareholders profiting off the exploitative use of people's data for personal financial gain can lead to data profiling and discrimination against demographic groups, particularly those already marginalised
Examples	Lloyd's Bank UK Digital Business Index 2018 found that 97,000 charities lacked basic digital skills, with scores for data analysis skills ranking lowest. https://resources.lloyds-bank.com/pdf/bdi-report-2018.pdf	"Fatal Journeys 4", from the International Organization for Migration's Global Migration Data Analysis Centre (GMDAC), in collaboration with the UN Children's Fund, UNICEF, highlights the need for better data on migrant deaths and disappearances, particularly for children; one of the most vulnerable groups of migrants." https://news.un.org/en/story/2019/06/1041521	Amazon tested a recruiting tool that used AI to score job candidates. In 2015 it realised the experimental tool was discriminating against women candidates. The tool 'taught itself' that male candidates were preferable, scoring down resumes with references to 'women' https://www.reuters.com/article/us-amazon-com-jobs-automation-insight/amazon-scraps-secret-ai-recruiting-tool-that-showed-bias-against-women-idUSKCN1MK08G

How Open is Open Data?

with Tom Sanderson

Defined as data that can be freely used, re-used, and redistributed by anyone, the term 'open data' came into currency in the early 2000s. During this time, institutions argued that making their data open to the public would increase democratic participation and civic empowerment. Since then the Open Data movement has been associated with promises of improvements in transparency, greater democratic scrutiny, and an effective mechanism with which citizens, communities, and organisations can hold the State to account.

→ Learn more about the Open Knowledge Foundation, an organisation dedicated to building 'a world where knowledge creates power for the many not the few' at www. okfn.org.

Open data is summarised by the Open Knowledge Foundation as "data that can be freely used, shared and built-on by anyone, anywhere, for any purpose" ("The Open Definition," n.d.). It is usually associated with government, public sector organisation, and researcher data, but any organisation can choose to open its data. Types of data range from big to small, include images, budgets, maps, and research results. Open data is available on everything from birth rates to bicycle lanes, from high tides to highly contractable diseases. Every day open data is used by journalists, policy-makers, advocacy groups, researchers, urban planners, and businesses of all kinds.

However, while there are thousands of innovative and inspiring uses of open data, there also remains a number of barriers to its widespread use. Despite the great potential of open data to empower citizens and communities, it remains inaccessible to many, especially those from disadvantaged backgrounds who are often the most directly affected by its collection and analysis.

As the Office of National Statistics case study below discusses, the discrepancy between the promises and reality of open data is often related to standards of data collection or presentation. While systems like '5-star Open Data' set best practice data publishing standards for institutions, such improvements often require major investment and structural changes, making uptake slow. In addition, complex database systems, jargon heavy taxonomies, PDF locked documents, and scattered datasets can make open data inaccessible, even when it has officially been made 'open' (Gurstein, 2011).

Make your stuff available on the Web (whatever format) under an open license

★☆☆☆☆

Make it available as structured data (e.g., Excel instead of image scan of a table)

★★☆☆☆

Make it available in a non-proprietary open format (e.g., CSV instead of Excel)

★★★☆☆

Use URIs to denote things, so that people can point at your stuff

★★★★☆

Link your data to other data to provide context

★★★★★

Data literacy researchers now argue that we must go beyond just making data public. In order to advance data literacies, we need participatory data architectures (Gray and Davies, 2015), infrastructures that can enable people to interpret and apply data in beneficial ways (Gurstein, 2011, Lawson et al., 2015). Better data skills can also help get around these barriers by embedding understandings of data types and file compatibility into workplace practice. Supplementary data acquisition skills, such as successful navigation of legal mechanisms like Freedom of Information must also be integrated into training to provide solutions to the problems around inaccessibility.

↳ Tim Berners-Lee, the inventor of the Web and Linked Data initiator, suggested a 5-star deployment scheme for Open Data. Above, we provide examples for each level of Tim's 5-star Open Data plan.

Case Study: The Limitations of Open Data on Disability

Recently the Office of National Statistics (ONS) in the UK recognised what they called a "burning injustice" facing disabled people in the country. Drawing from available data, the ONS reported that children with Special Educational Needs are more likely to be absent or excluded at school. As young adults, disabled people are less likely to be in further education, employment, or training. And while they note that a gap in employment has been narrowing, "disabled people are currently 29.9 percent points less likely to be in employment than non-disabled people."

The available data revealed large inequalities. But more worrisome was the lack of clear, robust data on these issues. While different data is currently collected in the UK by the ONS, as well as the Department for Education in England and the Department of Transport, each organisation collects data on different things and uses different kinds of measures to meet their own organisational or regional remits. While this makes sense from the perspective of each sector, it creates major challenges for those trying to figure out what stories of inequality might be in these datasets.

According to the ONS, more comprehensive statistics are needed so that they can be measured against the Equality Act 2010 and the UN Sustainable Development Goals agenda of "leave no one behind" that strives for every person to "have a fair opportunity in life," prioritise those that are furthest behind, and make sure that "every person counts and will be counted."

A press release on this new data initiative stated, "ONS will work closely with providers and users of statistics about disability to improve appropriate harmonisation of data collection and promote routine disaggregation of data by disability. By mobilising the power of data, we can deliver a clear, accessible and coherent understanding of the experiences of disabled people and enable Government and wider society to make better decisions and improve lives."

The press release mentions the importance of qualitative data to understand individual experiences and life courses. They call for disabled people and advocacy groups to get in touch to help them bring open data together in ways that can explore how to get the best outcomes.

Find out more about this initiative at https://blog.ons.gov.uk/2019/06/25/ending-a-burning-injustice-how-the-ons-will-inform-the-drive-against-disability-discrimination/

Mini-Exercise: Open Data on Disability Reflection Questions

Using the case study above, along with other material from this workbook and outside sources, answer the following questions:

1. How might the 5-star Open Data system be applied to these problems that the ONS is facing?
2. Thinking back to Chapter Two on Narrative Approach, how can we understand this data problem in relation to the idea that 'all data has a back story'?
3. Look at some existing open data on disabled people in the UK. How might you apply the lessons in data as character to tell data stories with these statistics?

Defining Big Data

with Phil Wilkinson

Big data is a relatively recent term, typically used to describe the challenges and opportunities of working with large datasets. The term 'big data' is widely considered to have been coined in 1997, though its exact origin is debated. In its contemporary form, big data is enumerated through a series of descriptors known as the 5 (plus or minus 2) Vs. Originally, in 2001 Doug Laney proposed three Vs—Volume, Velocity, and Variety—to capture the modern challenges of data management. Since 2001 this definition has been expanded and, depending on your taste, there are anywhere between the 3 and 7 Vs. To offer a consensus, the descriptors most commonly used are Volume, Velocity, Variety, Veracity, and Visualisation.

Volume: The challenge of managing the sheer amount of data created and collected.

For illustration, in May 2014 the National Security Agency (NSA) finished its new data centre, aptly named the 'Massive Data Repository,' estimated to be able to store five Zettabytes of data, or 5,000,000 Petabytes. In 2017, the 'Paradise Papers' data leak totalled a comparatively measly 1.4 Terabytes of data—13.5 million documents. Inconspicuously accessing, downloading, and transferring this volume of data creates significant pragmatic issues—before even considering the data analysis and journalistic reporting.

Velocity: The challenge of managing the increasing rate at which data is created.

Since 1959 the *New York Times* has published 2.9 billion words. Every day in 2019, 10 billion words are published on Facebook. In 2015, for the first time there were more Internet of Things (IoT) devices connected to the internet than people. In 2018, IoT devices generated 18 Exabytes a day—or 18,000,000 Terabytes. These IoT devices increasingly include real-time tracking of personally identifiable or private data through smart-home devices or wearable technology.

→ The Internet of Things includes appliances, devices, machines, or living creatures that are digitally connected to the internet and are programmed to transfer data and perform actions without human involvement.

Variety: The challenge of managing the multiple forms of data created and shared.

Every 60 seconds, 168 million emails are sent, 25 hours of video content is uploaded to YouTube, and ~66,000 posts are uploaded to Instagram. For a more specific example, the 2016 'Panama Papers' data leak contained 2.6 Terabytes of data—11.5 million documents. These documents consisted of 4.8 million emails, 3 million databases, 2.1 million PDFs, and

1.1 million images. Meaningfully integrating these documents such that they could be collectively analysed presented a significant challenge for the International Consortium of Investigative Journalists.

Veracity: The challenge of ensuring that data collected and analysed is both accurate and applicable.

There are 8 billion words published on Twitter every day. Sentiment analysis through computer algorithms can ascertain sentiment (positive, neutral, or negative) through a collection of tweets referencing specific topics (such as political parties). However, a persistent issue with sentiment analysis is its inability to detect sarcasm. Indeed, computers, like humans to a degree, are unable to reliably verify sincerity of communication.

Visualisation: The challenge of articulating insights from data that are both understandable and meaningful to a broader, typically non-expert, audience.

This includes both the reduction of quantitative data into graphical formats for easier consumption, as well as well as making sure that the visualisation maintains the integrity of the data. Effective data visualisations, however, can highlight and reinforce a point, often used today in persuasive communication by businesses, non-profits, charities, and activists.

Case Study: Florence Nightingale's Rose Chart

One of the earliest examples of using visualisation to present 'big data' came from noted social reformer and statistician Florence Nightingale. *The Causes of Mortality* illustrates not just the causes of death, but also the relative proportion of these causes. By using a visualisation to present this data, Nightingale helped persuade the Queen and Parliament to influence public policy, setting up a sanitary commission to improve army barracks and hospitals, thereby reducing the number of preventable deaths from disease and unsanitary conditions.

Drawing on Florence Nightingale's work from 1858 may seem anachronistic, but there are historical antecedents to big data that are worth noting. Though the term big data is new, the phenomena of information archiving, retrieving, processing, and articulation has a rich history.

→ For more on early 'big data' visualisations see: www.smithsonianmag.com/history/surprising-history-infographic-180959563

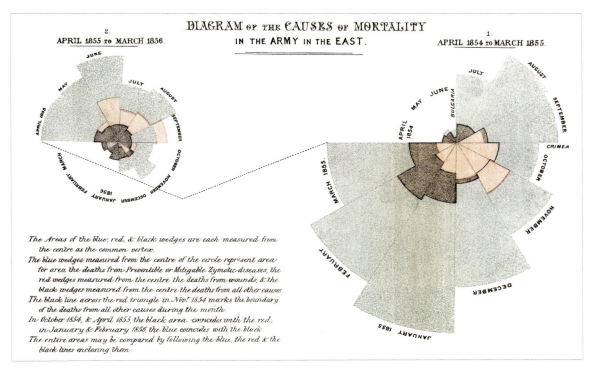

2.
APRIL 1855 ᴛᴏ MARCH 1856.

1.
APRIL 1854 ᴛᴏ MARCH 1855.

The Areas of the blue, red, & black wedges are each measured from
the centre as the common vertex.
The blue wedges measured from the centre of the circle represent area
for area the deaths from Preventible or Mitigable Zymotic diseases, the
red wedges measured from the centre the deaths from wounds, & the
black wedges measured from the centre the deaths from all other causes.
The black line across the red triangle in Nov.ʳ 1854 marks the boundary
of the deaths from all other causes during the month.
In October 1854, & April 1855, the black area coincides with the red,
in January & February 1856, the blue coincides with the black.
The entire areas may be compared by following the blue, the red & the
black lines enclosing them.

▹ **Florence Nightingale, "Diagram of the Causes of Morality in the Army of the East," 1858.** This polar area diagram uses size and colour to illustrate causes of death in the British Army.

Big Data Past and Futures

with Phil Wilkinson

Considering historical approaches in big data is important for two reasons. First, it acts as something of an inoculation against the uncritical way in which big data is sometimes used, as the term itself becomes increasingly vague through popularisation and overuse. As the popularity of big data is driven by commercial adoption, the term is often incorrectly used to refer to any aspect of data analytics, data sciences, or business intelligence. The second reason is that we can trace common issues from history that can provide additional context to our contemporary negotiations with a data-driven society.

In 1971, Arthur Miller, author of *The Assault on Privacy*, argued, "Too many information handlers seem to measure a man by the number of bits of storage capacity his dossier will occupy" (p. 256). In 1961, according to the Oxford Dictionary, the term 'information explosion' was coined to articulate the compounding increase of published information and the difficulty of managing this. In 1939, Henry D. Hubbard of the US National Bureau of Standards celebrated the "magic of graphs...the profile of a curve reveals in a flash a whole situation—the life history of an epidemic, a panic, or an era of prosperity. The curve informs the mind, awakens the imagination, convinces" (Brinton, 1939, p. 2).

Looking further back, in 1880 the U.S. Census was 'tabulated' using punch cards, repurposed from weaving looms, in an effort to reduce data processing time from 10 years to three months. Earlier still, in 1661 John Graunt presented his statistical analysis of the *Bills of Mortality*, an unwieldy collection of weekly mortality statistics in the City of London, as a few "perspicuous Tables" avoiding a "long series of multiloquicious Deduction" (Graunt, 1662, p. A3). Big data, then, should be viewed as a modern manifestation of historic issues. Though its challenges may not be entirely new, they are becoming increasingly significant in contemporary society and in the future.

→ Parkinson's Law refers to the idea that "work expands so as to fill the time available for its completion", coined by naval historian Cyril Parkinson in a 1955 article in *The Economist* that satirised bureaucracy in the workplace.

In 1980, I.A. Tjomsland argued that, like Parkinson's Law, data expands to fill the space provided. Regardless of how cheap data storage technology becomes, how much we have of it, or how many data centres we build, we will fill this storage capacity with data. In part this is driven by a presumed implicit value to data, as illustrated by the common adage of 'data is the new oil'—hence why nascent social media companies command market valuations in the billions despite not generating profit. There is a 'hoarding' of data by organisations because, as Tjomsland argues, "the penalties for storing obsolete data are less apparent than are the penalties for discarding potentially useful data" (Tjomsland, 1980).

There are of course penalties for this data hoarding, though those storing the data don't always feel them. On a global scale, data centres' energy demand is estimated to rise to 8% of global energy usage in 2030. As such, Greenpeace produces an annual report providing a scorecard, rating companies' usage of sustainable energy sources for their data centres.

→ Check out the Greenpeace score cards for different countries at www.clickclean.org.

Looking into the future for individuals, mass-collection of data by commercial and government entities makes it increasingly difficult to know who owns what data, where the data has come from, and, crucially, how the data is being used. Indeed, the recent Cambridge Analytica scandal in the UK and the revelations of NSA whistle-blowers in the U.S. provide a glance into a politicised, clandestine use of data to monitor and influence the broader public. The capacity for monitoring and influence will only increase in the future as mass-adoption of always-on smart devices and wearable technologies lead to real-time collection and analysis of private data and even biometrics.

Counting the Uncounted

While access to open data and the ability to collect and analyse big data can certainly diversify the kinds of narratives we tell with numbers, many important issues have no straightforward data source because the data is not gathered, or what is gathered is severely limited, redacted, or otherwise unavailable.

In cases where making information public could put governments at risk, data remains uncollected, kept hidden, or deemed too confidential to be made open. The major international controversies surrounding whistle-blowers like Chelsea Manning and Edward Snowden had to do, in part, with data that did exist, but was deemed to be a threat to national security when it was exposed. This can also be the case with smaller scale data collection where security issues at the individual or national level are concerned. Gary Marx (1984) described such practice as dirty data, referring to how texts that contain information that could be discrediting to government agencies get buried.

In other cases, data is missing because it is not in the interest of the government or organisation to collect such data. For example, as the case study below discusses further, there was no national policy in the United States for law enforcement officials to report officer-involved shootings. This meant that it was impossible to count—and thus to know—the scale of people killed by police. There remains no policy for police to systematically record and report uses of less lethal force. Likewise, there is no national or international policy that demands that the sale of less lethal weapons is tracked, even though their import and export often must go through government clearances. Thus, when journalists ask, 'How much tear gas is sold?' or, 'How many people died from tear gas in the last year?' our answer is, 'No one knows, because no one counts.'

As in the case of officer-involved killings and less lethal weapons, this lack of data raises concerns because it is about the health and human rights of people, and particularly of vulnerable populations (prisoners, detainees, migrants, children, those living in conflict zones). This issue of no data becomes even more complicated when it may be in the interest of those vulnerable people to stay invisible and uncounted because exposure could cause more harm than good.

For example, those who go uncounted in census data often do so because they feel that to be counted could expose them or put them at risk. In other cases people are uncounted because of difficulties understanding census questions. And in some cases, as with LGBT populations in the United States, populations go uncounted because the census does not ask questions that can produce representative data. Across these reasons for why data goes missing, the uncounted are most often children, ethnic and sexual minorities, those living in poverty and those living in urban, overcrowded housing.

Being uncounted in census data is not just a matter of representation. To go uncounted has effects for political participation, the allocation of public resources, and the gathering of data needed to make evidence-based cases for policy reforms. For example, in the United States children being counted in the census affects budgetary allocations for federal programs including the National School Lunch Program, Children's Health Insurance and the Head Start program that provides early childhood education, health nutrition, and parent support for low-income families. In the UK, The Royal British Legion started a campaign to get veterans counted in the 2021 Census. Their general director, Chris Simpkins told *The Telegraph*, "By adding questions to the 2021 UK Census we can help public bodies and charities to deliver the best services they can for our Armed Forces community where they are needed most" (Whitehead, 2016).

The census serves as a clear example of mass data collection and the problems produced when there is 'no data.' Because the census is a project of national governments, run by offices specialising in statistics, guided by teams of research experts, it serves as a perfect example of how complex the unequal terrain of data can be. Yet in some ways, this is an ideal case study of 'no data.' Scaling up this problem to international data collection on issues like undocumented migration, the arms trade, or domestic labour, comes with even bigger challenges associated with collecting, collating, and making contextual sense of what data is pieced together, bit by bit, in efforts to count the uncounted. Not all of these initiatives serve the interests of those counted. As data storytellers it is crucial to ask who is counting the uncounted and why?

Case Study: Citizen-Generated Data on Police Violence

In efforts to counter the problem of no data, many people turn to participatory data collection. This term refers to methodologies that generate data through civic participation. This can range from collecting water samples to look for contamination to sending tweets to journalists, as we see in "The Counted" project. This citizen-generated data can be used as an advocacy tool, putting pressure on organisations and governments to establish better public data protocols, and at times, shape new practices and policies (Gray et al., 2016).

Efforts in recent years to aggregate police killings in the United States are one prominent example of how data can be effectively generated as a response to the problem of 'no data.' As protests ignited by the uprisings in Ferguson, Missouri that followed the police shooting of unarmed black teenager Michael Brown on August 9, 2014 made national and international headlines, questions surrounding police violence, particularly against Black communities, came to the fore in America. Activists, advocacy groups, and journalists began to expose the poor state of official record keeping on officer-involved shootings.

Prior to Ferguson, the operational system in place for recording police killings was unsystematic and voluntary. Individual law enforcement agencies—of which there are more than 18,000 in the United States—could choose whether or not to submit their yearly stats on 'justifiable homicides,' which were defined as 'the killing of a felon in the line of duty.' Between 2005 and 2012, only 1,100 agencies reported justifiable homicides (Swaine et al., 2015). It was clear the police had a data problem.

→ You can view The Counted project archived at www.theguardian.com/us-news/series/counted-us-police-killings.

For an overview of citizen-generated data projects and their potential to influence policy see the report Changing What Counts at www.blog.okfn.org/2016/03/03/changing-what-counts.

Making this data problem visible on an international scale, major news projects began to aggregate, verify, and analyse incidents of police killing, distributing this information to the public through interactive graphics and data visualisations. These projects by *The Guardian* ("The Counted"), *The Washington Post* ("Fatal Force"), and earlier efforts begun by the "Fatal Encounters" project, marked a new era in police accountability. Their innovation and amplification was tied to the rise of collaborative social media technologies and platforms. Wiki-style websites, Twitter reports, encrypted emails, local news stories that could be shared at the click of a button, together with more traditional forms of reporting, made these data storytelling projects possible.

→ This section on police data is an excerpt from Anna Feigenbaum and Daniel Weissmann (forthcoming) What counts as police violence? A case study of data in CATO's Police Misconduct Reporting Project. *Canadian Journal of Communication.*

Data and Bias

People that support data-driven decision-making argue that one of its main advantages is its objectivity. Numbers often feel very depersonalised and computer operations such as algorithms are literally inhuman. This has caused many to conclude that data offers an objective viewpoint and that decisions that are data-led are more objective, rational, and evidence-based. Scholars taking on this view like Anderson and Anderson (2007) argue that math- and data-led programs minimize unconscious and conscious bias in human judgement. But this argument overlooks that the collection and interpretation of data always rests in human hands. This can significantly undermine the idea that data is objective. Researcher Kate Crawford (2013) refers to this belief as data fundamentalism, "the notion that correlation always indicates causation, and that massive data sets and predictive analytics always reflect objective truth."

When human influence is ignored, we risk producing bias. This can come in the form of creating inaccurate models for guiding policy, unfairly influencing opinion, or reproducing existing inequalities. Consider the following example: a major metropolitan area conducts a police satisfaction survey but only includes white participants. As a result, the survey outcome may be heavily skewed. This is not because racial groups have intrinsically different opinions, but because interactions with police differ depending on race. It is only by attending to these differences—of police brutality and poverty, for example—that we realise a single-race survey sample would produce highly misleading results.

Whenever we develop a research question, we do so with certain assumptions. In the example above, one assumption would be that race has no bearing on people's experiences with the police. If the research question became "How satisfied are white people with police?" this would more accurately reflect the types of conclusions that can be drawn from the data. Data becomes biased when researchers fail to account for the way that our assumptions can implicitly shape how we gather and interpret data.

This can have serious implications. In her book *Invisible Women: Data Bias in a World Designed for Men*, Caroline Criado Perez (2019) explores how history has systematically overlooked women and produced widespread bias across a number of industries. This happened in part because the majority of researchers and research participants have been men. She coined the term "gender data gap" (p. 13) to describe this phenomenon. She uses the example of the design history of car crash test dummies. First introduced in the 1950s, test dummies mimicked the average male's height, weight, muscle proportions, and spinal column. The data generated from these test crashes failed to consider the specific needs of women and how women might be differently affected by car crashes. This has produced major oversights in the automobile industry that continue to persist into the present-day. For example, women are at higher risk in rear-end collisions because they are up to three times more vulnerable to whiplash; but modern car seats, designed using a male test dummy, fail to account for these average differences. It was only in 2011 that manufacturers such as Volvo started using test dummies based on the female body—and they are still most often used in the passenger's seat. As in this example, there are many reasons why bias occurs, and overt prejudice is not always the cause. In the police survey example above, it is possible that the research team was all-white and thus failed to consider non-white perspectives. Or perhaps the research team only surveyed certain zip codes, effectively excluding certain groups.

→ **Volvo's pregnant crash test dummy.**
Copyright © Volvo Car Corporation.

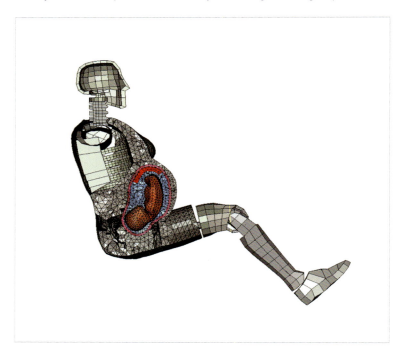

Standpoints Matter

Standpoint theory is one useful tool to identify and reduce bias in data. Standpoint theory was first introduced in the 1970s by feminist scientists and philosophers interested in articulating the relationship between knowledge and power. It argues that all knowledge is socially situated— that the knower's identities, perspectives, and experiences shape how they know what they know.

Critics of standpoint theory argue that it places too much restriction on who can study what. These critics argue that it is too limiting to say that people can only make knowledge-claims based on their own identities and experiences. But this is a misunderstanding. Standpoint theory is about seeing our situatedness as a resource for doing good research. It allows us to understand the assumptions we make when we ask a research question. Applied to data storytelling, it asks us to think about how our identities and experiences matter for how we go about gathering, analysing, and storytelling with data.

Standpoint theory has also been criticised on the grounds that it advocates for an epistemological relativism. These critiques ask, how can we make any claims to truth about the world if every knowledge-claim is relative to the speaker's social identity? But standpoint theorists (many of whom were scientists or had training in the sciences) do not claim that making evidence-based, testable observations is impossible; as Donna Haraway (2004) argues, "the alternative to relativism is not totalization and single vision" but "partial, locatable, critical knowledges sustaining the possibility of webs of connections called solidarity in politics and shared conversations in epistemology" (p. 89). What standpoint theory introduces is the possibility for a different kind of objectivity: one that eschews the totalizing 'god-trick' in favour of commitment to uncertainty and partiality in its claims.

→ Epistemological relativism is the idea that all knowledge is relative – that is, dependent on a specific context, society, culture, group, or individual. Extreme versions of epistemological relativism argue that one can't make any definitive claims about the world, because they are all dependent on the speaker. When Alex states that dirt is brown, Connor snidely remarks, "How do you know it's brown? To me all dirt looks purple."

In the previous section, we discussed the ways that bias can appear in research using the example of an all-white research team that conducts a police satisfaction survey. Their survey only collected data from white people, possibly skewing the results of their study. In this example, standpoint theory can help researchers understand their biases and produce stronger survey results by including respondents with diverse racial identities. How to best 'situate' one's identity in the data storytelling process is an ongoing discussion, but the first step occurs prior to any project being undertaken. Asking which perspectives are present (or absent) on a project, and how this may or may not affect the data storytelling process, will lead to stronger stories and more accurate evidence-based knowledge claims.

Worksheet: Addressing Data Bias with a Standpoint Approach

Using your own or someone else's data storytelling project, fill out this table to further explore the idea of standpoints and how they can benefit your data storytelling.

Stage of the Data Storytelling Process	What biases might emerge?	How could a Standpoint Approach help?
Coming up with your questions		
Data Collection		
Data Analysis		
Data Storytelling		
Sharing your data stories		

Data Discrimination

We live in a dataified world. Algorithms, machine learning, and social media are just a few technologies that have reshaped how data is collected, stored, and analysed. The rise of big data in particular has drastically changed decision-making in major sectors such as healthcare, education, insurance, and law (to name only a few). When bias is baked into data, it can have profound effects on the most important parts of people's lives. This has created a new type of discrimination, 'data discrimination', in which predictive algorithms, risk models, and other automatic processes exacerbate or reproduce existing inequalities.

In *Automating Inequality*, Virginia Eubanks (2018) notes that low-income people are dominated by data-driven systems, such as public assistance programs, that monitor and collect data on nearly every aspect of their lives. The instatement of these systems is built on political promises to lower the costs of welfare and reduce fraud, but the reality is often far different. Eubanks tells the story of a woman named Omega Young, who missed an appointment to recertify her Medicaid status because she was in the hospital due to terminal ovarian cancer. When she called the county Help Center to rectify the situation, she was told that her benefits had been terminated for "failure to cooperate" (p. 177). This decision was entirely automated.

Automation has also entered the world of employment, where data analytics are increasingly being used to determine whether a candidate should get a job. They're being used to determine everything from how high someone's car insurance premium should be set, to the likelihood that someone will have a heart attack. They're also being used to predict re-offending rates amongst people convicted of crimes.

The non-profit investigative journalism organization *ProPublica* critically examined a risk assessment product designed to score a defendant's likelihood of committing future crimes: the Correctional Offender Management Profiling for Alternative Sanctions, or COMPAS. Defendants are given a low, medium, or high risk ranking according to a set of scores generated from a 137-question survey given to defendants. This survey uses rankings based on nearly two dozen criteria that determine "criminogenic needs," including "substance abuse," "social isolation," and "residence/stability." COMPAS has been adopted by many jurisdictions across the United States. Judges often use it to determine sentences. If a defendant has a high-risk score, their bail may be higher or their sentence may be longer.

→ *ProPublica* host a Datastore that allows users to tell their own data stories using datasets provided by *ProPublica* and their collaborators. These datasets are on Health, Criminal Justice, Education, Politics, Business, Transportation, Military, Environment, and Finance. You can access them at www.propublica.org/datastore.

Advocates for the product argue that it will help decrease jail overcrowding by identifying low risk defendants. But in an independent analysis of COMPAS, ProPublica (Larson et al., 2016) found that "the score correctly predicted an offender's recidivism 61 percent of the time but was only correct in its predictions of violent recidivism 20 percent of the time."

In other words, 39% of the time, COMPAS incorrectly predicted that a defendant would commit another crime; for violent crime, it was wrong a whopping 80% of the time. That is a huge percentage of defendants who were given stricter bail terms or harsher sentences based on an algorithmic prediction – that turned out to be wrong. Most troublingly, ProPublica discovered that the tool's accurate prediction rate was equal for black and white defendants; but that when the tool got it wrong, it did so along racial lines: on average, white defendants' risk-score was underpredicted, while black defendants was over-predicted.

Unlike other forms of discrimination, data discrimination is uniquely dangerous for two main reasons. First, because it is based on automated processes, it carries the authoritative veneer of objectivity. This in turn makes data-driven outcomes appear rational and unchallengeable. Second, data tools are embedded within processes and technologies that are highly secretive and subtle. Complicated intellectual property laws make it difficult to uncover the exact mechanisms at work in many algorithms used by companies such as Facebook and Google. This makes them difficult to identify, let alone challenge or dismantle. As Eubanks (2018) notes, "With the notable exception of credit reporting, we have remarkably limited access to the equations, algorithms, and models that shape our life chances" (p. 5).

In order to prevent data discrimination, greater transparency is clearly needed, though transparency in itself is not enough. Data-driven systems are often highly technical, such that they may be confusing to people with no background in data science. What's needed is more empirical research into how discrimination emerges in data, more comprehensive law and policy around data and automation, and further collaboration between decision-makers and citizens into how data can best serve them in their lives.

Works Cited and Further Reading

→ Anderson, M., & Anderson, S.L. (2007). Machine ethics: creating an ethical intelligent agent. *AI Magazine*, 28(4), 15-58.

→ Andrejevic, M. (2014). Big data, big questions| the big data divide. *International Journal of Communication*, 8, 17.

→ Angwin, J., Larson, J., Mattu, S., & Kirchner, L. (2016, May 23). Machine bias. *Propublica*. Retrieved from https://www.propublica.org/article/machine-bias-risk-assessments-in-criminal-sentencing.

→ Ashery, S.F. (2019). *Micro-residential Dynamics: A Case Study of Whitechapel, London*. Cham, Switzerland: Springer.

→ Borgman, C. L. (2015). *Big Data, Little Data, No Data: Scholarship in the Networked World*. Cambridge, MA: The MIT Press.

→ Brinton, W. (1939). *Graphic Presentation*. New York, NY: Brinton Associates.

Crawford, K. (2013, April 1). The hidden biases in big data. *Harvard Business Review*. Retrieved from https://hbr.org/2013/04/the-hidden-biases-in-big-data.

Criado Perez, C. (2019). *Invisible Women: Data Bias in a World Designed for Men*. New York, NY: Abrams.

Eubanks, V. (2018). *Automating Inequality: How High-Tech Tools Profile, Police, and Punish the Poor*. New York, NY: St. Martin's Press.

Flint, S. (2017). Residential choices as a driving force to vertical segregation in Whitechapel. In A. Bregt, T. Sarjakoski, R. van Lammeren, & F. Rip (Eds.), *Societal Geo-innovation*. AGILE 2017. Lecture Notes in Geoinformation and Cartography. Cham, Switzerland: Springer.

Graunt, J. (1662). *Natural and Political Observations Mentioned in a Following Index, and Made upon the Bills of Mortality*. London: Thomas Roycroft.

Gray, J., Lämmerhirt, D., & Bounegru, L. (2016). Changing what counts: how can citizen-generated and civil society data be used as an advocacy tool to change official data collection?. *Available at SSRN 2742871*.

Gray, J., & Davies, T. (2015, May). Fighting phantom firms in the UK: From opening up datasets to reshaping data infrastructures?. May 27, 2015). Working paper presented at the Open Data Research Symposium at the 3rd International Open Government Data Conference in Ottawa, on May 27th 2015.

Gurstein, M. B. (2011). Open data: Empowering the empowered or effective data use for everyone?. *First Monday*, 16(2).

Haraway, D. (2004). Situated knowledges: The science question in feminism and the privilege of partial perspective. In S. Harding (Ed.), *The Feminist Standpoint Theory Reader: Intellectual and Political Controversies*. New York, NY: Routledge.

Larson, J., Surya, M., Kirchner, L., & Angwin, J. (2016, May 23). How we analyzed the COMPAS recidivism algorithm. *ProPublica*. Retrieved from https://www.propublica.org/article/how-we-analyzed-the-compas-recidivism-algorithm.

Lawson, S., Gray, J., & Mauri, M. (2015). Opening the black box of scholarly communication funding: A public data infrastructure for financial flows in academic publishing. *Available at SSRN 2690570*.

Marx, G.T. (1984). Notes on the discovery, collection, and assessment of hidden and dirty data. In J.W. Schneider, & J.I. Kitsuse (Eds.), *Studies in the Sociology of Social Problems* (pp. 78-113). Norwood, NJ: Ablex.

Miller, A. (1971). *The Assault on Privacy*. Ann Arbor, MI: The University of Michigan Press.

NCSA, The UK Civil Society Almanac 2017. Retrieved from https://data.ncvo.org.uk/a/almanac17/civil-society-data/

Swaine, J., Laughland, O., Lartey, J., & McCarthy, C. (2015). Young black men killed by US police at highest rate in year of 1,134 deaths. *The Guardian*, 31. Retrieved from https://www.theguardian.com/us-news/2017/jan/08/the-counted-police-killings-2016-young-black-men.

"The Counted." *The Guardian*. Retrieved from https://www.theguardian.com/us-news/series/counted-us-police-killings.

Tjomsland, I. (1980). Where do we go from here? In *Proceedings of Fourth IEE Symposium on Mass Storage Systems*. IEEE.

Whitehead, T. (2016, May 16). Call to count veterans in Census because UK knows more about 'Jedi Knights.' *The Telegraph*. Retrieved from https://www.telegraph.co.uk/news/2016/05/16/call-to-count-veterans-in-census-because-uk-knows-more-about-jed/.

Wilson, M. W. (2011). Training the eye: Formation of the geocoding subject. *Social & Cultural Geography*, 12(4), 357-376.

Spotlight:
The Journey of Jeans

Dr. Andrew Brooks is Senior Lecturer in Development and Environment in the Department of Geography at King's College London. He is the author of *Clothing Poverty: The Hidden World of Fast Fashion and Second-hand Clothes* (2015) and *The End of Development: A Global History of Poverty and Prosperity* (2017). Katelyn Toth-Fejel is an artist and PhD researcher at the London College of Fashion, University of the Arts. Her research draws from design, anthropology, and the visual arts to study the social practices of sustainability and community.

The Journey of Jeans highlights the political, social, and economic consequences of garment production around the world, using the iconic pair of blue jeans as its central model. The infographic visualises data sets from the UN Comtrade Database and the United Nations Environment Programme, as well as research from Dr. Brooks' book *Clothing Poverty*, to tell a vivid story of jeans from their production in countries such as Bangladesh, to their consumption in the Global North, to their recirculation in the Global South as discarded clothing.

The infographic uses the form of the biography to tell its story. By adopting this narrative structure, Dr. Brooks and Toth-Fejel transformed disparate data sets into a coherent narrative. The biographical form also makes visible the social relationships and historical themes that enliven the 'life' of the object. This recalls cultural anthropologist Igor Kopytoff's concept of "the cultural biography of things." For Kopytoff, commodities accumulate histories as they change hands and as they are transformed from raw materials to finished products ready for the market. *The Journey of Jeans* illustrates this 'cultural biography' by showing how a single pair of jeans acquires new meanings throughout the course of its 'life.'

For example, the infographic shows that while the consumer pays $35.00 for an average pair of jeans, the labourer makes only $1.67. The relative economic value of the jeans versus the labour required to make them reveals how objects take on changing degrees of significance.

In *The Journey of Jeans*, the form of the infographic is particularly effective in telling the biographical story of the object, as the structure of the graphic linearly guides the viewer's eye down the page. The infographic is also a modal format, which is reflected in the discrete graphs sequentially placed in the image. These blocks of information create pauses in the reading process, and offer the viewer moments of reflection and an opportunity to cognitively process what they are reading. *The Journey of Jeans* requires comparatively little data literacy and instead conveys meaning using aesthetic icons, colour, and a sequential format.

Perhaps most importantly, the infographic form offers a more accessible way for people to encounter the social sciences. By choosing this format, Brooks and Toth-Fejel invite the reader on an approachable, visually interesting journey: the journey of jeans.

→   Kopytoff, I. (1986). The cultural biography of things: Commoditization as process. In A. Appadurai (Ed.), *The Social Life of Things: Commodities in Cultural Perspective* (pp. 64-92). Cambridge: Cambridge University Press.

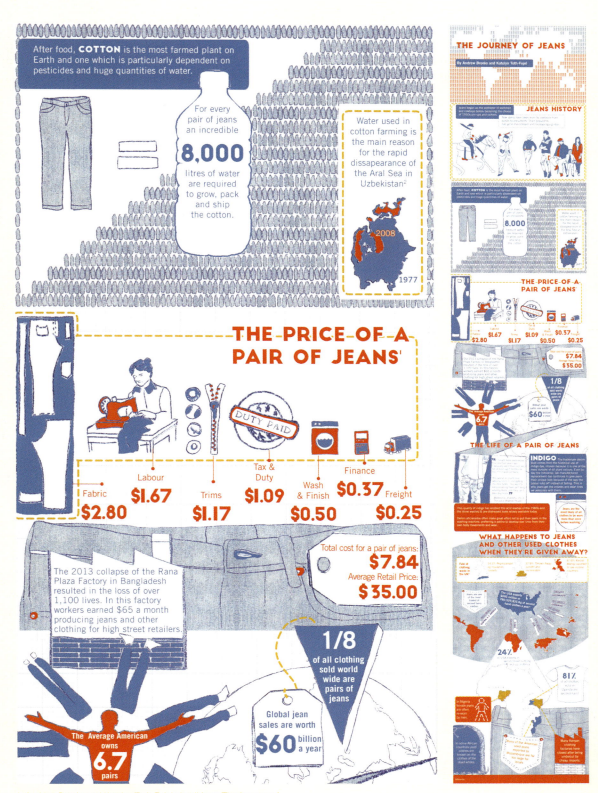

After food, **COTTON** is the most farmed plant on Earth and one which is particularly dependent on pesticides and huge quantities of water.

For every pair of jeans an incredible **8,000** litres of water are required to grow, pack and ship the cotton.

Water used in cotton farming is the main reason for the rapid dissapearance of the Aral Sea in Uzbekistan[2]

2008
1977

THE PRICE OF A PAIR OF JEANS[1]

DUTY PAID

Fabric **$2.80**
Labour **$1.67**
Trims **$1.17**
Tax & Duty **$1.09**
Wash & Finish **$0.50**
Finance **$0.37**
Freight **$0.25**

The 2013 collapse of the Rana Plaza Factory in Bangladesh resulted in the loss of over 1,100 lives. In this factory workers earned $65 a month producing jeans and other clothing for high street retailers.

Total cost for a pair of jeans: **$7.84**
Average Retail Price: **$35.00**

1/8 of all clothing sold world wide are pairs of jeans

Global jean sales are worth **$60** billion a year

The Average American owns **6.7** pairs

THE JOURNEY OF JEANS
By Andrew Brooks and Katelyn Toth-Fejel

JEANS HISTORY

THE PRICE OF A PAIR OF JEANS

THE LIFE OF A PAIR OF JEANS

INDIGO

WHAT HAPPENS TO JEANS AND OTHER USED CLOTHES WHEN THEY'RE GIVEN AWAY?

24%

81%

↳ Andrew Brooks and Katelyn Toth-Fejel, detail from *The Journey of Jeans*, 2015. Courtesy of the authors.

Spotlight:
The Centre for Investigative Journalism

The CIJ provides training in investigative journalism to journalists, researchers, and the public. They are based at the School of Journalism at Goldsmiths, University of London.

The CIJ is an experimental laboratory that teaches reporters new tools alongside the traditional craft of investigative journalism. We incubate promising new investigative projects and open out investigative journalism into fertile new territory.

Established in 2003 by the late investigative journalist and filmmaker Gavin MacFadyen as a response to the worrying decline of investigative reporting, our remit is like no other – we can take more risks than a conventional public interest publisher, be more radical than an advocacy NGO and be more innovative than either in championing new ways to do investigative journalism in the public interest.

We have been teaching data skills to journalists since the days when data journalism was known only as computer-aided-reporting or CAR, and were among the very first UK bodies to recognise the power of data analysis for public-interest investigations. With the help of the late data journalism pioneer, esteemed teacher, and multi-award winning journalist, David Donald, we were instrumental in bringing this technique across the Atlantic and establishing it as an important element in newsrooms across Europe.

Since those early days, we have trained thousands of journalists as well as NGO researchers, union campaigners, and human rights investigators in using data analysis for their work, always with our trademark investigative focus.

We have recently been working to address the narrowing demographics of investigative journalism through several initiatives: providing free skills training for new community-focused non-profit news organisations; funded bursary places to our annual Summer Conference for underrepresented groups; and a free masterclass programme to help those without connections in the media industry to overcome the barriers to entry faced by many.

In the era of "fake news", the CIJ wants to stimulate creative, critical and courageous thinking about what investigative journalism has become and where we want it to go from here. It's all the more pressing a task at a time when journalism is changing its form and where investigative journalism - the kind which holds power to account, and which shines a light on it at every turn - has to be nimble to survive.

By the Centre for Investigative Journalism

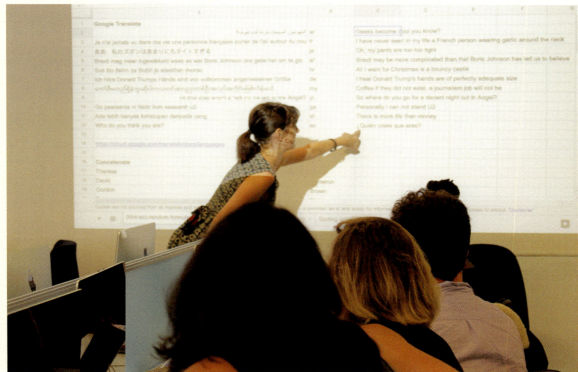

↳ Data skills training sessions at the CIJ. Courtesy of the Centre for
Investigative Journalism.

Spotlight:
Hasan Elahi

Hasan Elahi is an interdisciplinary artist whose work explores themes of migration, surveillance, and borders. He is currently Professor and Director of the School of Art at George Mason University. You can view *Tracking Transience* at www.trackingtransience.net.

In 2002, the FBI received a false tip associating artist Hasan Elahi with terrorist activities. Shortly after, he was detained at an airport, where he was subjected to invasive and relentless questioning by FBI agents. This would not be Elahi's last encounter with the FBI; the agency subsequently opened an investigation on him that lasted for six months. Although Elahi was ultimately cleared of suspicion, the experience catalysed the creation of his longest and most famous work to date: *Tracking Transience* (2003-present), an ongoing "project in self-surveillance" (Elahi, 2014). Since the project's commencement, Elahi has placed nearly every aspect of his life online: his real-time location (which is listed on the project website), transportation logs, and over 85,000 photographs documenting unmade beds he's slept in, airports he's travelled to, and half-eaten food he's recently consumed.

Before putting *Tracking Transience* online, Hasan sent reports of his whereabouts to the FBI agent that had been in charge of his case. The agent received long emails filled with pictures, as well as notes about daily activities and habits. Concealed inside this appearance of cooperation is a sharp rebuke. "You want to watch me? Fine," he writes. "But I can watch myself better than you can, and I can get a level of detail that you will never have" (Elahi, 2011).

Hasan notes that people's attitudes towards his project changed with the growth of social media use. "A few years ago, this project sounded like an artist's crazy idea. Now there are 1.6 billion people on Facebook doing the same thing, creating digital databases of themselves. You're all doing this, too" (Gerage, 2016). Although many of us object to large security apparatuses like the FBI or the NSA digitally monitoring us, we still participate in social media's data-hungry machinery by voluntarily putting gigabytes of personal data online. This isn't hypocrisy; it's the cost of living in contemporary society. *Tracking Transience* makes visible the compromises and contrivances inherent to these systems.

Although Hasan makes a large amount of data available, he controls what is shared and what is kept concealed. He is keenly aware of the half-truths present in the project and how these are reflected in the wider world of data collection. "I'm only telling one part of the story," he states (Elahi, 2014). He also purposefully designed his website to be non-user friendly, further undermining the appearance of openness. Its interface is confusing and anachronistic; photos aren't clearly labelled, and site navigation is poor. Amidst vehement public debate about big data and surveillance, Hasan's project offers a counterintuitive form of protest: show everything, reveal nothing.

→ Elahi, H. (2011, October 29). You want to track me? Here you go, F.B.I. Retrieved from https://www.nytimes.com/2011/10/30/opinion/sunday/giving-the-fbi-what-it-wants.html

→ Elahi, H. (2014, July 1). *I share everything. Or do I?* Retrieved from https://ideas.ted.com/i-share-everything-or-do-i/

→ Gerage, A. (2016, November 1). *Hasan Elahi Examines the Intersection of Technology and Art.* Retrieved from https://www.mccormick.northwestern.edu/news/articles/2016/11/hasan-elahi-examines-the-intersection-of-technology-and-art.html.

Spotlight:
Data Justice Lab

The Data Justice Lab investigates the social justice and political implications of datafication. The 'Data Scores as Governance' project maps and analyses where and how local governments are making use of data analytics for public services, with a particular focus on investigating uses of predictive analytics.

We started this project because we know that governments at all levels are making use of new data systems to try and improve their decision-making and service delivery, often as a response to being asked to do more with less. We also know that these systems are contentious, particularly when we are talking about uses of data systems to make predictions about people, needs, and funding. Our Data Harm Record provides a growing list of harms and risks that come with data systems. Given the risks and democratic implications that come with changing data systems public oversight and accountability is crucial. Yet we know very little about where and how data systems are being used despite recommendations that governments should be providing the public with lists of this. In the absence of this kind of list we set out to map and outline developments and practices across different contexts in the UK.

We used a multi-methods approach, one that enabled us to build a big picture overview of changing data practices and also enabled us to look at some examples in greater detail. We collected information by scraping government websites and filing freedom of information requests. We also held workshops to enable discussions between people across sectors. We did interviews with practitioners and civil society organizations working with impacted communities and service-users. In combination, this approach enabled the first systematic mapping of data systems across local authorities in the UK in combination with stakeholder perspectives.

The project to date has led to: 1) a map of data analytics systems across local authorities, 2) a research report that provides examples of different types of analytics systems and surveys civil society concerns, 3) an interactive online tool to facilitate greater research and debate and 4) a research article that situates findings in relation to changes in governance. We're also developing a video animation that will be posted on our website.

We found a rising trend of what we refer to as 'citizen scoring' with local authorities across the UK constructing numerous large and interlinked datasets, sometimes called 'data lakes' or 'data warehouses'. We found predictive analytics being used in child welfare, policing, fraud detection, public safety and transport. Applications differ from the use of data to assess changes at the level of the population and make planning and funding decisions, to applications that enable detailed profiling of individuals and families, to other applications that are being used to predict risk. Civil society organizations pointed to the potential for such data practices to lead to discrimination, stigmatisation, and surveillance, and stressed the need for greater public engagement, transparency, accountability, and regulation.

This project was funded by the Open Society Foundations. The project website, report and investigative tool can be found at www.datajusticelab.org/data-scores-as-governance. Further reading can be found at www.policyreview.info/articles/analysis/golden-view-data-driven-governance-scoring-society.

By Data Justice Lab

DATA JUSTICE
CONFERENCE

**Data
Justice
Lab**

21-22 May
2018
Cardiff University,
Cardiff, UK

↳ By Data Justice Lab

Spotlight:
Forensic Architecture

Forensic Architecture is a multidisciplinary research group based at Goldsmiths, University of London. Their investigations have explored cases of state violence and human rights violations using legal and digital media strategies. Their investigations have been used in courtrooms, cited at United Nations assemblies, and shown in art exhibitions around the world.

Forensic Architecture is a multidisciplinary research agency that combines digital technologies with investigative journalism to produce detailed inquiries into incidents of human rights violations. Their investigations address issues including environmental violence, police violence, and war-time human rights violations. The project 'Airstrikes on al-Hamidiah Hospital,' commissioned by Médecins Sans Frontières (Doctors Without Borders) in 2016, probed two airstrikes on a hospital in al-Hamidiah, Idlib Province, Syria. The bombings resulted in the deaths of twenty-five people and the destruction of the hospital. Russian and Syrian governments denied having any involvement in the attacks.

During the primary inquiry, Forensic Architecture collected photographs and video evidence, including satellite imagery, that showed Syrian and Russian planes departing from their respective bases at a time consistent with the bombings. They cross-referenced this information with first-hand testimony from survivors and witnesses to produce a timeline of events leading to the attack. Mégo Terzian, president of MSF France, acknowledges that "What Forensic Architecture has found is not 100 percent proof, but it is better than nothing. We want to find out the truth. I have no illusions that it will be difficult to obtain justice, but this work makes it possible to denounce the perpetrators of these criminal acts."

Within the agency, the project Forensic Oceanography works on investigations related to violence against migrants crossing the Mediterranean Sea. Their work on the 'left-to-die boat' event (2012) is a case study in

how researchers, artists, and scientists can use advanced data tools in their civic and social justice-oriented projects on the migrant crisis. The 'left-to-die' boat investigation critically probed an incident in 2011 in which a migrant boat was left drifting for two weeks in the Mediterranean, despite being within NATO's jurisdiction and surveillance zone. As a result of this negligence, sixty-three migrants died. As this case illustrates, it is not merely the turbulence of the sea itself which poses a risk to migrants; deaths occur even after state authorities become aware of boats. Charles Heller and Lorenzo Pezzani, co-founders of Forensic Oceanography, first became aware of this incident after the NGO *Groupe d'information et de soutien des immigrés* (GISTI) announced their intentions in June 2011 to file a legal suit against EU, NATO, and Frontex, the EU's border control agency, for failure to assist migrants.

In 2012, Forensic Oceanography published the results of their inquiry. They found "with certainty that the Italian and Maltese Maritime Rescue Coordination Centers, as well as NATO command, were informed of the location and distress of the migrants, and that there were several naval assets in the vicinity of the boat that had the ability to detect and assist it. None of these actors intervened in a way that could have averted the 63 deaths" (Pezzani, 2015, p. 129). To come to this conclusion, Forensic Oceanography conducted a comprehensive preliminary investigation "to build an overall understanding of the conditions in which maritime crossings were taking place" (Pezzani, 2015, p. 129). They interviewed migrants that had recently crossed the Mediterranean, representatives

↳ A composite of multiple satellite images above al-Hamidiah,
Syria, showing camera positions and lines of sight. Courtesy of
Forensic Architecture.

from the Coast Guard, and fishermen operating in the area. During the primary inquiry, they used a number of different computer and electronic tools to recreate the incident. They also interviewed survivors, the Eritrean priest who first received the vessel's distress call, as well as official statements and reports from government officials and Frotex representatives. The final report was submitted in a lawsuit on behalf of two survivors.

In these projects, data is not only visualized, but used as evidence in legal cases in order to establish culpability. By using tools that are usually employed to enforce dehumanizing surveillance regimes or to monitor airspace for wartime violence, researchers are able to identify human rights violations where the state bears fault or responsibility. Charles Heller describes this as a 'disobedient gaze': using the instruments of state violence to critically redirect the hegemonic gaze that seeks to "obscure the violence of the border regime" (Hinger, 2018).

Forensic Architecture can be thought of as a fugitive project, working from the 'inside' in order to operate authoritatively in varying contexts. By working from both inside and outside systems of power, Forensic Architecture is creating landmark interventions in the fields of journalism, documentary art, and human rights.

Forensic Architecture was founded by architect Eyal Weizman. Weizman also founded the Centre for Research Architecture at Goldsmith University's Department of Visual Cultures. Forensic Oceanography was launched in 2011 by architect Lorenzo Pezzani and researcher and filmmaker Charles Heller.

→ UNHCR (2012, January 31). Mediterranean takes record as most deadly stretch of water for refugees and migrants in 2011. Retrieved from https://www.unhcr.org/en-us/news/briefing/2012/1/4f27e01f9/mediterranean-takes-record-deadly-stretch-water-refugees-migrants-2011.html

→ Pezzani, L. (2015). Liquid traces: Spatial practices, aesthetics and humanitarian dilemmas at the maritime borders of the EU (Doctoral disseration). Retrieved from https://research.gold.ac.uk/12573/1/Redacted_ARC_thesis_PezzaniL_2015.pdf

→ Hinger, S. (2018). Transformative trajectories – The shifting editerranean border regime and the challenges of critical knowledge production. An Interview with Charles Heller and Lorenzo Pezzani. *Movements. Journal for Critical Migration and Border Regime Studies, 4*(1). Retrieved from http://movements-journal.org/issues/06.wissen/12.hinger--transformative-trajectories-the-shifting-mediterranean-border-regime-and-the-challenges-of-critical-knowledge-production-charles-heller-lorenzo-pezzani.html

→ 15 February 2017. Using technology to build evidence after a hospital attack. *Médecins Sans Frontières*. Retrieved from https://www.msf.org.uk/artic e/using-technology-build-evidence-after-hospital-attack.

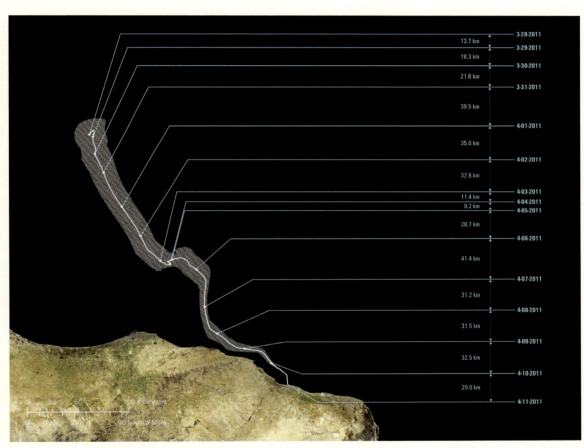

3-28-2011
13.7 km
3-29-2011
18.3 km
3-30-2011
21.6 km
3-31-2011
39.5 km
4-01-2011
35.0 km
4-02-2011
32.8 km
4-03-2011
11.4 km
4-04-2011
9.2 km
4-05-2011
28.7 km
4-06-2011
41.4 km
4-07-2011
31.2 km
4-08-2011
31.5 km
4-09-2011
32.5 km
4-10-2011
29.0 km
4-11-2011

0   25   50   100 Kilometers

0   12.5   25   50 Nautical Miles

↳ Hourly positions of the drifting vessel were calculated using daily Nucleus for European Modelling of the Ocean (NEMO) surface current data and hourly Lampedusa airport wind data. Sea surface currents were modeled by Istituto Nazionale di Geofisica e Vulcanologia (INGV) and the meteological data was provided by Euroweather. Courtesy of Forensic Architecture.

Spotlight:
Amnesty Decoders

Amnesty Decoders is a crowdsourcing platform inspiring a new generation of tech-savvy activists to become human rights monitors and help document human rights violations. The platform leverages micro-tasking technologies to engage tens of thousands of activists in processing large volumes of data such as satellite imagery, documents, pictures or social media messages that are used to showcase human rights violations patterns at large scale.

Amnesty Decoders started in June 2016 and uses crowdsourcing to engage digital activists in ground-breaking human rights research. Micro-tasking allows researchers to split large projects into small tasks that can be distributed over the Internet to many people. Micro-tasking "workplaces" like Mechanical Turk or ClickWorker connect business with "micro-workers" allowing them to outsource work like tagging photos, digitising receipts and invoices, etc. This technology is also used in the non-for-profit sector in order to solve complex problems that require many hands on deck or problems that machines and algorithms alone can't solve. Micro-tasking proved to be particularly useful for campaigning organisations that are looking to engage large amounts of people in their work.

Micro-tasking enabled Amnesty to engage activists in sifting through huge volumes of data, processing millions of "micro-tasks", such as pinpointing destroyed villages in small parcels of satellite images in Darfur, detecting online violence against women in social media messages, or extracting key information from handwritten oil spills investigation reports in Nigeria.

In addition to processing data for large scale research, microtasking is an opportunity to engage digital activists in meaningful ways. Going beyond "clicktivism", Amnesty Decoders leverages technology to bring together a global, diverse community of Decoders to contribute in very concrete ways to human rights monitoring.

Case study – How 3,500 digital activists took on Shell
The Niger Delta is Africa's most important oil-producing region, and one of the most polluted places on Earth.

Some of the corporations working in the Niger Delta publish investigation reports and photographs of oil spills, but most of the information that would allow organisations like Amnesty International to probe the credibility of this evidence is 'trapped' in handwritten and scanned documents.

To transform thousands of documents and photographs into structured data, Amnesty enlisted digital activists and used micro-tasking to channel their efforts. In total, 3,545 people from 142 countries took part in Amnesty's Decode Oil Spills project. They answered 163,063 individual questions and worked 1,300 hours, the equivalent of someone working full-time for eight months. The Decoders analysed 3,592 documents and photographs, helping create the first independent, structured databases of oil spills in the Niger Delta, covering spills from January 2011 to December 2017.

Step 1: Define the task and methodology
The first step in putting together the Decode Oil Spills project was to work with our researchers to define a task for our Decoders. The main goal was to extract key information from documents and photographs relating to oil spills that have been made public by two of the largest companies operating in the Niger Delta: Shell and Eni. But these documents were an average

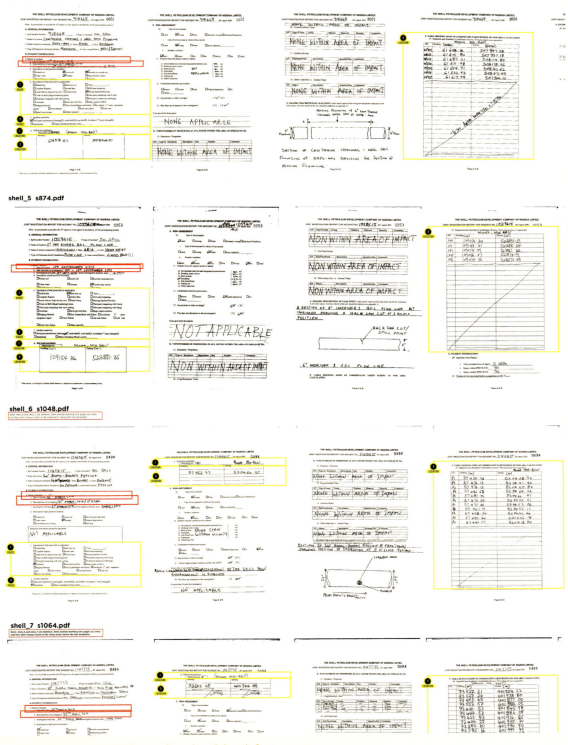

4 Shell changed their data collection template at least 9 times in 6 years. Courtesy of Amnesty Decoders.

of 8 pages long and extremely rich in details. We had to narrow down our research questions to make sure we collected the relevant data needed to hold Shell and Eni to account, while creating "micro-tasks" that were doable in a short time with limited training. After numerous workshops we narrowed down the tasks to extracting the cause, location, and size of spills from the documents. We also wanted Decoders to corroborate the information provided by the corporations with images taken at the spill.

Step 2: Get data, archive and pre-process

The next step was to gather all the data that the corporations made public, which included some structured data along with the documents and photographs for each spill. Before downloading the data, we had to check the companies' "Terms of Use" and consult legal advice to make sure we could use the documents as intended. While processing the data, we found that there were huge inconsistencies in the data collection forms used by the company and we had to find ways to mitigate these issues.

Step 3: Design and develop

To engage thousands of people, we had to focus on developing a tool that has both an extremely user-friendly interface and a strong database to collect all the contributions.

Step 4: Engage volunteers

We worked with campaigns and communications specialists on an engagement strategy which included media work, email campaigns, social media outreach and offline events organised by our sections.

To estimate the volume of Decoders we need to get a task done, we use a basic engagement model: 90% of the volunteers will review 2-5 documents, 9% will engage with an average of 20-40 documents and 1% of the volunteers will become super users, reviewing hundreds of documents and also helping others in the community. To engage the power users and make sure we answer their questions, we also have a community forum where Decoders can speak directly with Amnesty staff members.

Step 5: Verify, analyse, publish

The main verification mechanism of micro-tasking is ensuring that each task is completed by multiple Decoders—the exact number varies from project to project and is determined in a testing phase. To verify the data, we check for agreement between all the Decoders who complete a task, and also check if they agree with Amnesty researchers participating in the project. In this project we also consulted external pipeline experts to corroborate the findings.

The result was a wealth of evidence pointing to negligence on behalf of the companies. Decoders identified at least 89 spills about which there are reasonable doubts surrounding the cause provided by the oil companies. For example, Decoders highlighted photos wherein spills that appear to have been caused by corrosion were attributed to theft by the corporations. If confirmed, this could mean that dozens of affected communities have not received the compensation that they deserve.

Challenges and Opportunities

In the future, we are looking to combine this type of crowdsourcing with machine learning to scale research even further, building algorithms that automate tasks like feature extraction from satellite images, analysis of large databases of social media posts to identify potentially abusive messages, etc.

But challenges like access to data, developers and data scientists, together with securing dedicated budgets remain an obstacle for large scale adoption of these projects by non-profit organisations.

For more information on microtasking, go to: library. theengineroom.org/microtasking.

By Amnesty Decoders

□ Under water ☑ Swampy ☑ Exposed pipe surface
□ Well Plateform (on Water) □ Rig
e. Description of leak point (tick as applicable);
□ Drilled hole □ Hack saw cut □ Explosive tear,
☑ Complete Rupture □ Inward dent, □ Well head tampering
□ Failed Weld-on illegal hot tap valve, □ Missing Pipeline/Flowline
□ Crude oil theft (illegal) bunkering) point, □ Third party tampering with Clamp
□ Third party tampering with valve setting, □ Third party tampering with flange,
□ Corrosion □ Saver-pit over flow, □ Surge vessel overflow
□ Outward dent □ Flare System/Bund wall failure
□ Valve Failure □ com unit failure □ Cold vent
□ Relief valve failure □ Others (specify)_____

f. Incident caused by:
□ Third party interference ☑ Operational □ Mystery_____

g. Spill point coordinates
Measuring unit METER   (MINNA MID-BELT)

Northing:	Easting:
48207.85	429058.07

4. Incident caused by:
Please look at the highlighted section of the document and let us know which options are checked/ticked by choosing options below

Which option(s) are ticked/checked? (if any)

□ Third party interference
☑ Operational
□ Mystery

PREVIOUS   FINISH

🔍 View entire report
⚠ Issue with this task?

↳ Screenshot of Decode Oil Spills interface. Courtesy of Amnesty Decoders.

→ Example of social media message to recruit Decoders. Courtesy of Amnesty Decoders.

Amnesty West & Central Africa ✓
@AmnestyWARO

Got 30 seconds this morning?
Help us decode oil spills in the Niger Delta.
amn.st/60138UR5F

WHAT COULD THEY HAVE TO HIDE?

AMNESTY INTERNATIONAL

5:11 AM · Jul 9, 2017 · Twitter for iPhone

Spotlight:
Data Journalism Handbook

Drawing on the time that we have spent exploring the field of data journalism through the development of the *Data Journalism Handbook*, we propose twelve challenges for "critical data practice." These consider data journalism in terms of its capacities to shape relations between different actors as well as to produce representations about the world.

1. How can data journalism projects account for the collective character of digital data, platforms, algorithms and online devices, including the interplay between digital technologies and digital cultures?

2. How can data journalism projects tell stories about big issues at scale (e.g. climate change, inequality, multinational taxation, migration) while also affirming the provisionality and acknowledging the models, assumptions and uncertainty involved in the production of numbers?

3. How can data journalism projects tell stories both with and about data including the various actors, processes, institutions, infrastructures and forms of knowledge through which data is made?

4. How can data journalism projects cultivate their own ways of making things intelligible, meaningful and relatable through data, without simply uncritically advancing the ways of knowing "baked into" data from dominant institutions, infrastructures and practices?

5. How can data journalism projects acknowledge and experiment with the visual cultures and aesthetics that they draw on, including through combinations of data visualisations and other visual materials?

6. How can data journalism projects make space for public participation and intervention in interrogating established data sources and re-imagining which issues are accounted for through data, and how?

7. How might data journalists cultivate and consciously affirm their own styles of working with

data, which may draw on, yet remain distinct from fields such as statistics, data science and social media analytics?

8. How can the field of data journalism develop memory practices to archive and preserve their work, as well as situating it in relation to practices and cultures that they draw on?

9. How can data journalism projects collaborate around transnational issues in ways which avoid the logic of the platform and the colony, and affirm innovations at the periphery?

10. How can data journalism support marginalised communities to use data to tell their own stories on their own terms, rather than telling their stories for them?

11. How can data journalism projects develop their own alternative and inventive ways of accounting for their value and impact in the world, beyond social media metrics and impact methodologies established in other fields?

12. How might data journalism develop a style of objectivity which affirms, rather than minimises, its own role in intervening in the world and in shaping relations between different actors in collective life?

By Jonathan Gray and Liliana Bounegru

Edited by Jonathan Gray and Liliana Bounegru

THE DATA JOURNALISM HANDBOOK

Towards a Critical Data Practice

Amsterdam
University
Press

Spotlight:
Housing Justice Database Project

The Housing Justice Database project was an interdisciplinary collaboration between Concrete Action, The Centre for Investigative Journalism, and Bournemouth University's Civic Media Hub.

London housing is in a state of permanent crisis, with no beginning and no end. Many advocacy organisations, community groups, and journalists involved in housing justice struggles are using data to produce vibrant evidence-based campaigns that promote accountability and transparency in planning and urban development.

The Data for Housing Justice pilot project ran from January to July 2017. This initiative brought together campaign groups, researchers, and journalists working with data around housing struggles in the UK, to create a participatory data infrastructure that could offer ongoing and future struggles more accessible information for action. Following initial planning meetings, the team conducted a survey of people working with data for housing justice. Results from the survey helped us design a participatory workshop, run in London on 15th May 2017. Outputs from the workshop then fed into a prototype design process.

Prior to our participatory workshop, a short survey was sent to the participants to better assess their needs and expectations and to identify the common issues regarding the use of data in housing justice work. The survey consisted of 6 sections with a mix of multiple choice, open-ended and Likert-scale questions. The survey was shared with 33 invitees and was answered by 15 people. The respondents stated that they mostly used housing databases for academic research and advocacy work, and that they mostly use Excel and Google sheets as data management systems. A majority of the respondents obtain necessary data from their own research, from others' research reports, and from government websites. The housing data they work with is mostly stored in .XML, .DOC, and .PDF file formats.

The most pressing outcome of the survey is that there is a vast diversity in data skills of those working in this area. There was also no consensus on the types of housing data most used by the participants. However, a majority of respondents did share their struggles working with information that is redacted, buried, or not updated consistently. There was a shared frustration that a variety of possibly useful data is not accessible. It was also noted that the social and environmental costs of housing issues are not recorded as public data. A few participants stated problems with the response rates and quality of data provided by Freedom of Information requests. Respondents also indicated a lack of geolocative data and insufficient mapping of information according to the geographic areas that are affected. Supporting our initial motivations for running this project, the respondents reported that the datasets needed for housing justice work are difficult to integrate, aggregate, and cross-reference. The poor state of data on housing makes evidence-based analysis and advocacy challenging.

Workshop presentations and activities were organised to help us think about how we can create efficient and sustainable participatory data infrastructures that could be used by housing campaign groups, journalists, academics and the architectural profession.

Workshop Aims

1. Investigate the different data types that people encounter in their work around housing justice.

2. Foster participants' capacities for working with data for housing justice.

3. Use participants' insights to generate guiding principles for an open source Data for Housing Justice

↳ Mapping types of housing data: Workshop participants brainstorm different types of data used in housing justice work. Then they cluster those data types into categories based on where they come from.

interface prototype.

4. Lay the foundations for an effective Participatory Data Infrastructure, to be documented in a project report.

The Housing Justice Database workshop took place in the Amnesty Human Rights Action Centre on 15 May 2017. In the first part of the workshop, participants were given an introduction to participatory data structures and housing justice datasets. For the first activity, the participants were asked to write the types of housing data on post-it notes (timeline, housing data, repairs, locations etc.) according to their accessibility, and then try to group these different lists of data according to their usefulness to find emerging themes. According to the feedback from the groups, we then identified several issues regarding the accessibility and reliability of housing data. The most common problem was that data sources for housing data are not always included and there is a lot of fabricated or manipulated data, which jeopardises the reliability of the information. In addition, we identified that the social costs of housing issues are not recorded.

The second part of the workshop started with two masterclasses on working with data, where workshop participants were introduced to a range of ways that data can be collectivised and used to tell stories. The participants were also given an introduction to different tools and software that they can use to scrape, clean, analyse and visualise different types of data. After this we had a second activity that asked participants to prioritise the types of data they used in their work and rate the accessibility of that data. The key insights that emerged from this activity included:

→ Lack of standardisation in the recordings of data

→ Cleanliness of the data does not correlate to usefulness

→ Classifying data in relation to its relevance to certain stories and ease of use is more beneficial than dismissing data as 'dirty'

→ Looking at the variables within individual databases can be useful to identify or clarify useful data from 'dirty' databases.

The day ended with a group discussion on next steps. We established that the prototype should focus on individual councils and could be organised around the different types of data that emerge throughout the regeneration process. This place-based focus on the timeline of the housing regeneration process has a number of advantages:

1. Reflects the existing ways that organisations use data in their research and advocacy

2. Eliminates the need for technical knowledge around document types

3. Makes visible the links between different stakeholders involved in the regeneration process, and cross-references the data they produce.

Our project sought to bring data (and people!) together through the creation of a public database on housing, which can cross-fertilise community and industry projects. It can help these civic groups identify common points of reference, and prevent duplication of work, saving time and money. Linking data together helps generate data literacy, open information, and combat the fragmentation and lack of accountability that results from scattered data. In this way, generating such improved data tools can help address the housing crisis in London, working toward more affordable homes for UK residents.

↳ Plotting openness of data: Workshop participants plot the 'openness' of data on housing. In this activity there are two axes. The vertical runs from open to closed, and the horizontal runs from most to least useful. Then participants plot the sticky notes of data types onto the graph.

Activity:
Host a Hackday for Database Building

 Author

Name
Edward Apeh & Anna Feigenbaum

Affiliation
Bournemouth University

Biography
Dr. Edward Apeh is a Senior Lecturer in Computing at Bournemouth University and a member of the BU Civic Media Hub.

 Materials

→ Computers with internet access
→ White board

 Space Needed

Collaborative, computer lab.

 Aim

The aim of this hackday is to improve key word searching in order to refine information retrieval processes.

 Go Digital / Go Analogue

Go Analogue – This hack day is designed to be digital. However, you could develop keywords by reading printouts of sample documents and brainstorming on a flipchart.

 Group Size

A hackday works best with between 5 and 50 people.

 Top Tips or Additional Notes?

Use the white board to live document your key findings, as well as recording them digitally.

 Duration

1 day.

Task

To help sort out the messiness of many data retrieval tasks, we need more refined keywords. The following steps will help improve our keywords, which then improves our query strings. In other words, this hackday activity is designed to refine the process that brings us the information that we want to see.

Developing a keyword guide
For each type of sought after information, we need (a) keywords; (b) file names; (c) example url IDs

Fine tuning keywords
To enhance our keyword guide, go to a sample set of websites and investigate the text they are already using. This would involve the following steps:

1. Use your keyword guide to investigate what keywords and repeated phrases appear on the website's documentation around your issue.
2. Note down the keywords, any document names and url IDs.
3. This will be used to refine keywords currently in your keyword guide.

Fine tuning with JSON
To further refine our keyword guide, we can then retrieve JSON records to evaluate how well our API queries are doing. This would involve the following steps: For each returned record, perform an evaluation that includes the following: Relevance Check: Is the returned record relevant to the information type you are trying to retrieve? If not – Should it be assigned to a different type of information? Or is it not relevant at all? If yes – What are the keywords that appear in the record?

Sample Activity Plan

Based on a 6 hour hackday

30 min:	Introduction to the information retrieval problems and the task of improving them
1 hour:	Developing a Keyword Guide
30 min:	Feedback
30 min:	Lunch break
1 hour:	Fine Tuning Keywords
30 min:	Feedback
15 min:	Break
1 hour:	Fine Tuning with JSON
30 min:	Feedback
15 min:	Wrap up

Activity:
Digging for Financial Data

 Author

Name
Corporate Watch

Biography
Corporate Watch is a not-for-profit co-operative providing critical information on the social and environmental impacts of corporations and capitalism.

Twitter
@CorpWatchUK

 Materials

→ Computers with internet access

 Space Needed

Any space with a stable wi-fi connection.

 Aim

This activity is designed to teach participants the basic elements of digging through financial data in order to investigate corporate accountability.

 Go Digital / Go Analogue

Go Analogue – If you don't have stable wi-fi access, you can do this activity by printing out the financial accounts and searching for these figures by hand.

 Group Size

This module activity was designed for self-guided learning, but could be run in a group workshop format.

 Top Tips or Additional Notes?

For this activity to work, create a scenario prompt based on a UK registered company. If you want to search a US company, pick one that is publicly traded and you can find simlar documents on EDGAR which can be accessed through the Secruties and Exchange Commission website. www.sec.gov/edgar/searchedgar/companysearch.html

 Duration

1 hour.

Task

Scenario Prompt

You find out a company is not paying its worker a fair wage. The company says it cannot afford to pay more. But is this true? To try and answer this question a good first step is to look at the company's recent finances.

More than one company often have the same or similar names. For this reason, it is best to go to the company's official website. Often the full name of the company is in the lower banner or in a legal document on the website like the privacy policy or terms and conditions.

Note down the company number to be able to easily find information across sources for this company. Now go to Companies House https://beta.companieshouse.gov.uk/company and search by this number. Then click on filing history to see all the documents the company has submitted.

Now find the most recent financial accounts. These documents are long, so the trick is knowing where to look!
1. First, find the record of profits. Notice there are loads of different types of profit. Look at profit for the year.
2. Then look at how much the people at the top are making. Directors are the people running the company. You want to find out details on their pay or remuneration. This can appear in different places. Try looking for Director Remuneration.
3. Next look for how shareholders are doing. Money paid to shareholders are called dividends. By locating the cash flow statement you can see how much shareholders were paid out in the last financial year.

Sample Activity Plan

10 min:	Introduction to task and Companies House website
30 min:	Digging for financial data
20 min:	Feedback on exercise. If self-directed, have participants answer a set of follow-up questions online. In a workshop format, this can be a facilitated group discussion.

For example:
1. How does jargon make this task difficult?
2. What other barriers were there to locating the financial data you wanted?
3. How could this open access to financial information be improved?
4. How might you tell a data story using this uncovered financial data?

Activity:
Risk assessment for crowdsourcing projects

 Author

Name
Milena Marin

Affiliation
Amnesty International

Biography
Milena Marin works for Amnesty International on complex, large scale human rights investigations leveraging open-source information, crowdsourcing and data.

Twitter
@milena_iul

 Materials

→ Pens
→ Paper
→ Post-its and flip charts or whiteboard

 Space Needed

A comfortable, private room with stable wi-fi access.

 Aim

The aim of this activity is to assist teams interested in implementing crowdsourcing projects in assessing feasibility, evaluating risks, making a better-informed decision and producing a more robust product.

 Go Digital / Go Analogue

Go Digital – This exercise is great for in-person meetings but can easily be adapted for online collaboration. You just need a reliable video-conferencing tool and a shared document that allows all participants to collaborate and take notes.

 Group Size

The activity is designed for small groups of people directly involved in the project design. This activity works best with a diverse, inter-disciplinary team. Some roles you may want to include are issue specialists or researchers, campaigners, policy specialists or lawyers, project managers, beneficiaries, technical engineers, designers and cyber-security specialists.

 Top Tips or Additional Notes?

If your group is smaller than 10, you can run through all the criteria together. If the group is larger, split the team into 2–3 groups. Ensure diversity of expertise and opinions in each group.

This can be a hard exercise as you and the team will go through ways in which your project could fail. Be ready to think of ways to overcome risks but also to accept that some risks are not worth taking.

 Duration

1–2 hours depending on the size of the group.

Task

For each of the following criteria discuss and document:
(i) the intensity of risk (low, medium, high); (ii) the risk itself; and (iii) possible mitigation strategies.

Risk assessment criteria:
- → Sensitivity – look into the context of the project and the sensitivity of the data you want to analyse with the crowdsourcing project. Highly sensitive projects are not well suited for volunteers' participation.
- → Graphic nature – human rights research requires analysis of graphic material. While some levels of graphic content can be used with proper mitigation strategies, content like sexual violence, killings, torture or incidents involving children are never suitable for digital volunteers.
- → Risks of harming users – think of ways through which participating in your crowdsourcing project may harm users. For example, for people in certain countries, it may be dangerous to be associated with your organisation or working on your specific project. Assessing potential harm for users will also enable you to make decisions like: do you require registration for users or are people allowed to contribute anonymously? What data will you collect about your users? A data minimalist approach will minimise risks to users.
- → Ability to engage – collectively volunteers can dedicate hundreds and even thousands of hours of work to crowdsourcing projects but they will also require constant communications and follow up. Organisations need to consider their ability to engage with volunteers during and after the project. This may include the need to allocate dedicated staff or volunteers to oversee communications and engagement.
- → Degree of training required – crowdsourcing projects usually engage non-specialised audiences so it's critical to ensure that anyone can contribute by designing simple tasks that can be easily explained and exemplified. Projects that require lengthy or very specialised training are not suitable for crowdsourcing.
- → Transparency – a human rights risk assessment is conducted to determine whether the crowdsourced data can be shared. The data can be anywhere from private to shared with vetted partners to fully open based on the risks.
- → Data validation – planning for valid data is critical to the success of a project. Key considerations for data validity include: a well designed project with clear instructions; continuous engagement of volunteers making sure their questions are answered; redundancy in the data (ensuring each image is labeled by multiple volunteers); expert contributions; analysis of the accuracy of each labeller relative to their peers and the experts; inter-labeller validity analysis.
- → Risks of malicious attacks and misuse of data – crowdsourcing projects can become targets of malicious actors. Each project will face a different level of risks so these have to be assessed on a project by project basis.

Sample Activity Plan

Based on a 2 hour meeting

15 min:	Introduce the team and the task
60 min:	Assessment activity
30 min:	Feedback on risk assessments
15 min:	Takeaways and next steps

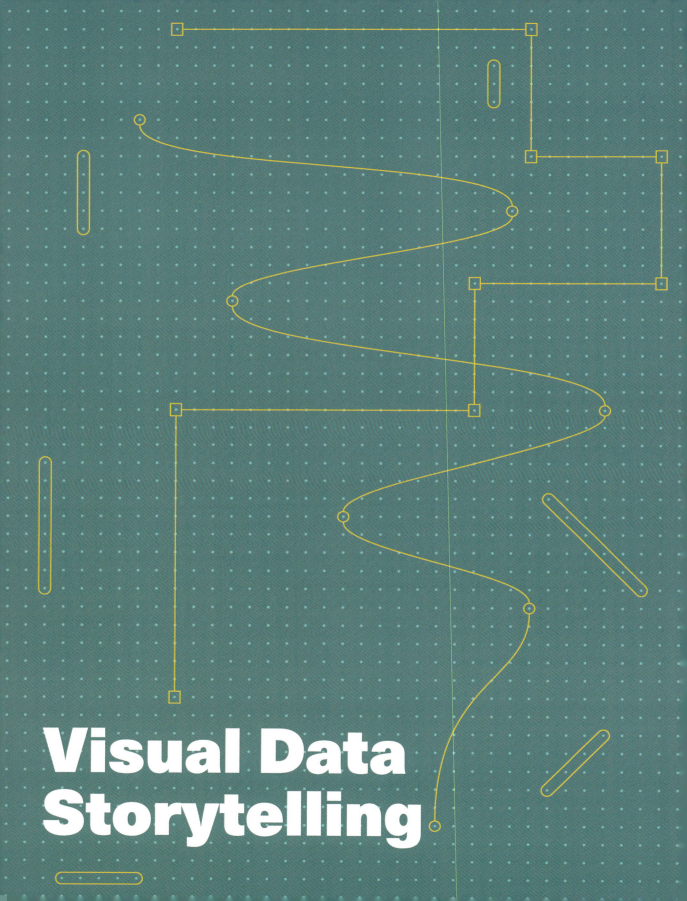

Visual Data
Storytelling

Visual Data Storytelling

During the 19th century visualising information came into what Michael Friendly (2008) calls the 'Golden Age of Statistical Graphics.' This accompanied the rise of state-run statistical offices collecting demographic data, alongside the increased use of statistics in the sciences, astronomy, urban planning, and commerce. Quantitative data collection and evaluative thinking gave way to a range of graphical developments for representing statistical information. While government institutions were the primary users of these new graphic techniques, this period also saw the employment of information visualisation for social campaigns, including John Snow's cholera map and Florence Nightingale's rose diagram on preventable deaths in the Crimea War.

Today, 19th century conventions for the graphical display of information continue to be used by data visualisation designers (Kennedy et al., 2016). Visualisation libraries like D3 and Gephi, as well as software programmes like Tableau, embed these conventions into contemporary design practice. There are many benefits to these platforms in terms of saving time and resources. First, these platforms make it increasingly easy to visualise data without needing to participate in other parts of the data process, i.e. its collection, cleaning, or even analysis. Second, templates are often already set up with 'best practice' chart design, colours, and caption placement. This frees users from needing to make these decisions. For audiences, the repeated use of templates can help build literacy through repetition. As they rely on dominant forms of graphical representation that have been in circulation often for over 100 years, the viewer's eyes are already trained to interpret what they are seeing.

At the same time, templates can also limit creative potential and opportunities for innovative data exploration and storytelling. In addition, because templates repeat dominant representational rules and forms, the content can get diluted by the sameness of the representation. In other words, when the same graphic symbols and colour schemes tell the story of fuel prices, animal shelters, political races, and sports statistics, the individuality of the data and its story can get lost. This template fatigue can lead to people seeing the data point but not connecting with the subjects of data. Too much use of the same template comes with the risk of creating visual data stories that get further and further abstracted from the question of 'what is at stake?'

Too much plugging data into templates without reflection can also make it difficult to answer the question 'Why does this visualisation matter?' When the process of designing a visualisation is detached from the process of data collection, preparation, and analysis, it can be hard to create a meaningful data story. Understanding the context, backstory, or potential biases of the data you are working with is important for adding meaning. Without this understanding, you are left with only the surface to work with.

→ You can learn more about John Snow's Cholera map in the section The Problem with Maps as Representations and Florence Nightingale's rose diagram in Defining Big Data.

→ D3 is a JavaScript library for visualising data using web standards. It can help visualisation designers produce dynamic, interactive data visualisations for web browsers. Gephi is a non-profit Open Graph Viz Platform that is widely used by academics and industry for both exploring and communicating data, particularly related to network analysis. Many of the data visualisations you see around the web are made with these popular resources. For more information, go to www.gephi.org and www.d3js.org.

→ Tableau is primarily designed for data analysts within businesses. However, while it is generally used internally by organisations, Tableau Public has point and click functionality that allows people to generate visualisations without the need for extensive coding. Many journalists, non-profits, political commentators and fan communities use this version of Tableau to easily create and share visualisations. Extensive galleries, online tips, and blog posts are available to explore at www.tableau.com.

This is why our BU Civic Media Hub approach aims to be more holistic. Along with many of the other data storytelling teams discussed in this workbook, we integrate visualisation into the process of our data story-telling. As visualisations are both representational artefacts and explor-atory tools, they can lead to richer understandings of the data you are working with. Thus, rather than treat visualisation as a separate design step that comes after all the data analysis is complete, it can function as part of a two-way communication system. Taking this approach, we find that often the most important questions emerge during the process of visualising for our data stories: What standpoints are being privileged? Who or what is missing? How can we better account for the biases and backstory in our datasets?

In order for data visualisation to be about more than making information beautiful, it must be approached with the same reflective and critical thinking as any other aspect of a data storytelling project. This is why we believe that people should be equipped with the conceptual and prac-tical tools needed to tell visual data stories that matter. These tools are what help us grapple with the challenges of graphic design and visual storytelling. They are what allow us to engage with the challenges of sen-sitive subjects, missing data, messy data, data biases, and all the other obstacles that working with data throws our way.

Feminist Data Visualisation

Our approach to visual data storytelling is indebted to recent work in fem-inist data visualisation. One of the main things that feminist data visualis-ation is concerned with is how biases in perception and representation can become embedded into design practice. These biases often get repeated in data visualisations without reflection or questioning. As a re-sult, negative stereotypes can be reproduced, marginalised voices can get erased or obscured, and many issues can get left out of visual data stories all together.

A basic example of how this happens in visual data storytelling comes with the represention of gender—one of the most common binary di-vides found in data. In infographics and other data visualisations, gender representations are often limited to the traditional bathroom sign iconog-raphy for man and woman. A long haired figure in a dress is contrasted to a short haired figure with straight legs. Imagine that you are creating a visual data story. If these are the only options available in a design tem-plate or icon set, yet you want to represent gender differently, what would you do? How could you go for a gender-neutral approach? A similar gen-dered bias occurs in visual symbols when, for example, all sports icons depict male figures doing activities or when icons for particular profes-sions are gendered exclusively male or female.

→ In visual culture, binaries refer to binary oppositions or two categories that are set in contrast to each other, such as man/woman, love/hate, nature/culture, straight/gay. Bina-ry oppositions are also often linked together, for example in dominant stereotypes of 'mother earth': woman-love-nature.

→ In the 2018 release of Streamline 3.0, one of the largest sets of icons available, designers added more diversity. Icon editor Vincent Le Moign wrote in an article posted to Medium, "With Streamline 3.0, almost all user and profession icons received a female variation. We've also added a gender neutral version for the user category." Find it at www.medium.com/streamline-icons/whats-new-in-streamline-3-0-1439d0951931.

Behind the scenes, problems of bias and representation also occur, limiting the kinds of data stories we can tell. For example, if the data being visualised does not include any demographic information about gender, then gender cannot be visualised at all. For example, a dataset our BU Civic Media Hub team worked with from CATO's National Police Misconduct Reporting Project, did not have gender attached to its data points. All acts of police misconduct in the dataset were recorded by general type (i.e. assault, drunk driving, perjury). So, while the dataset counted acts of violence, it did not record any information on whether that violence was gendered. This means that anyone visualising directly from the existing dataset would be unable to even begin to represent information on instances of gendered violence.

In this case, the information on gender was available in the recap summaries of the act of misconduct and in the linked newspaper stories (Feigenbaum and Weissmann, forthcoming). However, because it had not been recorded into its own column on the spreadsheet, it could not be visualised in any pre-programmed template. It was only after we noticed this pattern when reading through the recap summaries that we decided to add additional codes to the dataset. By doing so we found that violence against women, including sexual assault and domestic abuse, was a dominant form of police misconduct. This pointed to the need to tell an additional data story about the gendered nature of recorded police violence against women. To visually tell that story with statistical graphics, first we needed to notice that the information was missing.

While these examples discussed so far are about gender, the same principles hold true for how we visually represent race, age, disability, sexuality, class, and other categories that are important for addressing diversity, inequalities, and injustices. Thinking beyond the human, this is also the case for how we represent buildings, cars, dogs and trees—to name only a few representable nonhumans. In fact, all of the visual decisions that we make are influenced by existing cultural, social, and economic norms and practices. These kinds of dominant representations are embedded in the history of design and continue to be found in the modern-day visualisation software and templates we use.

For Catherine D'Ignazio and Lauren Klein (2016) a feminist approach to data visualisation addresses this issue head on. It challenges people to reflect on the decisions they make about the visual representation of information in order to enrich our current data visualisation practices. They argue that, while centred on design, a feminist approach to data visualisation "insists that data, design, and community of use, are inextricably intertwined." In line with our approach at BU Civic Media Hub, this means that we cannot separate the question of where data comes from and what audiences our data stories are for, from the processes of creating them. To help guide practitioners' work, D'Ignazio and Klein offer six core principles of Feminist Data Visualisation.

D'Ignazio and Klein Core Principles of Feminist Data		
D'Ignazio & Klein Core Principle	Summary from D'Ignazio & Klein	Consider...
Rethink binaries	Feminist data visualisation should emphasise representational strategies premised on multiplicity rather than binaries. This holds for visualisation, as well as data collection and classification.	How might we classify 'the multiple' in relation to gender categories, mixed race, sexuality spectrums?
Embrace pluralism	Move away from the single 'view from nowhere' toward designs that facilitate pathways to multiple truths.	How could a visualisation of people's job satisfaction, holiday travel, or use of social media be designed to incorporate and represent multiple perspectives or standpoints?
Examine power and encourage empowerment	Think about user communities rather than users as individuals, focus on design that can help communities advance their goals and build capacity to achieve them.	How could a visualisation about rental prices, school performances, or air pollution be designed to help empower community users to make decisions and take action?
Consider context	Knowledge is situated and design can try to better reflect the social, cultural, and material context in which that knowledge is produced. Participatory design for data collection and presentation can help enrich context.	What kind of participatory process might be used to generate and represent data on rental prices, school performances, or air pollution?
Legitimise embodiment and affect	Emotional and sensory ways of knowing can inform how visualisations are designed. This may include expanding types of data visualisation to include data sculptures, public walks, quilts, and other installations.	What might a walk to data visualise holiday travel look like? A sculpture on information about job satisfaction? Or a quilt about social media use?
Make the labour of the process of data visualisation more visible	Often when users only see an end product, the labour that went into making it is masked. Instead, making visible each step and who worked on it can help share credit for all stages of the work, making often invisible labour, visible.	What kind of meta data can you provide? Are there details on work that was done by interns, administrative assistants, or IT repair people? What might it look like to keep a data diary of all these aspects of work?

Challenges for
Data Visualisation

Overlapping in part with these feminist principles, in our work with clients and designers we have identified three key areas where current data visualisation conventions face their biggest challenges and limitations:

Exclusivity – People often think that data visualisation requires advanced skills, training, and resources, as well as institutional support and infrastructure. This is largely because the data visualisations we see circulating in the glossy pages of mainstream magazines and newspapers appear both beautiful and complex. Neon coloured radial diagrams can be daunting for data storytelling beginners. The thought of learning to code, understanding statistics, and wrapping your head around five kinds of tree diagrams (none of which look like trees) is overwhelming.

When data visualisation is presented to us as being about making complexity beautiful, rather than telling a story that matters, the task of data visualisation can feel out of reach. Starting from what the end product looks like can lead people to believe that they are not good enough artists, statisticians, or computer scientists to ever become visual data storytellers (Feigenbaum et al., 2016). This can make people feel excluded from practices of data visualisation before they have even begun to imagine what visual stories their data might tell.

Sanitisation & Impersonalisation – Data visualisations, especially when using templates and pre-existing libraries like D3, often prioritise formal structure and cleanliness over emotion and empathy, as D'Ignazio and Klein discuss in relation to feminist data visualisation. This can lead to visualisations that feel aloof, turning humans into clean lines and oversimplified icons without providing any sense of personhood. Sanitisation also sometimes involves a zooming out, as is common, for example, in social network graphs created from big data. Haraway refers to this as the "godtrick" of seeing from everywhere and nowhere (D'Ignazio and Klein, 2016; Kennedy et al., 2016).

Inability to Capture Complex Personhood – Following from this, data visualisations struggle to account for what Avery Gordon (2008) refers to as 'complex personhood,' the idea that people are always beset by contradictions, struggling to narrate their own lives. Gordon argues that people have changing senses of self and construct their identities with and between others. In other words, not only do people occupy multiple categories and have unique standpoints, but also, these categories and standpoints are always works in process. People change.

Qualitative research often makes efforts to capture such complexity by providing excerpts from interviews and focus groups that can offer narrative and context by making space for people's voices. Likewise, thick description in ethnography includes contextual details that help readers understand the social meaning behind human behaviour. But how can we turn these textual descriptions of complexity into visualisations?

Moreover, many of the issues facing the world today—from climate change to housing, from migration to mental health—all involve interplays between humans, animals, environments, objects, and systems. They are what archeology professor Ian Hodder (2012) calls human–thing entanglements. Similar to new materialists like Jane Bennett (2010), Hodder sees nonhumans as vital and vibrant. They are caught up in contingent relationships with humans, full of dependencies and co-dependencies.

Clay entanglements in the first part of the sequence of occupation at Çatalhöyük.
Originally published in *Entangled*, 2012.
Courtesy of Chris Doherty and Ian Hodder.

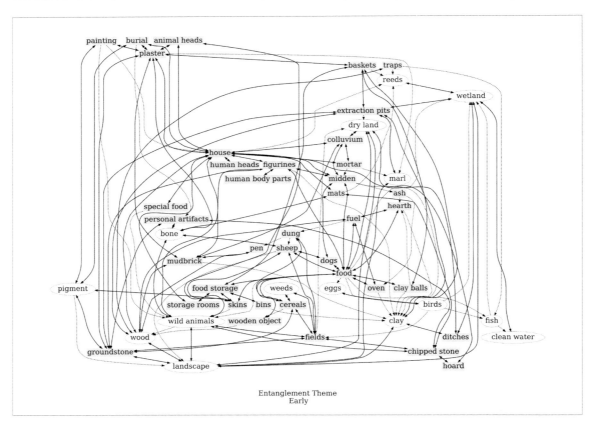

Entanglement Theme
Early

Using a tanglegram to illustrate this, Hodder and his colleague Chris Doherty tried to trace some of the threads of entanglement to make sense of the role of clay in the ancient proto-city settlement of Çatalhöyük. Lines with arrows connect nonhumans together, mapping out the threads of dependence and dependency surrounding the uses of clay. Each link is based on an interpretation of material evidence from archaeological research at the site. Reflecting on their process of creating this diagram, Hodder writes:

An important caveat about this diagram is that it cannot claim to be exhaustive. It is only a partial mapping. A real world mapping would be infinitely more complex ... The diagrams can only be a broad scheme for what people do and what they have to think about. They cannot claim to be complete or stable.

Reality is simply too messy and too complex to capture. But the process of visualising entanglement led to some important reflections. It helped to highlight which things were most entangled and to identify how humans had become dependent on particular nonhumans in ways that were both generative and constraining (Hodder, 2012, p. 181-184). In other words, it was the process of visually organising this information that revealed the data stories that mattered.

Working from a feminist approach to data visualisation, and taking account of these existing limitations, in the sections that follow we offer practical principles for turning data into evidence-based visual stories. We begin with a quick introduction to structuring your data, written for those of you who collect qualitative data, but may not have much experience with spreadsheets. We then introduce semiotics, a foundational set of concepts for understanding visual communication. This brief introduction to semiotics is provided for those of you who may be very familiar with spreadsheets, but are new to communication studies.

Following these introductions, we explore the finer details of putting together a visual data story by breaking down the visual representation of data into four componant parts or what we have called 'The Four Pillars': Symbol, Colour, Caption, and Editorial. We then delve deeper into the world of data visualisation, using Andy Kirk's CHRTS guide for selecting what graph best suits different kinds of data, based on the messages or meanings you want to communicate to your target audience.

A Quick Guide to Structuring Your Data

For those of you already working with spreadsheets or relational databases, structured data is something you will be familiar with. However, for those new to this terminology, understanding how data is structured (or unstructured) will lead to better data thinking and with it, better data visualisations. Becoming familiar with structured data can help you more efficiently and effectively record, store, and manipulate your data, making it much easier to tell visual data stories. This kind of basic data literacy will also help you get a better sense of what chart types to pick, how to troubleshoot when things go wrong, and how to know when anomalies are likely to be data input errors, rather than riveting data stories.

In our trainings with humanities researchers, journalists, and NGOs, we often find that people have vast, rich piles of data that could be visualised in charts or graphs, but they are stored in a format that makes it incredibly difficult to begin the task of data visualisation. For example, contacts and their affiliations may be typed up in one long list. Information on different people or organisations might be laid out in a table, but that table is in a Word document. Or someone might be using a spreadsheet, but each cell contains a bunch of random information that varies across the rows. Most often when working with these clients and collaborators, we find that data is not only recorded in unstructured ways, it is also spread across a number of different documents and file types (or in one case, across a drawer full of old Post-it Notes!). Before you can begin to visualise data, it is often useful to transform it into something more structured.

While some people are completely new to the idea of structuring data, others may rely on software programmes and dashboards to do the work of ordering, recording, or visualising data for them. In these cases, understanding what goes on behind the interface of the data tools you are using is important for increasing your data literacy and with it, the capacity to tell better data stories. Research software programmes like SPSS and Nvivo, as well as automated dashboards used by statistical offices, companies, and universities, often mask the actual processes involved in creating structured data. They limit what we can see and manipulate. In doing so, they are already shaping the kinds of stories we can tell. This contributes to data biases and absences, as discussed in the previous chapter.

As we become more and more reliant on computers to do the work of structuring and visualising data for us, we become less and less mindful of the importance of digging into the data in front of us. A pretty automated graph or pre-analysed sales figure may look good in a report, but when we cut and paste from dashboards without understanding how the graphs and numbers we are using got there, we are limiting our capacity to critically question data and the ways it shapes decision-making. This is why we encourage our students and clients to always seek out their data's backstory.

Case Study: From Archival Notes to Data Visualisations

Imagine that you are using historical materials to trace out the history of record shops in London. Each time you find a piece of archival information on a record shop, you note down the name, address, and what went on in the record shop (perhaps it hosted live gigs or had a recording studio in the back). As you go to enter this information into a Word document table, you implement a footnote style font to differentiate variables. This system works well for you as you are familiar with Word and you can search the text using the Find function when you need to look something up.

However, in order to create charts and graphs with this data, first it will need more structure. Moving this information from a Word document table into a spreadsheet is relatively simple, but like any data entry task, it is also time consuming and requires careful planning. Each record shop needs to be in its own row and then everything that describes that record shop needs to be in a column relating to that row. Addresses should be in their own cell, or multiple cells, depending on how precise you want to be able to generate coordinates. If you set the data up like this, then you can begin to make tables, maps, line graphs, etc., all using the same spreadsheet of your data.

To help ensure that you are consistently entering data, you can create data validations in each column. This functionality generates a drop-down list so that you can easily select from a limited set of variables that reoccur in your dataset. There are many books and tutorials online that offer introductory lessons in working with spreadsheets. You can also sign up for a course at a local university, library, or training centre. Learning how to work with spreadsheets is an important foundational skill for anyone wanting to become a data storyteller.

→ Data validation allows you to make rules for what one can enter into a cell on a spreadsheet. This is useful for maintaining consistency in data entry, as well as for guiding users, especially if multiple people are doing data entry on the same dataset.

Google Sheets offers extensive step-by-step guides in their online help centre at www.support.google.com/docs.

One of the biggest challenges when creating or modifying datasets is the tedious task of cleaning data. But the harsh reality is, the more structure you give to your data early on, the easier it makes your life, and the lives of others later. This means creating well thought-out spreadsheets in advance of moving or modifying your data, using data validation functions to ensure consistency (especially if you have more than one person inputting information), and becoming familiar with cleaning software like Openrefine, particularly for larger datasets.

→ Openrefine is "a free, open source, powerful tool for working with messy data." You can access Openrefine and tutorials on how to use it at www.openrefine.org.

Semiotics for Data Storytelling

While spreadsheets can feel like a familiar dialect to some, to others they are a daunting foreign language to learn. Likewise, those with backgrounds in communication studies may spot the meaning of a message instantly that would remain undetectable to someone else without any training in the field. Just as structured data is essential to those working with data, semiotics, or the study of signs, can help data storytellers better account for how people respond to visual representations (Hullman and Diakopoulos, 2011).

Perhaps the most well-known theory of semiotics comes from Roland Barthes. Drawing on the work of linguist Ferdinand de Saussure, Barthes (1972) argued that there are two basic levels of meaning. Denotation refers to the most basic description of an image. This may include things like shape, colour, and position. The second level of meaning, connotation, refers to the emotions, values, and associations that denotations give rise to. The level of connotation is where culture, background, and experience come into play. Lastly, for Barthes, there is what he calls myth. Myth refers to the broader ideological systems that give meaning to a sign, its context.

	1. Signifier	2. Signified	
Language MYTH	3. Sign I. SIGNIFIER		II. SIGNIFIED
	III. SIGNIFIED		

For example, a simple icon of a red rose may have the denotation of green line and red top. Then it may have the connotation of 'love' or 'gift'. At the same time, it also taps into a broader system of romance, bringing to mind entire narratives: a gift on Valentine's day for a new young couple. A man apologising for something he's done wrong. The Bachelorette selecting who gets to stay in the mansion. Depending on an individual viewer's background experiences, cultural context, and perspective or standpoint, interpretations will be different. The rose icon carries with it all of these possibilities, and a good semiotician can anticipate them and plan accordingly.

→ **Rose illustration**
By Loki Ba from the Noun Project.

Learning how to read denotation, connotation, and myth provides insight into how the simplest of images can be loaded with layers of meaning. When working with data visualisation, this is a crucial skill. It allows one to see a visual representation of data from a variety of perspectives, remaining aware of the diverse cultural meanings that come into play when interpreting a sign. In particular, thinking like a mythologist can help improve our decision-making around colour, shape, and emotion. This is important when visually representing sensitive subjects or creating icons that will travel across languages and cultures.

When applied to planning for visualisation, semiotics can help a data story-teller put questions about perspective at the centre of their process. Decisions about visual representation can be made according to the distinction between formal qualities (i.e. shape, colour, position), and how these come to take on meaning. Likewise, semiotics can help us better anticipate what to encode into visualisation, by helping us reflect on the different layers of meaning that the decoder or individual viewer may see. In this way, semiotics helps us understand the importance of perspective, of audience, and of different standpoints. Working from this introduction to semiotics for data storytelling, in the next section we turn to what we call the "Four Pillars of Data Visualisation": Symbol, Colour, Caption and Editorial.

→ Another terminology used in cultural studies to think about how communication works is Stuart Hall's notion of encoding and decoding. Encoding is the production of meaning in a cultural artefact and decoding is how a viewer understands or interprets the meaning of a cultural artefact. Contexts, standpoints and perspectives can make the encoded and decoded meanings different, and can explain differences in how individuals or communities decode meaning. These terms became popular in subcultural studies to explore things like punk.

Four Pillars for Data Storytelling

Reflecting in advance about the range of meanings an image can have, and about how different perspectives might lead to different interpretations of an image, is crucial for generating effective visual data stories for your audience. At the same time, there are also some universal design principles that can serve as a foundation for creating visual data stories. These principles hold whether you are making a network graph using big data, or an infographic that mixes personal testimonies with small-scale numeric data. To help make sense of the hundreds of universal design principles out there, we've organised those that we have found most useful in our visual data storytelling trainings into Four Pillars: Symbol, Colour, Caption, and Editorial.

Symbol

Just like data is defined differently across different fields, so too is the meaning of the word 'symbol.' In semiotics a symbol is differentiated from an icon and an index, which are all categorised under the heading of 'signs'. Web designer and author Stephen Bradley (2016) explains the differences:

→ An **Icon** has a physical resemblance to the signified, the thing being represented. A photograph is a good example as it certainly resembles whatever it depicts.

→ An **Index** shows evidence of what's being represented. A good example is using an image of smoke to indicate fire.

→ A **Symbol** has no resemblance between the signifier and the signified. The connection between them must be culturally learned. Numbers and alphabets are good examples. There's nothing inherent in the number 9 to indicate what it represents. It must be culturally learned.

Using a different definition, cartographers' symbols are the visual features used on a map to represent its features. In map symbolisation, no differentiation is made between what semioticians refer to as icons, images, or symbols. Instead they divide their symbols into points, lines and areas or polygons. The term symbol can refer to everything from the use of a straight line to represent a road, to the use of a rectangle to represent a type of building.

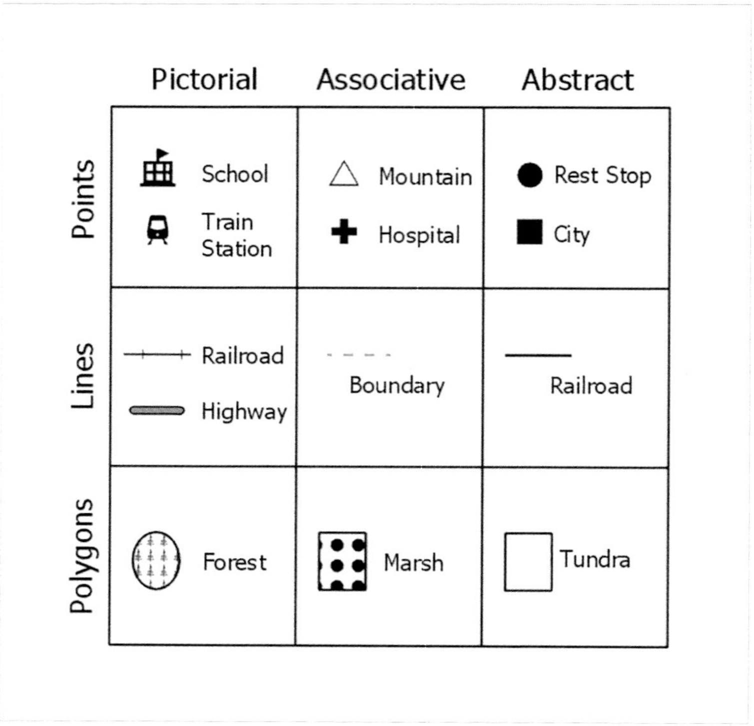

→ This chart shows examples of the types of symbols used in cartography.

	Pictorial	Associative	Abstract
Points	⊞ School / 🚆 Train Station	△ Mountain / ✚ Hospital	● Rest Stop / ■ City
Lines	┼──┼ Railroad / ▭ Highway	- - - - Boundary	─── Railroad
Polygons	Forest	Marsh	Tundra

To make matters even more complicated, in interface design, it is icons and not signs that are broken down into multiple types. Lidwell et al. (2003, p. 110) draw from previous work in the field to differentiate between four types of icons:

Similar – use images that are visually analogous to an action, object or concept. They are most effective at representing simple actions, objects, or concepts, and less effective when the complexity increases. For example, a sign indicating a sharp curve ahead can be represented by a similar icon (e.g., curved line).

Example - use images of things that exemplify or are commonly associated with an action, object or concept. For example, a sign indicating the location of an airport uses an image of an airplane, rather than an image representing an airport.

Symbolic – use images that represent an action, object or concept at a higher level of abstraction. They are effective when actions, objects or concepts involve well-established and easily recognisable objects. For example, a door lock control on a car door uses an image of a pad-lock to indicate its function, even though the padlock looks nothing like the actual control.

Arbitrary – use images that bear little or no relationship to the action, object or concept—i.e. the relationship has to be learned. Generally, arbitrary icons should only be used when developing cross-cultural or industry standards that will be used for long periods of time.

Looking across these different ways of understanding symbols provides insights that no single field alone could reveal. By thinking transdiciplinarily about symbols, two key principles emerge that can guide your use of symbols in data storytelling.

→ For the sake of offering a definition, in our trainings we use Cambridge Dictionary's broader definition of a symbol as "a sign, shape, or object that is used to represent something else."

1. **Symbols should be resonant** – When something is resonant it relates on an embodied level. One responds to it instantly. Whether simple like the symbols on a road sign, or more complex like the symbols for the 2020 Tokyo Olympics, as a data storyteller you want your audience to quickly get what it is you are trying to represent. Ideally, not only would they comprehend your symbol, they would also connect with it, opening up space for meanings to become stickier.

2. **Symbols should be relevant** – For symbols to resonate they need to be relevant. This means that the symbols you create or choose to use should be the right match for your audience. Of course, there are different audiences and differences within any audience segment. People are never all going to respond the same to an image. However, asking contextual questions about the connotation of symbols can help you consider their cultural and social relevance to your audience.

Mini Exercise: Symbols

Apply the distinctions between types of icons to the following symbols. Which ones are most resonant and why? Which ones might not be relevant across different cultures or geographies?

→ A pictogram refers to a pictorial symbol that stands in for a word or phrase.

Writing about their co-production project for creating better pharmaceutical pictograms, Barros et al. (2014) reflected, "Pictograms should be developed in accordance with the culture, beliefs, attitude and expectations of the target population" (p. 705). Research team Richler et al. (2012) came to a similar conclusion in their study of medical pictograms. They found that preferences for pictograms did not always differ, but when they did these differences would depend on an individual's country of residence, education level, and gender. "This suggests that when communicating specific health and medication information with patients, pictograms may be interpreted differently or understood with different clarity depending on the individual" (Richler et al., 2012, p. 224). Their team reflected that medical graphics "would be more beneficial if designed for a particular demographic" (Richler et al., 2012, p. 225).

These findings in health graphics research support a foundational idea in cultural studies—that representation systems are culturally shared (Hall 1997). To communicate people must have some sense of shared meaning and shared conceptual maps. Most obviously this would be a shared language like English or Chinese. But visual images are also part of our communication systems. Like fashion, facial expressions and even traffic lights, visual images have a 'language' of their own, and to understand each other we must share at least some knowledge of that language system. Importantly, whether spoken or visual, languages are learnt. This means that they can change and adapt (Hall 1997, p.22).

Colour

Like symbols, for colours to be effective in visual storytelling, they must be resonant and relevant. Colour perception is studied across a range of disciplines from art history to psychology to optometry. Information designers pull from all these areas of study to understand the connotations and functions of colour. In *The Information Design Handbook*, authors Jen and Ken Visocky O'Grady (2008) highlight the importance of cultural considerations for how we employ colour:

> Our interpretations of a color's meaning are highly influenced by culture. Numerous influences mold these interpretations, from religion to politics, linguistics to popular trends ... For clear communication and unambiguous information delivery, it is essential to understand the needs, customs, and attitudes of the end user. Therefore, investigations into cultural perceptions of color are essential whenever designing for a new audience, market or global campaign (p. 114).

For example, while white is the most common colour for bridal gowns in Western cultures, brides in India traditionally wear red (Visocky O'Grady, 2008, p. 114). The cultural meaning of colours is particularly important when designing pictograms or creating more illustrated visualisations.

Creating Colour Contrasts – When selecting colours, keep in mind how contrast can be used to highlight significance or show difference. Contrast can be created through your choices of colour hue (type of colour), colour value (lightness or darkness of a colour), and colour saturation (purity of a colour).

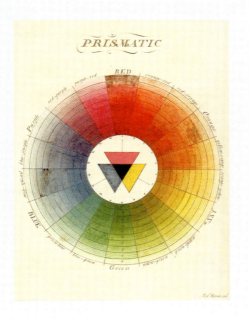

→ **A colour wheel created by Moses Harris, from *The Natural System of Colours* (1766).** "In a color palette, complimentary colors are two colors directly across from each other. For example, red and green are complimentary colors. Tetradic color palettes use four colors, a pair of complimentary colors. For example, you could use, yellow, purple red and green. Tetrad colors can be found by putting a square or rectangle on the color wheel." From www.commons.wikimedia.org/wiki/File:Moses_Harris,_The_Natural_System_of_Colours.jpg.

→ Nominal data refers to variables that represent different categories where there is no order or measure between the categories. For example, eye colour is an example of nominal data.

For example, if you have nominal data and you want to make one category standout as the subject of your data story, you may choose to create a contrast in its saturation or value. This is particularly useful when the point you are trying to make is not that this category is the largest or smallest, but where it falls in relation to the others. For example, if your data story is about the experiences of Nigerian students in the United Kingdom, you may choose to highlight the data for Nigerians across a range of graphs that compare different international students experiences. This would help guide the reader along your data story. At the same time, you may not want to use a different colour entirely, as this may be too much contrast and feel like you are stealing the spotlight, overshadowing the supporting characters in your data story.

You may also want to use contrast to highlight variables in your data if you are trying to point out a pattern that is not necessarily going to stand out on its own. For example, when creating visualisations from our additional coding of data from CATO National Police Misconduct Reporting Project, we wanted to highlight the pattern we found around gendered violence and violence against women. This led us to make the decision to use a bold colour only for those categories that related to women and gendered violence. As we wanted to draw attention away from the other data, in efforts to make the pattern emerge, we coloured the other categories in a dull grey. Here we focused on hue and saturation to tell a story with this simple bar chart made with Datawrapper.

→ For more on the CATO NPMRP project see the section on Feminist Data Visualisation.

→ Anna Feigenbaum and Daniel Weissmann augmented the CATO NPMRP dataset to account for gender and age variables. Using orange as a highlight colour and fading the other bars to a light grey, this bar chart was designed to direct readers to the issue of gendered violence in reported police misconduct.

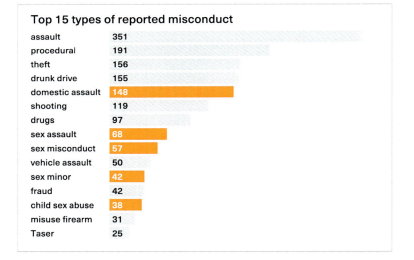

→ There are a number of free online tools to help you check if your colour contrast passes the Web Content Accessibility Guidelines, such as www.webaim.org/resources/contrastchecker.

These international standards were created primarily to improve interface design for people with disabilities, as well as those limited to accessing the web by only mobile phone.

Although preferences for a favourite colour may be subjective, there are some colour contrasts that are easier for most people to comprehend. Taking colour blindness and aging into account, the American Disability Act suggests that best practice is to provide a 70 percent contrast between type and background. Visocky O'Grady (2008) suggest making sure that the contrast you select works well in greyscale and avoids eye strain (p. 119). Working with online tools, as well as old fashioned colour wheels, can help you make informed decisions on what colours to use and when.

Colour metaphors and gradients – The other main way that colour is primarily used to tell visual data stories is with colour metaphors and gradients. Here colour is used to represent scales or increases and decreases in values. Colour metaphors refer to the use of different colours that carry particular meanings or connotations in a shared cultural context (i.e. green for go, red for stop). A colour gradient refers to a range of colour transitions that is often gradual and blends together as it progresses (i.e. from blue for cold to red for hot). As in the example of hot and cold, gradients can also be metaphors. These can be applied to anything from housing statistics to population density, from income levels to attitudes toward migration.

When you have ordinal data, a colour metaphor may be useful for telling your data story. For example, the Monash University guide to FODMAP diet-friendly foods uses a green, yellow, red scheme to make distinctions between for foods that are good to eat, foods that can be eaten in small quantities, and foods that should be avoided. This kind of scheme is common in health graphics, as discussed below. For interval data, colour gradients are a common choice to represent change, rankings, or intensity. The same metaphor of red, yellow, green can also be employed as a gradient where the data you have uses numeric values. For example, Energy Performance Certificate ratings in the United Kingdom use a gradient colour scheme going from green to red along seven bands. These bands are based on numerical rankings from 1–100. The band for the most energy efficient homes is shown in a bold green, while the lowest ranking band is assigned a rich red hue. Here metaphor and gradient work together to create a resonant and relevant representational system.

→ In statistics, ordinal data refers to variables where the order matters but there is no precisely determined meaning or difference between values. Satisfaction levels are an example of ordinal data.

→ Interval data refers to variables where differences are standardised and meaningful. Temperature is an example of interval data.

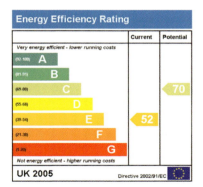 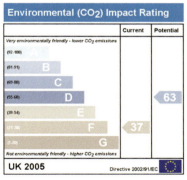

→ **The UK Energy Performance Certificate** uses gradient colour to create contrast between rankings.

In relation to colour metaphors and interpreting colour gradients, Arcia et al (2016) found that their study participants "responded well to symbolic and colour analogies" (p. 179). By looking across three of her team's studies on participatory infographic design for low health literacy communities (that addressed general health, dementia, and asthma control) Arcia (2019) and her team were able to pull out some recurrent themes around preferred imagery. In relation to colour, the team found that colour analogies worked well when paired with a human figure to help represent gradations of scale. For example, the green to red stoplight spectrum worked well whether coupled with BMI categories, caregiving burdens, or the experience of an asthma attack.

→ Arcia caregiver burden green to red

Using the stoplight analogy is often discouraged because they are diffi-cult for people with colour blindness to read. Arcia's team took this into account:

> We were concerned about potentially disadvantaging people with color blindness, but could not ignore how effective stoplight colors were at conveying the intended messages across a wide variety of health topics. We compensated by ensuring that all information en-coded with color is also encoded with text (2019, p. 4).

→ Read Andy Kirk's post on designing for colour blindness at www.visualisingdata. com/2019/08/five-ways-to-design-for-red-green-colour-blindness

→ Chroma.js Color Palette Helper is also a useful tool for providing colour suggestions based on how many different colours and the type of hue you want for your design. See more at www.gka.github.io/palettes.

Andy Kirk addresses this issue in his blog post, "Five ways to design for red-green colour-blindness." These include: using red/green variations, opting for a non red-green variation, using a second encoding such as shapes or text to help with comprehension, or (when budget allows) of-fering two versions of a colour scale for the user to choose between.

As Arcia (2019) notes, the use of these colours alone did not always lead to comprehension. When colour was attributed to symbols that were not metaphorically resonant, the image failed to make a connection. This is shown in the example of balloons standing in for lung capacity, a meta-phor most participants did not like and therefore had no resonance. Col-our scales also failed to connect with users when the colour metaphor was unfamiliar. For example, a warm red to cool blue scale was used to signify how controlled a person's asthma felt. The scale was paired with an icon for lungs. Many participants could not relate.

While an audience that spends a lot of time looking at heat maps may have found this type of scale highly relevant, the participants in this study did not connect with this visualisation. However, when the team showed the image of a tree to represent feelings of overall health that went from bare to fully in leaf, this familiar image resonated with participants. These findings further support other researchers around the importance of the cultural relevance. Importantly, they conclude that, while it comes with additional costs, working directly with target audience communities through participatory infographic design, is the best way to create graphics that can enhance health literacy (Arcia, 2019, p. 6; Barros et al., 2014; Richler et al., 2012).

→ Arcia tree metaphor

Captions

Returning to our semiotic toolkit, the importance of good captions can be thought about through the concept of polysemy. Polysemy literally means 'many signs'. In semiotics it refers to how words can have more than one meaning. However, polysemy captures more than just the linguistic phenomenon of multiple meanings (i.e. a letter of the alphabet or a letter we post in the mail). In *Semiotics for Beginners* Daniel Chandler (1994) explains that the connotations of signs are more open to interpretation than their denotations. As we covered earlier in this chapter, denotation is the basic description of an image, whereas connotation refers to the emotions, values, and associations that denotations give rise to.

Because our emotions, values and associations differ according to culture, background, and experience, the meanings visual images take on will likewise be varied. In other words, our standpoint matters for how we interpret signs. For some people red roses are an expression of thoughtfulness and love. For others, they are a capitalist marketing ploy. Or perhaps, they have both of these meanings for someone at once. What we bring from our previous associations to the present will shape how we decode a sign's connotations. So even when we share a conceptual map that understands that roses can mean both of these things, our individual relationship to the image of a rose can be different on an emotional level. This makes the resonance and relevance of a visual image vary across viewers.

So what does this have to do with captions? As the same visual image can mean different things to different people, we need to guide viewers to the intended message of our data story—our Think, Feel, and Do. This means that we need to limit the possible meanings a visual image can have. For example, ever year people in the United States spend millions of dollars on red roses for Valentine's Day. Imagine you have a dataset about the export of red roses to the United States. The conflict you are trying to express in your story is: humans vs. the environment. Your goal is to get people to think that the red rose trade has damaging environmental impacts. You want them to feel alarmed by the scale of this international enterprise, and act on this feeling by joining a petition for florists to only stock locally produced flowers on Valentine's Day. If this is your Think, Feel, and Do, then the way you caption your graphs of export data, supply chain routes, and the environmental impacts of packaging, industrial shipping, etc. need to help tell this story.

On the other hand, if the story you want to tell is about how Latin American businesses have developed through their participation in the export of red roses to the United States, then you will want to frame your visuals differently—even if you are using exactly the same datasets and visualisation types.

→ Daniel Chandler explains that the metaphor of an anchor is used in semiotics to explain how captions can be used to constrain the reader's interpretation of an image. The term comes from Roland Barthes' book *Image-Music-Text* (1977).

Captions work to guide audiences toward your Think, Feel, and Do. By crafting carefully worded text that anchors the images in your data story, you can stop viewers' interpretations drifting away from your intended messages.

When creating your captions think about the other possible interpretations of your visual images—including charts, graphs and other illustrated elements of your data story. Then brainstorm how best to use captions to steer the viewer along the narrative of your data story. Captions can also be used to highlight details and spotlight elements essential to your data story.

Editorial

The fourth and final pillar of data storytelling is editorial layout. Editorial layout refers to how the different visual elements of your data story are strategically arranged onto a page, screen, poster or whatever platform you are using in order to effectively and efficiently reach your target audience. The layout you choose should work well to get across your intended message—the Think, Feel, Do of your data story.

In today's cross-platform, digital/analogue hybrid world, you will often be designing a data story for multiple platforms, making it even more important to consider editorial layout from the start of your data storytelling process. How many elements you choose to include, your colour scheme, the size and detail of your symbols, and other illustrated elements all depend on the amount of space you have to work with. Often a fantastic data story is designed for a webpage, but ends up far too detailed to work on a smartphone screen. If most of your audience is reading off their smartphones, you will need to think about this when making decisions about the design details of your visual data story.

This is why we advise our students and clients that layout should come at the start of the planning process. Before you even begin to select symbols, fonts or chart types, ask: What different screen sizes does this layout need to work for? This question is as important for print-based data stories as for digital ones. If you are designing an infographic for educators that would ideally be printed at a poster size of A1, but most teachers will be using office printers that only go up to A4 (US letter size) or A3 (US legal size), you need to make sure your layout is still readable and functional at a smaller scale. In fact, today many design experts suggest that you begin by planning for the smallest display size and then increase the scale and level of detail for larger versions (Babich 2017). This is what people working in user experience and web design refer to as optimisation, meaning, to create a layout that works best for each differently sized display.

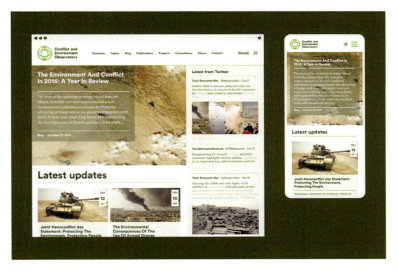

→ **Conflict and Environment Observatory.**
Responsive website design by Minute Works. Best viewed at www.ceobs.org.

A modular layout is often a good starting place for editorial layout design. This is where the page or screen is divided into smaller parts that fit together in a grid system, and can be a good starting place for designing your visual data stories. Based on best practices in design around using grid layouts, we created the '6 card design' challenge. Working with restricted layout templates can help guide your design process. For our '6 card design' challenge we give each group of participants a set of index cards or cut rectangles of paper and a sheet of paper, along with the brief that they must design a 6 element visual data story that can work on a smart phone screen (either by swiping through the story or as stand-alone mini-narratives), and be fitted together to form a printable poster. This challenge helps guide people's creative process from the start, highlighting the importance of layout to the decisions we make about charts, graphs, symbols, captions and other editorial story components.

Mini Exercise: Modular Design Challenge

Using 6 equally sized cards, try to create a modular layout for a visual data story that would work both on a mobile phone and as a printed poster. Before you begin, make sure you have selected at least one target audience and done the Think, Feel, Do exercise for them. In your editorial layout, try to include:

→   A headline and introductory text
→   Four charts or graphs with captions on individual cards
→   A 'take action' card designed particularly to try and turn your 'think and feel' into a 'do'

Another task we do with clients and students uses a 6-panel template laid out sequentially, following the way comic narratives are read. You can find details on this challenge in the Learning from Comics and activities sections.

→ See the sections on Types of Narrative and What is Conflict in Data Storytelling.

While these design principles are a good starting place for improving and reflecting on the process of laying out a data story, it is also important to embrace the experimental and break out of these proscriptive structures. A spin on this same activity asks participants to take their modular 6 card design and then redesign it, throwing out all the rules of grids and order to see what else they can create. We sometimes do a modified version of this creative activity by supplying participants with printouts from a template-based visualisation software programme, like Tableau, and then having them use scissors and glue sticks to reconstruct the existing data story. This task can be paired with thinking about types of conflict or the seven basic plots in order to practice figuring out how storytelling structures and visual layouts fit together. It is this process of strategically arranging your visual elements to tell your data story that creates a powerful editorial.

In their study of 58 data visualisations taken from online journalism, business and data visualisation research, Segel and Heer (2010) found that there were seven commonly employed genres of narrative visualisation. Informed by the work of comic Scott McCloud, they described these different uses of space as: magazine style, annotated chart, partitioned poster, flow chart, comic strip, slide show, and film/video/animation (p. 7). Importantly, these genres can be mixed, and while it may be more traditional to see an annotated chart in a boardroom and a comic strip in a classroom, there are no rules on what genre is necessarily best for your audience. What matters is how each of these different styles of layout supports some narrative structures, while limiting others.

→ Scott McCloud's books *Understanding Comics* (1993), *Reinventing Comics* (2000) and *Making Comics* (200€) have now become canonical reading for data visualisation designers. His simple breakdowns and explanations of visual narrative offer a good starting place for thinking about how story structure, symbol, caption and layout work together.

Seven
Genres of
Narrative
Visualisation

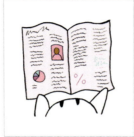
↳ **Magazine style**

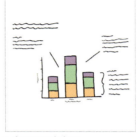
↳ **Annotated chart**

↳ **Partitioned poster**

↳ **Flow chart**

↳ **Comic strip**

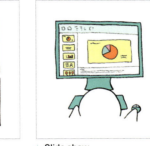
↳ **Slide show**

↳ **Film/Video/Animation**

For example, a magazine layout may be more useful for a data story that requires lengthy text to contextualise accompanying data visualisations, whereas a slide show may work better for a series of graphics, presented as visual evidence, leading the viewer to a final argument or action point. Importantly, Segel and Heer (2010) also found across their research sample an "under-utilization of common narrative messaging techniques such as repetition of key points, introductory texts, and final summaries and syntheses" (p. 7).

↳ Seven Genres of Narrative Visualisation. Adapted from *Narrative Visualization: Telling Stories with Data*, by E. Segel & J. Heer, 2010. Illustrations by Alexandra Alberda.

SYMBOL

ARE USEFUL AND EASILY UNDERSTOOD

BUT THEY ARE NOT NEUTRAL

 ← ARE ICONS GENDERED?

EXAMINE PURPOSE:

GRAPHIC ELEMENTS VS GRAPHIC EMBELLISHMENTS

EDITORIAL

LAYOUT OF PAGE

WHERE IS THE DATA VIZ EMBEDDED?

ADDITIONAL

TEXTUAL

-AND-

VISUAL

ELEMENTS

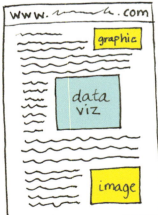

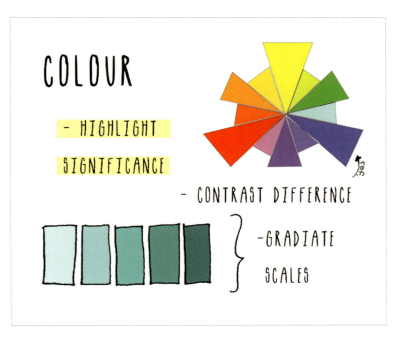

COLOUR

- HIGHLIGHT
SIGNIFICANCE

- CONTRAST DIFFERENCE

-GRADIATE SCALES

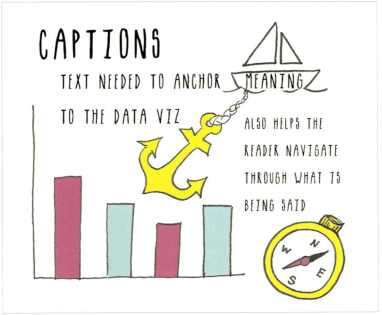

CAPTIONS

TEXT NEEDED TO ANCHOR MEANING

TO THE DATA VIZ

ALSO HELPS THE READER NAVIGATE THROUGH WHAT IS BEING SAID

Whatever genre and layout style you choose, a final important part of creating effective and efficient designs is to avoid unnecessary features. While some illustrative icons or added details may enhance a data story, making good editorial decisions requires learning how to differentiate between functional flourishes and ornamental embellishments. These unnecessary add-ons are what Edward Tufte infamously labelled chartjunk.

Chartjunk

'Chartjunk' is by now a well-used and hotly debated phrase in data visualisation circles. Coined by Edward Tufte in his canonical 1983 book, *The Visual Display of Quantitative Information*, chartjunk refers to what Tufte calls "the interior decoration of graphics [that] does not tell the viewer anything new" (p. 107). Causing decades of controversy, he argued that such embellishments, found across technical papers, commercial ads, and media graphics, might at first appear to add value to a visualisation, but in reality were a distraction. They were lazy and superficial, overshadowing "the hard work required to produce intriguing numbers and secure evidence" (p. 107).

Based on his own review of hundreds of data visualisations, Tufte identified three main kinds of chartjunk: unintentional optical art, the dreaded grid, and the self-promoting graphical duck. He coined these with comical names to capture practices of visual embellishment that commonly occurred in data visualisations of the time.

Unintentional optical art – Discussing the early rise of software programmes that allowed for patterned fills, unintentional optical art refers to the cross-hatching and ruled lines that became used to differentiate data types, particularly in black and white visualisations. Tufte argued that this "eye-straining" and "illusive" use of moiré effects had "no place in data graphical design." Today the moiré method of creating visual contrast is largely obsolete. However, contemporary versions of this kind of eye-straining optics can be seen in the overuse of 3-D effects, colour gradients, and the use of images in place of more simple shapes.

The dreaded grid – For those of us who went to school in the era of graph paper, 'the grid' may evoke memories of creating hand-drawn graphs for school reports. The small squares serve as a visual guide, allowing one to measure lines and areas. But in Tufte's eyes, once the grid line has served its purpose of helping to make the graph, it should disappear from view, "lest it compete with the data." Tufte argues that gridlines carry no information, and therefore constitute chartjunk. If a grid is needed in order to follow how information is plotted on a graph, then the lines should be muted, ideally in a very pale grey.

While it is less common for gridlines to be automatically included in a graph produced by a software programme today, it is useful to always ask oneself if gridlines are necessary. If so, can they be further faded into the background? This principle can also be applied to extra numbers or variables in a graph. If there seems to be too many interval figures, consider what might be removed or condensed without skewing the information you want to present.

The self-promoting graphical duck – Tufte's final pet peeve is what he termed the 'the duck,' named after a large architectural building designed—for no instrumental reason—to look like a big duck. Applying this to data visualisation, Tufte argued against the practice of building an entire structure as a decoration. Under this category of chartjunk Tufte included: the use of fake perspective, unnecessary additions of colour, and visualisations that show off what software can do instead of what data can say. Terming this practice 'We-Used-A-Computer-To-Build-A-Duck Syndrome,' Tufte argued, "Occasionally designers seem to seek credit merely for possessing a new technology, rather than using it to make better designs" (p. 120).

This 'big duck' category of chartjunk is perhaps most immediately relevant to the present. As software for data visualisation becomes capable of creating ever more complicated and colourful graphical representations, people can fall ill with Build-A-Duck Syndrome. Readers are offered up multi-coloured neon smorgasbords of data that say very little of any importance, or are based on weak evidence made to look beautiful. At the BU Civic Media Hub, we share Tufte's distaste for data ducks. Not only do these practices obscure the significance of data, they can also hinder data literacy and alienate beginners from seeing themselves as data storytellers, as we discussed earlier in this chapter.

Edward Tufte's notion of chartjunk continues to be the subject of visualisation trainings, keynote conference talks, and heated Twitter discussions. Offering a different perspective, data visualiser, consultant, and educator Stephen Few argues that Tufte's view may be too dismissive. In a newsletter about a 2010 study on chartjunk, Few (2011) wrote, "Embellishments can at times, when properly chosen and designed, represent information redundantly in useful ways, and even when they aren't information in and of themselves, can meaningfully support the display of information." In particular, Few notes the potential effectiveness of properly (or professionally) designed embellishments that work memorably or metaphorically, immersing readers in the data presented.

→ The full study Few refers to is Bateman, S., Mandryk, R. L., Gutwin, C., Genest, A., McDine, D., & Brooks, C. (2010, April). Useful junk?: The effects of visual embellishment on comprehension and memorability of charts. In *Proceedings of the SIGCHI Conference on Human Factors in Computing Systems* (pp. 2573-2582).

Used as a tool for visually editing one's work, 'chartjunk' can help differentiate between those visual elements that are needed to tell your data story, and those that are embellishments. But eliminating chartjunk does not have to mean excluding illustrative elements from your visual data stories. As we will discuss further in the sections on the Learning from Comics and Graphic Medicine, introducing extra information to a graph or chart can also, at times, help create context and humanise data.

Both the Four Pillars and Tufte's critique of chartjunk offer principles that will be applicable no matter what visualisations you may decide to create with your data. More importantly, being equipped with these principles can help get you thinking visually from the very beginning. This will help you navigate challenges and limitations in the chart design process. For example, if you are working with a low data literacy audience, you may want to select a basic chart that is more familiar to lay readers, or that incorporates symbols rather than just numbers. Perhaps you are publishing in an academic journal and are restricted to using black and white. Or maybe you are working to very limited budget and cannot make full use of the colour spectrum. When telling visual stories all kinds of issues, beyond the data you have in front of you, will limit the scope of what chart makes the most sense to create. In addition, understanding the principles of good visual design—and the seductive allure of fancy software—can help you engage with charts more confidently, expanding your literacy of their potentials and their pitfalls.

Storytelling with Andy Kirk's CHRT(S)

Today there are hundreds of charts and graphs to choose from. The options available can feel overwhelming and it can be difficult to know which selection is best for your data and the story you are trying to tell. To help with the daunting task of selecting the best graphical form for representing the data you have, designer and educator Andy Kirk came up with a simple mnemonic: CHRTS. As the name suggests, CHRTS provides a taxonomy for thinking about what kind of chart is best for your data. Like any classification system, Kirk notes that there are exceptions and outliers, examples that span multiple categories, as well as other possible ways to divide up these different kinds of graphs. But as an easy to use guide, the CHRTS system provides an excellent starting place to navigate through the hundreds of options available.

→ For a much more detailed version of this guide see Andy Kirk (2019) *Data Visualisation: A Handbook for Data Driven Design*, 2nd Ed. London: SAGE

Andy has also created a directory based on this categorisation system that provides information on what software can help you create different kinds of charts. You can find it at www.chartmaker.visualisingdata.com.

Understanding Andy Kirk's CHRT(S)

Type of Chart	What is it For?	Common Examples
Categorical	Comparing categories and distributions of quantitative values	Bar chart, clustered bar chart, pictogram, bubble chart, spider diagram, polar chart, word cloud
Hierarchical	Revealing part-to-whole relationships and hierarchies	Pie chart, waffle chart, stacked bar chart, tree map, Venn diagram, dendogram, sunburst,
Relational	Exploring correlations and connections	Matrix chart, network diagram, Sankey diagram
Temporal	Plotting trends and intervals over time	Line chart, slope graph chart, area chart, horizon chart, GANTT chart
Spatial	Mapping spatial patterns through overlays and distortions	Heat map, proportional symbol map, dot map, flow map, area cartogram

These different clusters of charts are based on the types of data you have. Within each cluster the decision of what particular graph to use will often depend on the number of variables you have in the data you are trying to visually represent.

To help think through when and why to use certain charts in visual data stories, imagine you are writing a report about the most recent election in the country you currently live in. Your primary dataset is an exit survey of how people voted in the most recent national election. The dataset is divided into basic demographic categories: gender, age, and formal education level. Each of these different demographic categories is a variable. In addition, you have a dataset of results organised spatially by geographic areas; a chronological or time-based dataset that looks at voter turnout across past elections; a dataset based on a survey that asked people what issue they felt was most important in the same year as the election took place; a dataset of each of the main parties' manifestos and campaign pledges; and data available on party donations and financing. Importantly, the samples in these datasets are not the same, so you cannot combine them together directly. Each one can inform your story, but any visualisation must account for the different context and backstory of each dataset. Depending on what data stories you want to tell, different aspects of these datasets can be visualised using a wide variety of graphs.

In the following overview for using different charts, the examples are all based on the kinds of election datasets commonly made available as open data. Since the following chapter covers data storytelling with maps, we've excluded the 'S' for spatial data visualisations here, making this our Guide to Data Storytelling with Andy Kirk's CHRT(S).

According to the OECD glossary for statistical terms, a variable is a characteristic of a unit being observed that may assume more than one of a set of values to which a numerical measure or a category from a classification can be assigned (e.g. income, age, weight, etc., and "occupation", "industry", "disease", etc.

See more definitions of common statistical terms from the Organisation for Economic Co-operation and Development at www. stats.oecd.org/glossary.

A sample refers to the group of people, objects or other living things taken from a larger population for measurement.

Different disciplines and industries have different standards and practices for sampling when gathering data.

Applying Andy Kirk's CHRT(S) to UK Election Data

You can follow along using real datasets. As an activity, choose one graph from each CHRTS type and try to create a visualisation using real data. You can use Excel or simple visualisation software like datawrapper.de to create many of the graphs discussed in this section.

2017 Election Results by Region
https://researchbriefings.parliament.uk/ResearchBriefing/Summary/CBP-7979

Voter turnout by age in the last 10 elections
https://researchbriefings.files.parliament.uk/documents/CBP-8060/CBP-8060.pdf

2017 Manifesto guide from the BBC
https://www.bbc.co.uk/news/election-2017-39955886

Information on donors to political parties
http://search.electoralcommission.org.uk/

A Guide to Using Andy Kirk's CHRT(S)

Categorical Charts	Good to Use When	For Example	In terms of storytelling, this could
Bar chart	You are comparing numeric values where there is a single variable category	You are looking at how people voted by age	Highlight significant differences in voting behaviour across generations
Clustered bar chart	The categories you would be comparing in a standard bar chart can be further divided into additional categories that you want to show	Within different age ranges you also want to show education level	Highlight any trends between education level and voting behaviour across generations
Pictogram	You want to display similar information as you would in a bar chart but using more emotive or humanising symbols	You want to depict education level using an icon for a diploma, with colour showing differences in what party people voted for	Add emphasis to a story about formal education levels and voting behaviour
Bubble chart	You want to use shapes rather than a standard grid to show value differences and variables between categories	You want to breakdown the votes for each party by age	Draw out the significance of how many older people voted for one party, and younger people voted for an opposing party, in a quick, eye-catching way
Spider diagram	You want to show the scale of value differences across three or more variables, usually for a single category	You want to show the percentage of people that found different issues of the most importance in a given year	Place emphasis on the issues that may have informed voters' choices
Polar chart	You want to show value differences across three or more variables, usually for a single category	You want to show how many people found each issue important in a given year	Highlight how one or two issues were of particular importance in a given year
Word cloud	You want to show frequency of word use in textual data	You want to see what words are used most often in election party manifestos	Highlight differences in terminology between parties

Hierarchical Charts	Good to Use When	For Example	In terms of storytelling, this could
Pie chart	Comparing the percentage breakdown of a category into two or three parts	You want to compare white and BME (Black and Ethnic Minority) voter turnout	Spotlight BME voter behaviour in the most recent election
Waffle chart	Showing the proportion of a single part to a whole	You want show how BME votes were distributed across parties	Highlight proportion of BME vote for a particular party
Stacked bar chart	You want to show part to whole breakdowns across specific major categories	You want an overview of how each age group's votes were distributed across parties	Highlight how differences in vote distribution for parties changes with age
Tree map	You want to compare how parts make up a whole when you have many different parts or sub-divisions of parts	show votes for each party broken down by region	Get an overall picture of vote distribution
Venn diagram	You want to show relationships between multiple sets	show where parties fall on major issues	Investigate overlaps and divergences around major issues in party pledges
Dendogram	Displaying hierarchical relationships where elements belong to a larger category	show what party elected officials belong to	Provide overview of all newly elected officials and what party they belong to
Sunburst	Displaying both parts of a whole and the hierarchical relationships within each part	show breakdown of votes by part and list all newly elected officials	Highlight differences in numbers of newly elected officials by part

Relational Charts	Good to Use When	For Example	In terms of storytelling, this could
Matrix chart	Showing values at the intersection between two categories	You want to summarise campaign promises on key issues found across party manifestos	Show which parties have certain issues as priorities in their campaigns
Network dia-gram	Showing the connections between different entities	You want to create an over-view of major campaign contributes	Spotlight the major donors to each political party
Sankey dia-gram	Display flow between two categorical states or stag-es (i.e. now and then)	You want to show changes in election results between the 2017 and 2015 elec-tions	Highlight shifts in voter behaviour across different demographics between two elections
Temporal Charts	**Good to Use When**	**For Example**	**In terms of storytelling, this could**
Line chart	Showing trends over time	changes in voter behaviour over time	Highlight a major change in voter turnout over the last 10 elections
Area chart	Same as line chart with the area below the line filled in to show the volume of change	changes in voter behav-iour over time by different demographic subgroups	Highlight differences in changes in voter turnout over the last 10 elections broken down by age group.
Slope graph chart	Showing changes in a single category over two stages in time (i.e. now and then)	changes in voter behaviour between two stages in time	Highlight a major increase or decrease in voter turn-out between the last two elections

→ See Spotlight: Seeing Data Project for more.

In addition to Andy Kirk's *Data Visualisation: A Handbook for Data Driven Design*, there are a number of excellent resources as part of the Seeing Data Project that can be found on their project website http://seeingdata. org/. We also highly recommend the Storytelling With Data website. It breaks down technical jargon and showcases a wide range of amateur and professional visualisations as part of their #swd challenges series. You can find their resources at www.storytellingwithdata.com.

An illustrated summary of Andy Kirk's CHRT(S)

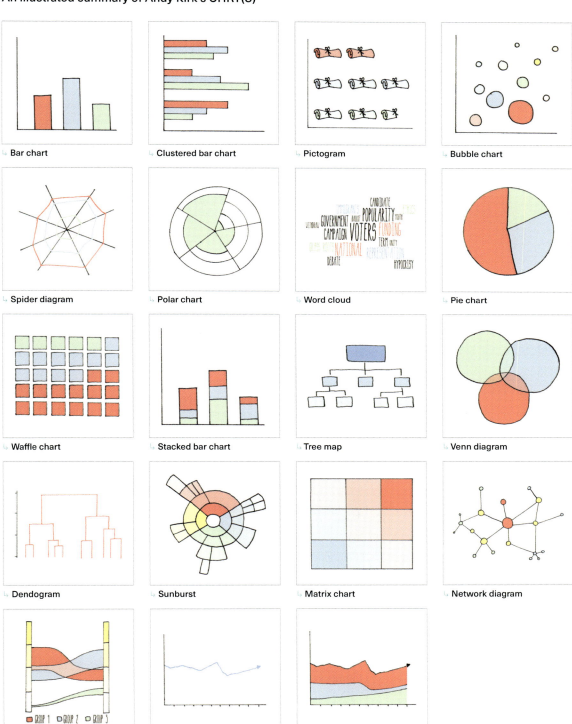

↳ Bar chart

↳ Clustered bar chart

↳ Pictogram

↳ Bubble chart

↳ Spider diagram

↳ Polar chart

↳ Word cloud

↳ Pie chart

↳ Waffle chart

↳ Stacked bar chart

↳ Tree map

↳ Venn diagram

↳ Dendogram

↳ Sunburst

↳ Matrix chart

↳ Network diagram

↳ Sankey diagram

↳ Line chart

↳ Area chart

The Power of Trees

In his preface to *The Book of Trees: Visualizing Branches of Knowledge*, Manuel Lima points out that the tree has been a powerful visual archetype for many centuries. The most well-known 'tree' visualisation is the genealogical tree, in which branches are metaphors for parents and leaves for their children. This familiar tree structure is effective for two reasons. First, it uses the symbol of a tree to help the viewer quickly grasp the concept of the family (leaves come from stems, stems come from branches). Second, it represents the information in a hierarchical format, providing the viewer with an ordering system that shows how different pieces of information relate to each other. Such tree structures used to construct family trees and other taxonomic visualisations are called tree diagrams.

Case Study: Creating a Tree Diagram for the RiotID Pocket Guide

In the RiotID project, Anna Feigenbaum collaborated with the Omega Research Foundation and design studio Minute Works to create an infographic about Impact Munitions, a form of 'less lethal' ammunition and projectiles used by law enforcement to cause pain and compliance, while reducing the risk of causing death. Clarity was the most important consideration in the design of this RiotID guide. The team knew that the infographic would be translated into multiple languages and used by people from a range of cultures, with varying technical literacy.

Faced with these challenges, the designers decided to use a tree diagram. The diagram shows the different types of Impact Munitions at the top of the graph. The second order of information indicates the type of discharge (spray, explosion, or ejection) and the third layer of information details what kind of ammunitions are released. For example, using this tree diagram, a citizen on the ground in Palestine or Brazil can easily identify a grenade. The graph tells us that a grenade 'explodes,' whereas a 37mm cartridge 'ejects' various ammunition including pellets, beanbags, or baton rounds.

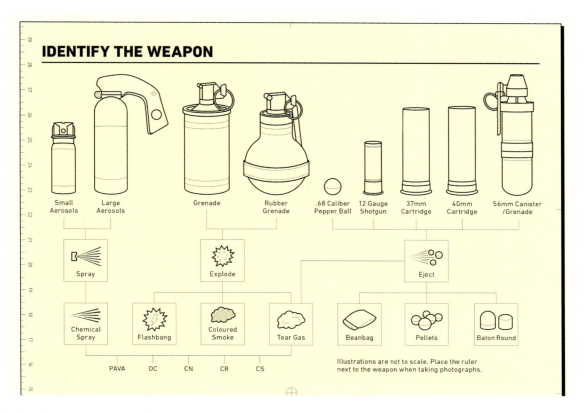

IDENTIFY THE WEAPON

| Small Aerosols | Large Aerosols | | Grenade | Rubber Grenade | .68 Caliber Pepper Ball | 12 Gauge Shotgun | 37mm Cartridge | 40mm Cartridge | 56mm Canister /Grenade |

Spray

Explode

Eject

Chemical Spray

Flashbang

Coloured Smoke

Tear Gas

Beanbag

Pellets

Baton Round

PAVA   OC   CN   CR   CS

Illustrations are not to scale. Place the ruler next to the weapon when taking photographs.

The other common type of tree graph is the treemap, though you might not think to call it a tree based on its appearance alone. The recursive algorithm used to produce computerised treemaps was originally developed by computer scientist Ben Shneiderman in the 1990s as a way to visualise nested file folders on a computer. Treemaps display information hierarchies by representing data categories as nested rectangles. The area size of the rectangle is generally proportional to its quantity or value. If there are subcategories, they are visualised as smaller rectangles that are nested inside the larger rectangle groups. Treemaps are space-constrained, which means that they are more compact than other visualisations. In addition to the area size, rectangles can also be distinguished by colour.

Treemaps are a good way to display a large quantity of information. They are especially useful if you want to show how a system or entity is divided. For example, let's say that you're working on your personal budget. You want to be able to easily visualise where your pay check goes each month. With a treemap, you can create categories (such as housing, food, or entertainment), and subcategories (for housing, subcategories might be rent, utilities, and internet; for food, they might be groceries and eating out). You would then allocate values to these categories depending on how much you spend each month.

Tree Diagram from RiotID Guide. Design by Minute Works. Available to download at www.riotid.com.

→ According to Khan Academy, the idea behind a recursive algorithm is "To solve a problem, solve a subproblem that is a smaller instance of the same problem, and then use the solution to that smaller instance to solve the original problem." Using the metaphor of a Russian doll, you can imagine each recursive case to be opening up the smaller doll inside, until you reach the smallest doll that has no more dolls inside. This is the 'base case' problem that the recursive algorithm eventually wants to solve.

The Khan Academy is a free resource that offers lessons in computer programming, finance and maths (among other subjects), which can be very useful training tools for those looking to gain statistical and coding skills. You can explore their courses at www.khanacademy.org.

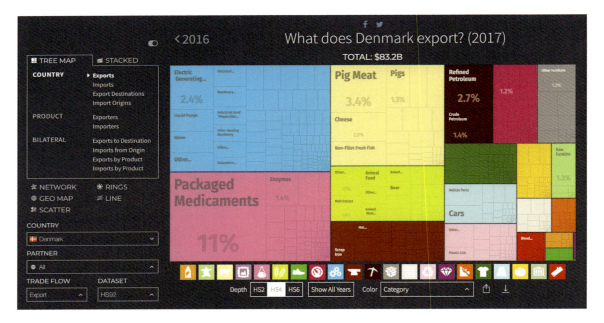

What does Denmark export?
The Observatory of Economic Complexity uses the treemap to build visualisations of countries' imports and exports. On the left, the user can customise the chart type, compare countries, view export destinations, and more.

The Observatory of Economic Complexity, developed by Alexander Simoes, is "a tool that allows users to quickly compose a visual narrative about countries and the products they exchange." On the Observatory's website, users can view visualisations that show various countries' imports, exports, trade balance, and more. There are multiple ways to customise the display; not only can the viewer see export and import information, but this data can be broken down by item (i.e., you can see which countries export specific goods, such as horses or melons) and users can 'partner' countries to see specifically what, for example, the United States exports to the United Kingdom and vice versa. By hovering over the treemap's rectangles, the user can view more specific information about that data point. While the treemap lets the user quickly and easily grasp the basic contours of information, the interactive functions make the level of detail scalable according to the user's needs. These features make treemaps powerful narrative tools for the data storyteller.

Narrative Networks

Another type of visualisation that is very useful for data storytelling is the network graph. Recently, Liliana Bounegru and her colleagues (2017) wrote that "the narrative or storytelling potential of networks is just beginning to receive more sustained attention from researchers" (p. 700). Network graphs are used to illuminate associations or relationships between data points. In a network graph, relationships are displayed as nodes (or vertices) connected by links (or edges). Both the links and the nodes convey information about the data. For example, the thickness of the links can indicate the strength of an association between nodes. The size of the nodes can be adjusted to indicate the frequency of connections to other nodes. This method for creating visual networks is based on link analysis or social network analysis. Associations between nodes are observed and recorded, then visualised as links to help the investigator see where influences and connections are the strongest or most frequent.

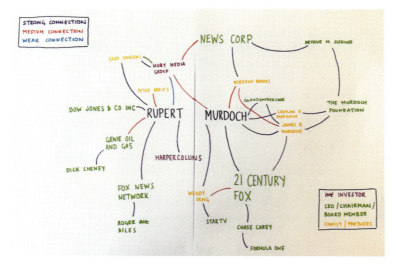

→ **A power map of Rupert Murdoch.**
A power map made by students in Dr. Feigenbaum's Media, Journalism & Society class at Bournemouth University, seminar C, 2018.

A basic network graph can be drawn by hand or created as a collage. At Bournemouth University, our undergraduate students make 'power maps' of media ownership structures by hand. This is a simple exercise that uses bottom-up social network analysis, drawing on publicly available information to uncover the actors that control media institutions. One graph focuses on Rupert Murdoch. The student developed two colour-coded keys: one to distinguish the strength of the connection between Murdoch and the institution, and the other to delineate the kind of relationship he had with each node. Using this additional information, the viewer can clearly see how Murdoch is linked to a dense and diverse web of media companies.

→ The term 'bottom-up' refers to information processing that works from the individual parts or details, connecting them together to form a bigger picture. In contrast, a 'top-down' approach begins from the big picture and then focuses in on details.

This kind of network graph is sometimes pictured in police procedural television shows or films. A bulletin board in the background of a police department might show suspects in a network (nodes) connected to each other with string (links). In the UK Home Office (2016) *Social network analysis: How to guide* written for police forces, the aim of social network analysis is described as a way "to understand a community by mapping the relationships that connect them as a network, and then trying to draw out key individuals, groups within the network, and/or associations between the individuals" (p. 3).

In this guide, focused on mapping out gang networks, users are advised to code for social relationships (friends, business, romantic, etc.), as well as criminal offences (antisocial behaviour, drugs, firearms supply, etc.). Looking at intelligence logs for these connections, those entering data are instructed to record whether criminal activity is done 'to,' 'for,' or 'with' another person. After these connections are gathered and recorded,

→ Kumu is a platform dedicated to helping people and organisations make sense of complicated relationships. Founded by brothers Jeff and Ryan Mohr as an alternative to overly academic and difficult to use visualisation tools, Kumu (which means 'source of wisdom' in Hawaiian), aims to help people "work through the complexity and create thoughtful, sustainable solutions." We use Kumu in our trainings because it is accessible to learn and embodies many of the principles for creating strong visual narratives that are foundational to our approach to data storytelling. You can read the Kumu manifesto at www.kumu.io/manifesto and explore the platform here: www.kumu.i.

→ Oligrapher is a tool developed by LittleSis. It comes from the word Oligarch, meaning a small group of people controlling a country or organisation. LittleSis is a free database that "brings transparency to influential social networks by tracking the key relationships of politicians, business leaders, lobbyists, financiers, and their affiliated institutions." You can explore Oligrapher online at https://littlesis.org/oligrapher and LittleSis at https://littlesis.org.

→ Graph Commons is a collaborative platform for building interactive social network maps. They offer very useful and easy to follow tutorials online to help you get started with social network analysis. Find them at www.graphcommons.com/help.

questions can be asked of the dataset, such as, "Which individuals are linked together in the network? How are they linked?" as well as, "Who may be vulnerable to increased involvement in gang activity?" and "Who is a 'gatekeeper'"? When teaching journalism students, we call this "interviewing your dataset." The same questions police officers would ask a suspect in person, they can ask of their dataset.

This process of recording nodes and how they are linked works the same whether one is a police officer looking at a gang network, or a researcher looking at a police network. In 2016, using the platform Kumu, Anna Feigenbaum created a social network graph for *Waging Nonviolence* to visualise the relationships between speakers, sponsors, and affiliates to the Illinois Tactical Officers Association conference held in Chicago that year. Community groups and organisations including AFSC-Chicago, CAIR-Chicago, Assata's Daughters, Black Lives Matter-Chicago, the Arab American Action Network and War Resisters League formed a coalition under the banner #StopITOA to protest the use of public resources being put toward the use of force training for police officers. They argued that government officials should prioritise spending for human needs over more police militarisation and violence.

Investigative journalists, NGOs, think tanks, investors, activist groups, and academic researchers, among others, commonly use this method of 'bottom-up' social network analysis. In addition to Kumu, software tools like Oligrapher and Graph Commons offer easy to use platforms that do not require coding and can be used for researching, recording and visualising networks.

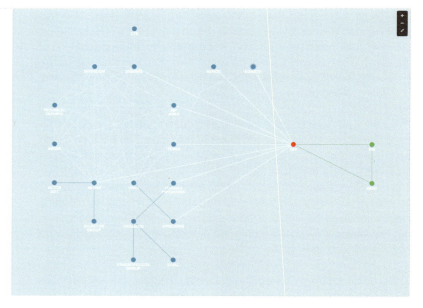

Our report finds that these entities in Greece participated in a **public tenders construction cartel**, in which participants allegedly conspired to win contracts via a practice of fixing prices and passing costs on to the public.

The CEO of **Ellaktor Group** is subject to a European Arrest Warrant for corruption. He recently paid 1.8 million euros to escape jail time for tax evasion and money laundering.

5'9 →

'Risky Business' by Bankwatch.
Designed and built by Minute Works using Kumu. View the interactive presentation at www.bankwatch.kumu.io/risky-business.

With the advance of data analytics and social media platforms, the possibilities for social network analysis have proliferated. Imagine that you have access to all the data on Facebook. In your hands is a mass of information about what people like, who they talk to, and what kinds of news articles they're more likely to read. All of this social media usage can become subject to data mining, analysed and visualised using top-down social network analysis. Such analyses yield insights into what people will like, who they might be friends with, and what products they may want (or be told they want) to purchase. This kind of information can then get sold on to marketers, making Facebook billions of dollars in the process.

Whether making hand-drawn network graphs of media ownership or visualising large-scale networks on social media, Bounegru and her colleagues (2017) propose the notion of a 'network story' to enliven the ways that network visualisations can yield narrative insights. As mentioned above, variables such as node size and link thickness can be powerful indicators of information; the position of nodes, their colour, and whether or not the edges are directional are other important ways that researchers can use network graphs to construct meaning. These choices ultimately form the narrative reading of the network.

In their analysis of over 40 pieces of journalism that use network graphs, Bounegru and her colleagues point out that the text accompanying the graphs—headlines, labels, captions, and articles—are a key part of constructing narrative meaning. This is what we refer to as 'caption' and 'editorial'—two of the 'Four Pillars' essential for telling visual data stories. These pieces of written information help frame the data story and cue the reader toward what to look for and pay attention to. Depending on the complexity of the visualisation, accompanying text can also help make network graphs more accessible to less statistically minded readers.

When network graphs are used to analyse very large data sets, they are often presented in an interactive format that allows the user to manipulate the graphical display, zoom in on individual nodes, or otherwise 'move' through the visualisation. Data visualisers can also introduce a temporal dimension to a network graph in order to show how associations change over time. Gephi and Cytoscape are two open-source programs that are useful for visualising these kinds of larger or more complex networks.

→ You can explore Gephi at www.gephi.org and Cytogscape at www.cytoscape.org.

Tinkering with Timelines

Another particularly important graphical form for data storytellers is the timeline. Timelines have existed for thousands of years. In fact, they are one of the oldest forms of information visualisation. Used in ancient societies to record important people, events, and inventions, timelines were key tools for keeping track of culture, histories, and heritage. Employing chronological time as a structuring device, information can be neatly ordered and presented. This linear structure lends itself well to storytelling, as laying out events over time makes them ripe for narrative. In fact, many of the events people choose to record on a timeline already contain elements of conflict (i.e. a major battle, policy decision, relationship milestone, etc.) and character (an elite person, record-setting achievement, or world shaping invention), so that timelines are often rendered as stories in themselves.

Yet, while timelines provide an excellent means of reducing complex information and stripping down details into easy to process chunks of historical information, there are also limits to what these linear representations can do. Most notably, timelines are full of absences. Deciding what events, people, or moments in time to include on a chronological map involves a process of elevating some things, while eliminating others. Very few data points can make the cut and claim a spot in a timeline's data story. What gets left off the timeline becomes visually absent from the history being presented.

In this sense timelines are ruthless. They force data storytellers to make difficult decisions about what data points should be emphasised and why. Having a clear approach to how you are making your selections can help negotiate biases and standpoints. For example, when we created our timelines for tear gas and impact munitions infographics as part of the RiotID project, we wanted to highlight the international nature of these weapons' development, expansion, and use. This meant that in addition to including key moments of technical invention, we also included major international conflicts where the weapons had been deployed in particularly harmful or unlawful ways. We marked locations as the bold heading to highlight the geographical influences of key events, sometimes using the label 'international' to stress that less lethal weapons are a global issue. At the same time, the United States is the market leader in manufacture and export. This was important for us to highlight by having multiple entries for the US to represent the extent of their involvement.

→ **Timeline from RiotID Impact Munitions**
Design by Minute Works. Available to download at www.riotid.com.

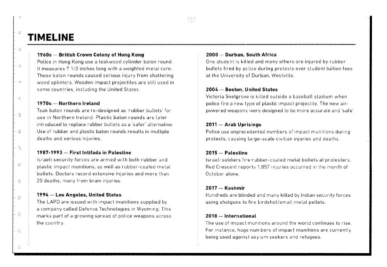

TIMELINE

1960s — British Crown Colony of Hong Kong
Police in Hong Kong use a teakwood cylinder baton round. It measures 7 1/2 inches long with a weighted metal core. These baton rounds caused serious injury from shattering wood splinters. Wooden impact projectiles are still used in some countries, including the United States.

1970s — Northern Ireland
Teak baton rounds are re-designed as 'rubber bullets' for use in Northern Ireland. Plastic baton rounds are later introduced to replace rubber bullets as a 'safer' alternative. Use of rubber and plastic baton rounds results in multiple deaths and serious injuries.

1987-1993 — First Intifada in Palestine
Israeli security forces are armed with both rubber and plastic impact munitions, as well as rubber-coated metal bullets. Doctors record extensive injuries and more than 20 deaths, many from brain injuries.

1994 — Los Angeles, United States
The LAPD are issued with impact munitions supplied by a company called Defence Technologies in Wyoming. This marks part of a growing spread of police weapons across the country.

2000 — Durban, South Africa
One student is killed and many others are injured by rubber bullets fired by police during protests over student tuition fees at the University of Durban, Westville.

2004 — Boston, United States
Victoria Snelgrove is killed outside a baseball stadium when police fire a new type of plastic impact projectile. The new air-powered weapons were designed to be more accurate and 'safe'.

2011 — Arab Uprisings
Police use unprecedented numbers of impact munitions during protests, causing large-scale civilian injuries and deaths.

2015 — Palestine
Israeli soldiers fire rubber-coated metal bullets at protesters. Red Crescent reports 1,857 injuries occurred in the month of October alone.

2017 — Kashmir
Hundreds are blinded and many killed by Indian security forces using shotguns to fire birdshot/small metal pellets.

2018 — International
The use of impact munitions around the world continues to rise. For instance, huge numbers of impact munitions are currently being used against asylum seekers and refugees.

In addition to the difficulties around choosing what goes onto a timeline, other limitations have to do with its linearity. Linear, chronological representations generally can only depict forward movement. It is difficult to use them to compare and contrast information or accounts of events, to show multiple perspectives, or tell stories about entanglements or networks. For this reason, timelines often work well as an accompaniment to other forms of data storytelling. In our RiotID examples, the timeline forms just one part of the story, providing a historical background for the more public health and humanitarian information that is the focus of these infographics. It serves as an anchor, rather than an overarching explanation or history. Applying the Four Pillars of Visual Data Storytelling to timelines, caption, and editorial layout are key.

Putting timelines to creative use, some people have experimented with this form to add storytelling layers to more traditional timelines. For example, in Kate Evan's graphic biography *Red Rosa* (2015), a timeline is used to tell the story of how Rosa Luxemburg researched the 1905 Moscow Uprising of the Russian Revolution. The events are presented as patches on a patchwork quilt. Rather than linear, the dates are connected together by stitching, giving a sense of time moving, but also of the multiplicity of factors and layers of context that go into any singular event. On the following page the quilt continues. This time the patches comprise elements from Rosa Luxemburg's revolutionary theory. Images of empowered workers accompany the snippets of text, "The mass strike does not produce the revolution: the revolution produces the mass strike" (p. 74). Borders sewn between the rows of patches contain slogans and key words from the revolution: *Seventeen hour days, Starvation wages, Freedom*. Rosa is pictured in the upper-right hand corner of the page, laying the quilt onto a bed, giving the timeline a material form and purpose.

A quilted timeline.
An excerpt from Kate Evans, *Red Rosa*, 2015. Courtesy of the artist.

A Timeline of Timelines

Developed from Daniel Rosenberg and Anthony Grafton's Cartographies of Time: A History of the Timeline.

Time Period	Milestone
264/3 BC	Oldest surviving Greek timeline is a chronological table listing rulers, events and inventions.
4th C AD	Eusebius develops table structure to organise and reconcile chronologies from different historic sources
15th C	Vespasiano da Bisticci and others revise the Eusebian model during the Renaissance. This form of information visualisation helped facilitate the organisation of chronological data, was easy to produce, correct and print.
18th C	The Eusebian 'spreadsheet' model for recording chronological data remains the popular choice for scholars. The rise of cartography introduces more precision to day and time keeping.
1765	The publication of the *Chart of Biography* by Joseph Priestley provides the first visual vocabulary for a time map, using a horizontal axis to map out the chronology of when scientists lived.
1860s	French Engineer Joseph Minard creates new infographics techniques that map variables, in addition to time, by using graphical notations and variations in line thickness.
20th–21st C	Timelines remain a popular choice for visually representing chronologies. At the same time, artists interrogate and subvert classical timelines, pointing out the shortcoming and conceptual difficulties of chronological representation.

Case Study: Life Course Narratives

Life course models offer a way to individualise people's health situation by creating contextual, personal narratives. This comprehensive perspective on health takes into consideration biological, socio-economical, and psychological factors that expose risks to health, highlighting transitional periods in an individual's life. Such modelling enables people to look back reflexively onto their life story. This can reveal insights into decision-making, factors that contribute to behavioural changes, and signal points for preventative intervention both to individuals and health care providers. These life course models are considered more empathetic, and can therefore be more effective as forms of health communications than presenting data and clinical information alone.

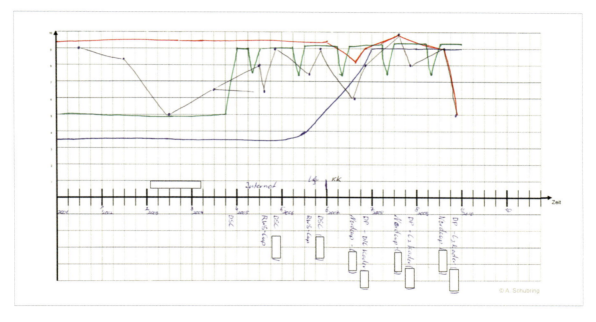

At present, the data storytelling potential of life course narratives is underutilised. The visual presentation of life courses is often disconnected from the underlying data, leading to a separation of evidence-based information and personal narratives. From a data storytelling perspective, bringing together broader, quantitative or statistical data with personal stories can maximise the impacts of evidence and interventions by displaying data points chronologically, situated in the larger context of what was going on in someone's life. By relating health patterns to people's lived realities, and empowering people through reflecting on their own lives, this data storytelling approach could then enhance buy-in from a range of stakeholders and the public. Astrid Shubring et al. (2019) argue, "The biographical mapping approach possesses great potential for qualitative research, the visualization of research results, as well as for practical application" (p. 10).

↳ This life course drawing is a 'biographical mapping' created by a youth athlete in a research project on adolescents' health and illness experiences in elite sport (see Schubring et al., 2019). When creating the mappings, the participating athletes were asked to draw multi-thematic development lines representing their performance (red), health (black), the relevance of health (green) and nutrition (blue) over time. Confidential information has been blinded.

Visualising Absence

If you work with data over a long enough period, it's inevitable that you will come across data sets that contain missing values. This is particularly the case if you are working with data that concern vulnerable populations or underrepresented groups. However, even in the case of seemingly uncomplicated data sets, rarely are we able to perfectly capture all the information we'd like. The task of the data storyteller is not to throw up her hands and say 'Oh well' to missing data, but to find ways to include it in the narratives she tells.

In his popular webinar "How to Visualise Null and Zero," Andy Kirk explores best practices around visualising 'nothing.' He makes the powerful insight that gaps in data are often just as revealing as the data that's available. Kirk outlines three different ways that 'nothing' can appear in data. First, data sets often contain zero values. In this case, the data is available...it's just a zero amount. Let's use a straightforward example: a small business owner has collected data on daily revenue figures for the past three months. Her business is not doing so well, so there are a few days in each month where the revenue figures are zero. If she wants to tell a data story about why some days generate more value than others, paying attention to these zero values is key. Ignoring these gaps in her data set would mean missing out on an opportunity to better understand her business and would lead to an incomplete data story.

The second instance of 'nothing' that Kirk describes is cases where parts of the data simply aren't available. In these instances, the data isn't zero—it's non-existent, or 'null.' Data sets about sensitive subjects are rife with null data. In a blog post for *Behind the Numbers*, part of the Canadian Centre for Policy Alternatives, researcher Katherine Scott makes the important point that measures of gender inequality, such as wage gap data, don't tell the whole story of women's lives if data about, say, Indigenous women's experiences are missing. She writes, "...we don't have a good sense of what is happening at the community level because—with the exception of the Census—there are few reliable, consistent or public data sources available for neighbourhoods or municipalities which disaggregate the population by gender identity, disability, racialized group or Indigenous status" (2019).

The final instance of 'nothing' relates to data visualisation design. Kirk points out that blank spaces can be deliberately introduced into a data visualisation in order to tell a more compelling story about the data. Blank spaces can be used to heighten tension, call attention to an issue, or to show gaps between two or more amounts.

Learning from Comics

with Alexandra Alberda

In recent years, our team at the BU Civic Media Hub began to explore different ways to communicate with data comics for storytelling. Across different fields, researchers find that the comics medium is an effective way to communicate complex information (Czerwiec et al., 2015). Comics combine words and images, using sequential story panels to take the reader through the narrative. As data visualisation researcher Benjamin Bach and his colleagues argue in a recent paper (written as a comic), "Although comics are familiar to everyone, they are vastly underexplored for data-driven storytelling" (Bach et al., 2017). While research repeatedly shows that familiarity with comics can help comprehension, it should be noted that not all readers will have the same literacy level when it comes to reading comics. Some will be more familiar than others with more experimental features in comics.

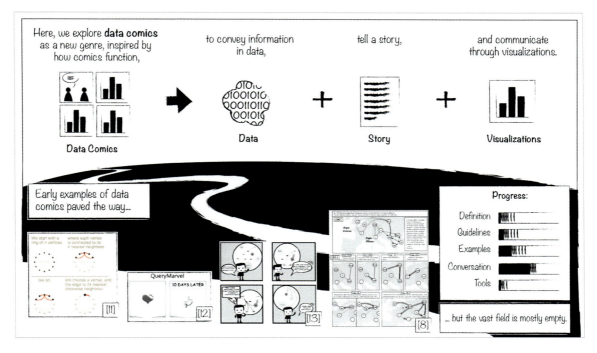

At the BU Civic Media Hub, we summarised the reasons for why comics work well for data storytelling around three principles. Comics are: approachable, accessible, and relatable. These three principles are useful in thinking about how graphics reach out to audiences, especially when trying to connect people with complex or sensitive data, such as health data. The use of graphics to represent decision-making in health has repeatedly been proven useful in patient communication (Chuang et al., 2010; Green and Meyers, 2010; Hawley et al., 2008). Comics can communicate both risk factors and social issues surrounding an illness. Readers

↳ Excerpts from *The emerging genre of data comics*, by B. Bach, N. H. Riche, S. Carpendale, & H. Pfister, 2017. Courtesy of the authors.

can relate to events and experiences, connecting them to their own and creating empathy (McAllister, 1992).

Although comics have different histories and take on different aesthetics throughout the world, they are a cross-cultural medium, prevalent in popular cultures. The familiarity of the medium makes comics approachable. Comics are also approachable as the reader has control over how long they engage with the work. As sequential art, comics express messages through words and images. As opposed to videos or television, in sequential art we process the message at our own speed (Karp, 2011). In terms of connecting with storytelling in comics, Green and Myers hypothesised that comics may make people feel "more focused and in control" and "less isolated and more hopeful" through this individual pacing (Green and Myers, 2010). This sequential aspect of comics also contributes to its potential for enhancing data-driven storytelling. Bach et al. (2017) suggest that making use of panels can help break complex processes into less complex units, helping guide the reader through transitions. For example, panels might be used in a data-driven comic story to move from detail to broader context, or as a way of drilling-down from broader picture to smaller detail.

Comics are likewise accessible in that they are usually presented in an easy to understand format. They often connect with readers by employing iconography that has a local, regional, or national identity, using recognisable images that can often get closer to meaning than text alone. For this reason, comics are often used in language classes to provide visual reinforcement by pairing text and image. Because of their familiarity and ability to make information more comprehensible, comics are also a useful medium for getting information out to the general public (McNicol, 2017, p. 25).

The combination of words and images often make comics more relatable than other graphic forms. In the case of health, "[c]omics can offer patients and family members opportunities for self-awareness, reassurance, empathy, companionship and ways to explore the impact of illness on family relationships" (McNicol, 2017, p. 20). Not only is it important that the disease and health data is depicted accurately, but that patient and family experiences are also represented fairly (Green and Myers, 2010). Through the use of emotive stories, people can make stronger connections with the data, helping them to make sense of their own personal experiences with the specific topic.

Much of the reason for the approachability, accessibility, and relatability of comics is that, as a medium, comics are often characterised by the presence of multiple messages. Subtext, performative encounters, and conflicted feelings can be represented graphically in comics. For example, in *Mom's Cancer*, Brian Fies accomplishes something that is almost impossible to do with pure text: the representation of a conversation along with the hidden, unspoken meaning behind the words. Depicting a telephone call between himself and his stepfather, Fies reveals in each of eight panels both the spoken conversation and the unspoken subtext of what those words really mean (told in separate boxes below each illustration). In this way, the reader simultaneously has access to both the words and the thoughts of the characters. This view inside of someone's inner thoughts illustrates that what we say out loud is not always what we feel inside (Green and Myers, 2010)

In data comics, this layered storytelling style can help capture the uncertainty of data—both as a claim to truth, as well as in relation to the experience or issue it captures. Consider the subject of illness. As different people respond to diagnoses and treatments differently, the plurality of meaning in comics can work to convey a diversity of experiences, as promoted by feminist designers calling for a more humanising data visualisation (McNicol, 2017, p. 21; Lupi, 2017).

↳ **An excerpt from** *Mom's Cancer*.
Courtesy of Brian Fies.

→ A graphic pathography is a memoir told in the comics medium that is specifically about one's experience of illness.

Case Study: DataComicsJS tool

In an effort to test how the introduction of the humanising element of comics contributed to readers' experiences of data visualisation, researcher Zhenpeng Zhao and colleagues at the University of Maryland created a piece of software that created comics frames as explanatory text for visualisations. In addition to keys and captions, a comic character would point to important elements in the data visualisation, adding emphasis, directing the viewer, and helping to show how the visualisation should be read.

Using a sample of data visualisations created through this tool, they set up an experimental trial in efforts to test its efficacy over more traditional data visualisation presentation forms, such as PowerPoint slides. They had 12 students, aged 21 to 30, compare the comics versions to the more traditional visualisations. Quantitative findings from their small-scale study suggested that engagement and enjoyability were higher for the data visualisations presented with the comic. This was supported by qualitative findings in which participants reported that the comics-style presentation helped them comprehend the story as a whole. Speech bubbles provided focus and the sense of an interactive dialogue, while the presence of the comic figure helped them become more immersed in the scenario.

Read the Study: Zhao, Z., Marr, R., & Elmqvist, N. (2015). Data comics: Sequential art for data-driven storytelling. Technical Report. Human Computer Interaction Lab, University of Maryland.

Graphic Medicine

with Alexandra Alberda

Graphic medicine sits at the intersection of the comics medium and healthcare. In 2007, the term 'graphic medicine' was coined by Dr. Ian Williams, a physician, writer, and comics artist (Green and Myers, 2010). Today, 'Graphic Medicine' refers to both a graphic genre and a critically acclaimed organization. The phrase provides an umbrella term to bring together a growing number of comics that engage with healthcare, illness, disability, patient education, treatment and patient experiences, and practitioner experiences. Some comics cover issues including climate change and animals, looking at how they affect our health as well. Works classified as graphic medicine cross a variety of comics genres, including webcomics, graphic pathographies, informational comics, comics strips, single panels, and video/audio installations.

In 2015, Graphic Medicine scholars, artists, and practitioners published the seminal text *Graphic Medicine Manifesto*, an interdisciplinary collection of comics and essays that laid out how comics serve as a way of communicating knowledge and experience to medical practitioners and students. The manifesto looks at the inclusion of health data and the power of self-representation to explore how numerical information impacts patient experience. Advocates of graphic medicine see the potential of enhancing effective communication through the direct, collaborative involvement of patients, practitioners, and artists.

Graphic memoirs specifically bring out the participatory and humanising elements of graphic medicine. These memoirs, or graphic pathographies (Green and Myers, 2010), involve acts of personal storytelling about the lived experience of illness or disability. This often involves representing how people encounter and make sense of data in relation to illness, and in doing so, exploring complex personhood and stigmatized health identities. Christina Maria Koch (2016) writes, "The visual-verbal medium of comics is particularly apt in showing how intricately mental states are bound up with lived bodily experience and an embodied sense of self" (p. 29). In the comics medium, hyper-visualisation allows artists to represent the somatic and psychological experience of one's changing health

→ For an example of hyper-visualisation see the Spotlight: Ken Dahl.

identity. From what it feels like to receive a diagnosis to the fear of telling others about your illness, comics can express the feelings that may not be visible on the surface in a way that no other medium can.

For example, in M.K. Czerwiec's *Taking Turns: Stories from HIV/AIDs Care Unit 371*, a line graph is combined with elements from the memoir to link the total death rate of victims of the HIV virus to moments in the story. The graph and the story begin with the icon of the HIV virus, symbolising for the reader that it is this virus, and not the stigmatised people, that is the cause of these deaths. Towards the climax of the story, pills are used to represent the medication needed to treat the disease that often too many people cannot access. The pill bottles, included in the image as the death rate decreases, are a link to a panel at the denouement of the story, stating "And Then Hope Arrived," referring to when a new medication was introduced that helped save many lives. This line graph not only provides numerical information about the number of victims that died of the disease, but also serves as the story arc for Taking Turns and a guide for readers.

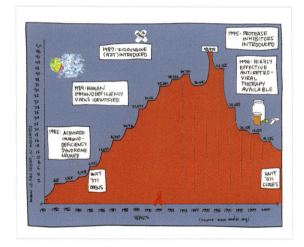 

Including quantitative data in graphic medicine often is a way of connecting the clinical definition of what the artist is experiencing (either their own or someone in their life's illness or disability) and juxtaposing it to the actual lived experience with the illness or disability. Graphic medicine works reclaim the human side of health experiences from the clinical lexicon upheld by healthcare systems, much like the work of graphic pathographies (Charon 2006; Farthing and Priego 2016; Priego 2016; Czerwiec et al., 2015).

⌐ **Left: Hand-drawn amfAR line graph.**
An excerpt from M.K. Czerwiec, *Taking Turns*, 2017. Courtesy of the artist.

⌐ **Right: H.A.A.R.T. medication introduction.**
An excerpt from M.K. Czerwiec, *Taking Turns*, 2017. Courtesy of the artist.

Graphic Social Science

The growing field of graphic social science uses comics and other graphic mediums, such as data visualisations, to illustrate social scientific information in an approachable and accessible way. The term was first coined by Mark Carrigan and arises out of the longer history of graphic medicine and the Medical Humanities. In June 2017, the Graphic Social Science Research Network was established to provide a communications network for scholars, artists, and publishers interested in the practical and theoretical implications for conjoining graphics and the social sciences.

Graphic social science emphasizes interdisciplinarity and collaboration. According to Katy Vigurs (Priego, 2016), comics are innovative tools to increase engagement with social scientific research. Engagement is an important factor when communicating research findings to the public, who may come from non-technical backgrounds. Although comics, illustration, and other graphic mediums are not traditional academic disciplines, they can help scholars reach wider audiences than they would otherwise. In cases where social science directly affects decision-making, such as in health care, it is all the more important that laypeople understand the research undergirding policy and law.

→ Vigurs, K., Jones, S., Harris, D., Zito, A., Sharples, B., Moore, E. & Wightman, J. (2016). *Higher Fees, Higher Debts: Greater Expectations of Graduate Futures? A Research-Informed Comic.* London: Society for Research into Higher Education.

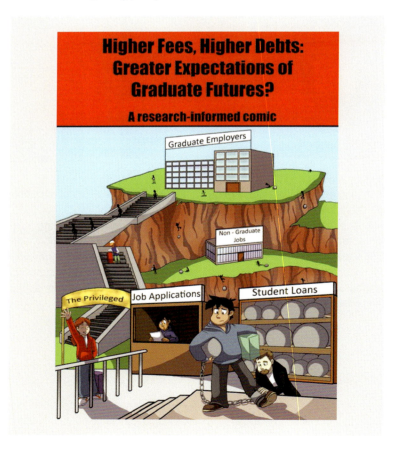

Illustrations are not only tools for disseminating research findings; increasingly, they have become the academic output itself. More and more scholars are experimenting with producing original research in a visual, rather than textual, format. Vigurs' original comic *Higher Fees, Higher Debts: Greater Expectations of Graduate Futures?* is based on a report for the Society for Research into Higher Education. This is one example of a comic that is both a representation of a research report and a valid academic output in its own right.

Many of the practitioners of graphic social science have a background in comics, which is reflected in the emphasis on hand-drawn aesthetics and the panel format. In this way, graphic social science can be interpreted as a reaction to the formal conventions of contemporary data visualisation: its emphasis on computer graphics, its 'clean' aesthetic, and the data literacy required to read and interpret complex graphs.

Graphic social science is still a relatively new field, and there is much to explore. For example, how can the peer review process adapt to the increase of graphics in social science publishing? How can we create new avenues for artists and quantitative researchers to meet and collaborate? With its greater emphasis on narrative, structural flow, and the use of iconography to capture sensitive subjects, graphic social science can enhance the ways that we communicate quantitative data and embed this data in human stories. As numbers are given narratives, stats come to tell complicated—and contested—stories.

Multisensory Data Storytelling

with AM Kanngieser

When we encounter the world, we are always encountering it through all of our available senses. Sight, touch, smell, taste, and sound shape how we perceive and engage our environments. Put another way, we inhabit the world through our bodies, and how we inhabit the world continually changes it. Responding to this reality, artists and researchers have started to incorporate sound, taste, touch, and smell into their representations of numerical data. These "multisensory data visualisations" offer experiences and interactions with data, rather than relying on a passive visual experience.

By thinking about the ways in which our senses and bodies affect and are affected by our day-to-day experiences, multisensory approaches are concerned with bringing new insights to traditional research practices, which often assume a singular, universal subject position. Rather than assume that everyone experiences and inhabits the world in the same ways, multisensory methods are reflexive and experimental; that is to say, they stress that the creation and representation of knowledge, whether it is about culture, society, politics, or communities, is always based on the experiences and position of the person doing, or participating in, the research.

One type of multisensory data visualisation is multisensory maps. Multisensory mapping centres on techniques and approaches to mapping spaces and places through bodily experiences and knowledge. The significance of multisensory mapping for data storytelling is manifold. It means that a larger range of people's experiences and voices can come to bear on research practices and knowledge production.

In 2010, artist/researchers AM Kanngieser and Manuela Zechner undertook a project in Shanghai, China, speaking with young people about their experiences of precarious labour in the cultural industries as part of the Transit Labour project. Alongside interviews and participant observation, the project organised a mapping session in which participants were invited to map out the ways in which their work affected their everyday lives. They developed a combination of maps: a body map on which participants were asked to indicate what body parts experienced particular work-related stress and illness; a city map, to demarcate travel routes taken around the city for work and the time it took; and time maps, broken into hourly brackets for participants to show their activities over a day and to chart the allocation of their time to work-related tasks, social interaction and self-care. What these combined maps showed in detail was the often hidden and overlooked toll taken on the lives of young workers struggling with under-employment despite national discourses celebrating a market boom.

At the same time as illustrating what is often invisible, multisensory data visualisations can expand the field of what comes to count as data. Artist Kate McLean has developed what she calls "smellmaps" of cities around the world. She argues that "smells form part of our knowing," and that by including the sense of smell in cartographic practices we can develop a richer and more complex construction of a place. In her work and other multisensory data visualisations, the emphasis is on phenomenological experience: experiences that are directly related to or manipulated by our existence as bodied people, rather than disembodied brains.

The more acute awareness that smell mapping brings to understandings of how people live in space and experience their environments is complemented through paying attention to sound. Sensory mapping in general encourages a wider spectrum of investigation into how environments are made and how people interact with them. Documenting space through sound, for instance, generates new perspectives into the values people place onto the sounds they hear. A user-contributed project featuring thousands of sound recordings from around the world, Radio Aporee was one of the first online digital sound maps (a map onto which sounds are plotted) to provide a global platform onto which people can upload recordings of their surroundings. From towns to villages, forests to deserts, small island nations to huge metropolitan cities, bedrooms to protests and demonstrations, Radio Aporee offers insight into how people listen to the world and what captures their 'ear.'

→ Kate McLean, *Spring Scents & Smells of the City of Amsterdam*, 2014, Digital Print, 1000 x 1000mm. Courtesy of the designer.

Aside from revealing how people interact with their environments, platforms such as Radio Aporee and the long running immersive exhibition "Dialogue in the Dark," demonstrate how mapping space through the senses can foster different ways of representing and communicating research. Founded in 1998 to open discussion with, and build empathy towards, visually impaired and blind communities, "Dialogue in the Dark" provides an interactive experience of what it is like to navigate urban environments without full sight. Participants are led around a series of reconstructed settings—home, market, street, café—and encouraged to feel, hear, and smell their way around the space. Staffed by guides with low vision or blindness, participants learn about their skills and experiences. By being invited to explore familiar and mundane spaces, participants are able to get a very material idea of how space might be experienced differently.

A simple way to introduce multisensory experience into your data story is by incorporating interactivity: inviting the user to play or manipulate with the data in real time. This is beneficial because it allows the user to compare different trends in data, explore how variables interact, or simply allow for free and open exploration. Interactive data visualisations highlight the dynamism of data by showing how user choice influences what the data shows.

Artists Moritz Stefaner and Susanne Jascheko's project *Data Cuisine* is both interactive and collaborative. Their 'data dishes' are based around research question such as, "Have you ever tried to imagine how a fish soup tastes whose recipe is based on publicly available local fishing data?" Or, "What a pizza would be like if it was based on Helsinki's population mix?"

The result is a collective research experience-slash-cooking class that results in a public meal of 'data foods.' *Halal Internet*, made by Majid Albunni, Christine Liehr and Marketa Hulpachova, uses a meal of saffron risotto with barberry chutney and turmeric chicken to illustrate Internet access in Iran. Arber Hajrizaj and Zana Sherifi's *Seeds of Courage* represents corruption in Kosovo via seeded muffins. Although viewers experience these visualisations as purely visual artefacts, they are produced using a methodological process that incorporates all five of the senses.

→ *Halal Internet*, Data Cuisine MiCT Berlin, 2015, Photo by Uli Holz. Courtesy of the artists.

Majid Albunni, Christine Liehr and Marketa Hulpachova

Halal Internet

In Iran, half of the world's top 500 websites are blocked.

But, 70% of young internet users circumvent the barriers by using proxy servers.

Accessible websites

Accessed via proxy

Blocked websites

Saffron risotto with barberry chutney and turmeric chicken

These projects radically challenge not only the definition of data but the definition of a data visualisation. By combining one or more of the other senses, researchers transform numerical data from information to experience. The collection, translation, and communication of data is enlivened when senses and bodies are taken into account, bringing about opportunities for discussions and interactions that might otherwise remain invisible in academic and activist work.

→ *Seeds of Courage*, Data Cuisine Pristina, 2017, Photo by Majlinda Hoxha. Courtesy of the artists.

Arber Hajrizaj and Zana Sherifi

Seeds of Courage

2015

2016

Future

1137 reported corruption cases

2005 reported corruption cases

Every corruption case is reported

Works Cited and Further Reading

→ Arcia, A. (2019). Colors and imagery in tailored infographics for communicating health information to patients and research participants. OSF Preprints.

→ Arcia, A., Suero-Tejeda, N., Bales, M. E., Merrill, J. A., Yoon, S., Woollen, J., & Bakken, S. (2016). Sometimes more is more: Iterative participatory design of infographics for engagement of community members with varying levels of health literacy. *Journal of the American Medical Informatics Association: JAMIA*, 23(1), 174-183. Retrieved from https://www.ncbi.nlm.nih.gov/pmc/articles/PMC5009940/.

→ Babich, N. (2017). Designing for different screens and devices: 7 steps to creating a great UX. Adobe. Retrieved from https://theblog.adobe.com/designing-for-different-screens-and-devices-7-steps-to-creating-a-great-ux/

→ Bach, B., Riche, N.H., Carpendale, S., & Pfister, H. (2017). The emerging genre of data comics. *Computer Graphics and Applications, IEEE Computer Society*, 6-13. Retrieved from https://aviz.fr/~bbach/datacomics/Bach2017datacomics.pdf.

→ Barros, I.M., Alcântara, T.S., Mesquita, A.R., Bispo, M.L., Rocha, C.E., Moreira, V.P., & Junior, D.P.L. (2014). Understanding of pictograms from the United States Pharmacopeia Dispensing Information (UsP-Di) among elderly Brazilians. *Patient Preference and Adherence*, 8, 1493.

→ Barthes, R. (1977). *Image-Music-Text* (S. Heath, Trans.). New York, NY: Hill and Wang.

→ Barthes, R. (1972). *Mythologies*. London, UK: J. Cape.

→ Bennett, J. (2010). *Vibrant Matter: A Political Ecology of Things*. Durham, NC: Duke University Press.

→ Bounegru, L., Venturini, T., Gray, J., & Jacomy, M. (2017). Narrating networks. *Digital Journalism*, 5(6), 699-730.

→ Bradley, S. (2016, April 5). Icon, index, and symbol—three categories of signs. *Vanseo Design*. Retrieved from https://vanseodesign.com/web-design/icon-index-symbol/.

→ Chandler, D. (1994). *Semiotics for Beginners*. Self-published. Retrieved from http://www.visual-memory.co.uk/daniel/Documents/S4B/index.html.

→ Charon, R. (2006). *Narrative Medicine: Honoring the Stories of Illness*. New York: Oxford University Press.

→ Chuang, M. H., Lin, C. L., Wang, Y. F., & Cham, T. M. (2010). Development of pictographs depicting medication use instructions for low-literacy medical clinic ambulatory patients. *Journal of Managed Care Pharmacy*, 16(5), 337-345.

→ Connolly, W. E. (2013). 'The 'new materialism' and the fragility of things. *Millennium: Journal of International Studies*, 41(3), 399–412.

→ Czerwiec, M., Williams, I., Squier, S. M., Green, M. J., Myers, K. R., & Smith, S. T. (2015). *Graphic Medicine Manifesto*. University Park, PA: The Pennsylvania State University Press.

→ D'Ignazio, C. & Klein, L.F. (2016). "Feminist Data Visualization." Conference Proceedings of IEEE VIS Workshop on Visualization for the Digital Humanities, Baltimore.

→ Evans, K. (2015). *Red Rosa: A Graphic Biography of Rosa Luxemburg*. London, UK: Verso.

→ Farthing, A., & Priego, E. (2016). 'Graphic medicine' as a mental health information resource: Insights from comics producers. *The Comics Grid: Journal of Comics Scholarship, 6*(3).

→ Feigenbaum, A. & Weissmann, D.G.B. (forthcoming). From copwatching to data aggregating: Understanding police violence through CATO's Police Misconduct Reporting Project. *Canadian Journal of Communication, 45*(1).

→ Feigenbaum, A., Thorsen, E., Weissmann, D., & Demirkol, O. (2016). Visualising data stories together: Reflections on data journalism education from the Bournemouth University Datalabs Project. *Journalism Education, 5*(2), 59-74.

→ Few, S., & Perceptual Edge. (2011). The chartjunk debate. *Visual Business Intelligence Newsletter*, June, 1-11.

→ Friendly, M. (2008). A brief history of data visualization. In *Handbook of Data Visualization* (pp. 15-56). Springer, Berlin, Heidelberg.

→ Gordon, A. F. (2008). *Ghostly Matters: Haunting and the Sociological Imagination*. Minneapolis, MN: University of Minnesota Press.

→ Green, M. J., & Myers, K. R. (2010). Graphic medicine: use of comics in medical education and patient care. *BMJ*, 340, c863.

→ Hall, S. (1997). "The work of representation." In S. Hall (Ed.), *Representation: Cultural Representations and Signifying Practices* (pp. 13-74). London: SAGE Publications.

→ Hawley, S.T., Zikmund-Fisher, B., Ubel, P., Jancovic, A., Lucas, T., & Fagerlin, A. (2008). The impact of the format of graphical presentation on health-related knowledge and treatment choices. *Patient Education and Counselling*, 73(3), 448-455.

→ Hodder, I. (2012). *Entangled: An Archaeology of the Relationships between Humans and Things*. Chichester, UK: John Wiley & Sons.

→ Home Office. (2016). *Social Network Analysis: 'How to Guide.'* Retrieved from https://assets.publishing.service.gov.uk/government/uploads/system/uploads/attachment_data/file/491572/socnet_howto.pdf.

→ Hullman, J., & Diakopoulos, N. (2011). Visualization rhetoric: Framing effects in narrative visualization. *IEEE Transactions on Visualization and Computer Graphics*, 17(12), 2231-2240.

→ Kanngieser, A.M., & Zechner, M. (2010). Future functions: Aspiration, desire and futures. In C. Kernow, B. Neilson, N. Rossiter, & S. Zehle (Eds.), *Transit Labour Digest #2* (pp. 11-13). Sydney: Blood and Thunder Press.

→ Karp, A. (2011). Jews in America: A cartoon history, and: Jews and American comics: An illustrated history of an American art form. *Shofar: An Interdisciplinary Journal of Jewish Studies*, 29(2), 174-177.

→ Kennedy, H., Hill, R., Aiello, G., & Allen, W. (2016). The work that visualisation conventions do. *Information, Communication and Society, 19*(6), 715-735.

→ Kirk, A. (2016). *Data visualisation: Handbook for Data Driven Design*. London: SAGE Publications Ltd.

→ Kirk, A. How to visualise null and zero [Webinar]. *Tableau*. Retrieved from https://www.tableau.com/learn/webinars/visualise-null-zero.

→ Koch, C.M. (2016). "When you have no voice, you don't exist"?: Envisioning disability in David Small's Stitches. In C. Foss, J.W. Gray, & Z. Whalen (Eds.), *Disability in Comic Books and Graphic Narratives* (pp. 29-43). Basingstoke, UK: Palgrave Macmillan.

→ Lidwell, W., Holden, K., & Butler, J. (2003). *Universal Principles of Design: 100 Ways to Enhance Usability, Influence Perception, Increase Appeal, Make Better Design Decisions, and Teach through Design.* Gloucester, Mass: Rockport Publishers.

→ Lima, M. (2014). *The Book of Trees: Visualizing Branches of Knowledge*. New York, NY: Princeton Architectural Press.

→ Lupi, G. (2017). "Data Humanism, the Revolution will be Visualized." Retrieved from https://medium.com/@giorgialupi/data-humanism-the-revolution-will-be-visualized-31486a30dbfb.

→ McAllister, M.P. (1992). Comic books and AIDS. *The Journal of Popular Culture, 26*(2), 1-24.

→ McCloud, S. (1993). *Understanding Comics: The Invisible Art.* Northampton, Mass: Kitchen Sink Press.

→ McCloud, S. (2000). *Reinventing Comics: How Imagination and Technology are Revolutionizing an Art Form.* New York, NY: HarperCollins Publishers Inc.

→ McCloud, S. (2006). *Making Comics: Storytelling Secrets of Comics, Manga and Graphic Novels.* New York, NY: HarperCollins Publishers Inc.

→ McLean, K. About. Retrieved from https://sensorymaps.com/about/.

→ McNicol, S. (2017). The potential of educational comics as a health information medium. *Health Information & Libraries Journal*, 34(1), 20-31.

→ Merleau-Ponty, M. (1962). *Phenomenology of Perception* (C. Smith, Trans.). London, UK: Routledge.

→ Priego, E. (2016). Comics as research, comics for impact: The case of higher fees, higher debts. *The Comics Grid: Journal of Comics Scholarship*, 6. Retrieved from https://www.comicsgrid.com/articles/10.16995/cg.101/.

→ Richler, M., Vaillancourt, R., Celetti, S.J., Besançon, L., Arun, K.P., & Sebastien, F. (2012). The use of pictograms to convey health information regarding side effects and/or indications of medications. *Journal of Communication In Healthcare*, 5(4), 220-226.

→ Schubring, A., Mayer, J., & Thiel, A. (2019). Drawing careers: The value of a biographical mapping method in qualitative health research. *International Journal of Qualitative Methods*, 18,

→ Scott, K. (2019, March 5). Who's missing: Data gaps undermine our efforts to track gender gaps and push for meaningful change. *Behind the Numbers*. Retrieved from http://behindthenumbers.ca/2019/03/05/datagaps-gendergaps/.

→ Segel, E. & Heer, J. (2010). Narrative visualization: Telling stories with data. *IEEE Transactions on Visualization & Computer Graphics, 16*(6):1139-1148.

→ Tufte, E.R. (1983). *The Visual Display of Quantitative Information.* Cheshire, CT: Graphics Press.

→ UK Home Office, Social network analysis: How to guide. Retrieved from https://www.gov.uk/government/publications/social-network-analysis-how-to-guide

→ Visocky O'Grady, J. & Visocky O'Grady, K. (2008). *The Information Design Handbook.* Cincinnati: How Books.

→ Zikmund-Fisher, B.J., Witteman, H.O., Dickson, M., Fuhrel-Forbis, A., Kahn, V.C., Exe, N.L., Valerio, M., Holtzman, L.G., Scherer, L.D., & Fagerlin, A. (2014). Blocks, ovals, or people? Icon type affects risk perceptions and recall of pictographs. *Medical Decision Making: An International Journal of the Society for Medical Decision Making*, 34(4), 443-453. Retrieved from https://www.ncbi.nlm.nih.gov/pmc/articles/PMC3991751/.

Spotlight:
Patil Tchilinguirian

Patil Tchilinguirian is a multidisciplinary designer and artist who uses stories to explore political and social circumstances. She uses various methods and materials in her work, including silkscreen, embroidery, collage, and data visualisation.

Patil Tchilinguirian's installation *Shelter-Me-Not* (2015) combines data analysis with cultural craft-making traditions to explore the experiences of Syrian refugees in the aftermath of the Syrian civil war. Using data from a UNHCR March 2014 shelter survey, the work looks at how access to basic needs, such as housing, water, and sanitation, are threatened by the precarious effects of displacement and forced migration.

For the installation, Tchilinguirian embroidered seven monochrome visual representations of these basic needs and suspended them from the ceiling at eye level. She left the embroideries unfinished, their black threads spilling off the back of the embroidery hoop and onto the floor. Statistics corresponding to the images on the hoops were printed in circles and placed on the floor. For example, the embroidered image of a toilet hangs over a sign on the floor that states "23% lacking latrines." By juxtaposing these elements, the artist draws a literal correlation between the numerical data and its textile representation.

At the centre of the embroidery hoops hangs a larger hoop depicting a typical Syrian household, which often contains multiple cohabiting families. The faceless figures are rendered in fabric, rather than embroidery. Their anonymity generalises them to the viewer, while the portrait's placement in the center of the installation symbolises how access to basic needs now revolve around their daily existence. In an interview with the artist, Patil emphasises her use of embroidery as a way of invoking powerful cultural histories, as well as creating a particular aesthetic experience beyond the transmission of numerical data. She stated, "The artisanal aspect of textile art juxtaposes a layer of honesty and ingenuity to the meanings negotiated" (email interview, February 15, 2018). This aesthetic intervention expands the framework of interaction to offer a broader understanding of the experience of displacement and cultural loss felt by Syrian refugees.

According to the artist, this representational format uses differing kinds of information "order to arrive at a compelling story that is factual yet has a strong visual component" and that "stirs emotions, builds empathy and conveys new knowledge" (2018). These informational layers leverage the tension between the numerical data set on the floor and the handmade textiles that hang over them.

For Tchilinguirian, design is a means of connecting data to culture in impactful, socially relevant ways. She cites her research into Palestine culture, particularly the sociocultural importance of embroidery threads and patterns, as an influence for her practice. Yet she acknowledges that artists and designers must often navigate difficult terrain when referencing cultural narratives and political events in their work. "As designers, we tend to want to solve complex social issues through data visualization but I think the real negotiation happens when we acknowledge that it's not about solving a particular problem but rather to pose questions that allow a certain discourse to take place," she states. "To open up a space for dialogue that recognizes these sensitive topics and makes them accessible to a larger audience" (2018).

↳ Patil Tchilinguirian, *Shelter-me-not*, 2015. Photos by Ieva
Saudargaité Douaihi. Courtesy of the artist.

Spotlight:
Heather Dewey-Hagborg

Heather Dewey-Hagborg is an artist and educator whose work treads the intersections of art and science. Her work combines scientific methods with a creative practice to explore issues in genetics, biopolitics, technology, and surveillance.

Since its founding in 2008, the biotechnology company Parabon NanoLabs has provided DNA phenotyping services to police and other law enforcement organizations. Their "Parabon Snapshot" advanced phenotyping service uses a suspect's DNA to create a composite sketch of that individual, including details like eye colour, whether or not the suspect has freckles, and face and skull shape.

But how accurate are these technologies in predicting a person's appearance? How much should law enforcement rely on them when investigating crime? Artist Heather Dewey-Hagborg's projects *Stranger Visions* (2012-2013) and *Radical Love* (2015) address these questions by using a subset of phenotyping technology to produce 3-D printed facial portraits constructed from DNA samples. *Stranger Visions* used DNA information taken from strangers' discarded detritus (cigarette butts, hairs, and chewing gum); while *Radical Love* was produced in collaboration with whistleblower Chelsea Manning, who provided cheek and hair cells.

These works critique the way that phenotyping technologies are premised on reductive categorizations of sex and race. According to Dewey-Hagborg, phenotyping classifies "types of bodies into socially constructed categories like gender and race" by using a process that quantifies one's ancestral background and translates it into a set of visual characteristics. These characteristics, however, are built on statistical assumptions as well as the motives of the designer. Although Parabon NanoLabs use confidence measures alongside their DNA portraits, which indicate which characteristics they are more or less certain about, in actual practice Dewey-Hagborg argues that the pictures are "presented as objective, neutral, and

certain" (Hagborg, Probably Chelsea).

Radical Love continues the artist's critical exploration of phenotyping. The concept for this project began when *Paper Magazine* contacted Dewey-Hagborg in 2015 to create a DNA portrait of Manning, who was incarcerated for whistleblowing. At that time, the only available portrait of Manning was from 2010 — three years prior to her public announcement that she was transgender. The prison's restricting policy on visitors meant that there were no up-to-date photographs of Chelsea, making her new identity *as* Chelsea effectively invisible in the press and news media.

Using a DNA sample from cheek and hair cells, Dewey-Hagborg created two portraits: one with an 'algorithmically neutral' gender and one 'algorithmically female.' On her website, the artist writes, "The exhibition of both these possible faces side by side draws attention to the problem of utilizing chromosomes or birth assigned sex to assign gender as well as a larger issue of what it means to rely on stereotyped ideas of what a gendered face is 'supposed' to look like."

Dewey-Hagborg's work makes clear that we urgently need to reimagine the potentials and pitfalls of genetic data visualizations. Articulating the limits of new genetic technologies will facilitate new ways of visualising what it means to be human, chromosomes and all.

→   Cascone, S. (2017, August 4). The strange and troubling science behind the 3-D printed portraits of Chelsea Manning. *Artnet News*. Retrieved from https://news.artnet.com/exhibitions/chelsea-manning-1041596.

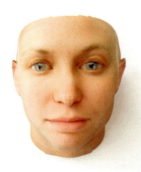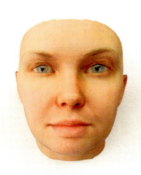

↳ Installation view of *Stranger Visions in You Must Change Your Life*, Artefact Expo, STUK Kunstencentrum, February 2015. Photo by Joeri Thiry. Courtesy of the artist and Fridman Gallery

→ Heather Dewey-Hagborg, *Radical Love*, 2016; Genetic materials, custom software, 3d prints, documentation. Portrait dimensions: 8 x 6 x 6 inches. Photo by Thomas Dexter. Courtesy of the artist and Fridman Gallery.

→   Dewey-Hagborg, H. Sci-fi crime drama with a strong black lead. *The New Inquiry*. Retrieved from https://thenewinquiry.com/sci-fi-crime-drama-with-a-strong-black-lead/.

→   Dewey-Hagborg, H. *Radical love: Chelsea Manning*. Retrieved from https://deweyhagborg.com/projects/radical-love.

→   Dewey-Hagborg, H. *Probably Chelsea*. Retrieved from https://deweyhagborg.com/content/6-projects/6-probably-chelsea/probably-chelsea-essay.pdf.

Spotlight:
Catherine D'Ignazio

Catherine D'Ignazio's multidisciplinary work straddles the fields of design, technology, and the humanities. She is interested in data visualisations as tools to increase civic participation and to empower communities. She is an Assistant Professor of Urban Science and Planning and Director of the Data + Feminism Lab at MIT. This is an abridged interview conducted in June 2018. It has been edited for clarity. You can find out more about the "Make the Breast Pump Not Suck Hackathon" at www.makethebreastpumpnotsuck.com.

→ **Why is participation an important component of design in your work?**

Participation is important as a way of broadening one's own perspective. We come into the world as one person: we have one person's body, one person's history, one person's experiences. A lot of the training of a designer is in ways to expand beyond that. But I think the key thing is always putting yourself in situations where you're trying to expand your knowledge and your own conception of things in your world view. I think participation is maybe the best way to do that. If you're able to and have the ability to actually involve the people with whom or for whom you are doing the work, I think in most cases it produces a better outcome. Often it lengthens the process and that's why sometimes it's just not feasible.

But I think that more participation, the better. There's that trading of worldviews that happens. The participants become more aware of the affordances of design as well. The expertise of the designer or storyteller is then shared with them.

→ **It's like a two-way learning process.**

Absolutely. And relationship building - not just designing for somebody that you think about in the abstract, but really being in relationship with those somebodies, I think can be in some cases transformative.

→ **That reminds me of a project you co-founded in September 2014, "Make the Breast Pump Not Suck Hackathon."** You had women contacting you with very well-thought-out ideas for ways to improve the breast pump, but no designer or engineer had ever thought to ask them.

Totally. All they needed was someone to invite their participation. We got long Google documents. We got ten-point plans. Some were just like, 'Let me pump while sleeping.' But there were people who had clearly been thinking about this for a really long time.

→ **What makes 'feminist hacking' feminist and how do you think it's different from other hacking practices or hacking subcultures? For example, there were so many children present at the breast pump hackathon, which is so different from other hacking events.**

Yeah, I like to say that we got the Guinness Book of World Records for the most babies at a hackathon. I think there are multiple things. Of course, there's the subject matter. In a certain way we thought about this as a hack of the MIT Media Lab, which was an institution we were a part of as well. The Media Lab and most traditional hacking practices are about creating the future and innovating for the better. But what often what happens in those future visions of technology is that they don't include women. They don't include women's bodies. They don't include babies. So, in a way, just the choice of focusing on breast pumps was an intentional feminist choice.

There are also things around process. I think we modeled a very feminist process. It was organized by a

MAKE THE BREAST PUMP NOT SUCK HACKATHON

↳ Make the Breast Pump Not Suck Hackathon, 2018. Photo by Ken Richardson.

→ Participants at the Make the Breast Pump Not Suck Hackathon, 2018. Photo by Ken Richardson.

group of us. We had the luxury of having a grant to put the second one [in April 2018] together, where we focused on racial equity and socio-economic equity. We had a year of lead-up time and we really involved a lot of people who face the most barriers to breastfeeding. We involved them as innovators. In our original conception, we wanted to interview them. Then we got told very explicitly by a really awesome woman who runs the Black Mother Breastfeeding Association, hey, you guys are being extractive because the main value of what you're doing is to have black designers come to the table and have black moms participating.

So we flipped our research model based on her feedback. I think for us that was a learning opportunity but also what made it a feminist process. It's not always doing everything perfectly and knowing how to perfectly design for equity, but it's being adaptable enough in the process that when you learn something you're doing in a hegemonic way, that you can shift that practice and being open to hearing that. I feel that's part of the feminist process as well.

→ **How do we include a sense of uncertainty in our work while still maintaining a strong advocacy message?**
It's an interesting tension. Lauren Klein and I wrote a paper, "Feminist Data Visualization," that does talk about legitimizing affect and embodiment. We talked about some of the forms of data visualization that are alternate to, say, screen-based 2-D presentations. But it wouldn't be to say that to do feminist data visualization you have to do a tactile form or something like that. I think those experiments are really useful for interrogating the boundaries of what qualifies.

I'm trying to think through how we build more embodied experiences of data, but on the other hand, for certain kinds of goals – advocacy goals, activist goals – the best solution might be a Google map. We don't always have to innovate the form of presentation. I do think there's a lot of potential and power in the classic data presentation methods because you can wield the authority in a political way. You can critique the authority, and certainly that's what a feminist position does. We can also use that. You can deploy neutrality intentionally as a strategy.

↳ Participants at the Make the Breast Pump
Not Suck Hackathon, 2018. Photo by Ken
Richardson.

→ Make the Breast Pump Not Suck Hackathon,
2018.

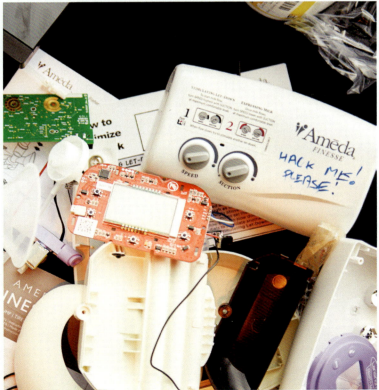

Spotlight:
Herald/Harbinger

Jer Thorp is an artist, writer, and teacher living in New York City. He is the co-founder of The Office for Creative Research and is an adjunct Professor in New York University's Interactive Telecommunications Program. Ben Rubin is an artist and designer. He is the Director of the Center for Data Arts at The New School in New York City, where he is also an Associate Professor of Design.

In 2002, Eugene Stoermer and Nobel Laureate Paul Crutzen proposed that the effects of human activity on the Earth have been so significant that they have propelled us into a new geological epoch: "the Anthropocene." Anthropogenic effects are seemingly everywhere: from the rapid acidification of the world's oceans to the dissemination of plastics in the biosphere, human activity has permanently shaped the world in undeniable ways.

Perhaps the most visible symbol of the Anthropocene is the glacier. Artists Jer Thorp and Ben Rubin's *Herald/Harbinger* is one recent work that uses glacial activity to explore the relationship between humans and the natural environment.

Herald/Harbinger combines visual and aural elements to bring the Bow Glacier, a site approximately 160 miles west of Calgary in Canada's Banff National Park, to Brookfield Place, a 56-story office building located in downtown Calgary, Canada. To create the work, Thorp and Rubin built a solar-powered seismic observatory near the glacier. They also installed a permanent sensor system on the body of the glacier, allowing them access to its activity. This data is then uploaded via satellite and transferred in real-time to Brookfield Place. There, a visual LED installation and an immersive soundscape relay the relentless real-time changes to water and ice that play out in and on the glacier's immense form.

Herald/Harbinger is a new way of visualising data, one that creates a sharp break in the everyday of city life. Against the bustle of traffic and the noises of pe-

destrians, passersby will hear a glacial symphony, as water and ice resonate across the building plaza. The sounds are a constant reminder that glaciers are living things – not conscious, perhaps, but certainly animate. Even minute temperature changes can produce expansions and contractions in the ice. According to Thorp, the soundscape creates a sense of having "one foot in the Pleistocene, the other in the Anthropocene" (Thorp 2018). The noises become a two-way conversation between radically different and yet irreparably conjoined landscapes.

This work powerfully illustrates the ways in which our comprehension of a phenomenon like climate change is severely limited by numbers alone. It is not the real-time data transfers that make this work compelling, but the engagement of our senses. The visual pulsations of the LED lights combine with the fragments of sound in the plaza, bringing the object of the glacier ever closer, in an intimate reckoning that defies physical distance.

→   Crutzen, P. and Stoermer, E. (2000, May). The "Anthropocene." *Global Change Newsletter*. Retrieved from www.igbp.net/download/18.316f18321323470177580001401/1376383088452/NL41.pdf

→   Thorp, J. (2018, June 25). Sounding the Bow: How we moved a vanishing glacier to the center of Canada's fastest growing city. Retrieved from www.medium.com/@blprnt/sounding-the-bow-628f92beb0b7

↳ Ben Rubin and Jer Thorp, *Herald/Harbinger*, 2017. Photo by Brett Gilmour. Courtesy of the artists.

→ Solar-powered remote sensing station, Bow glacier, Banff National Park. Courtesy of the artists.

Spotlight:
Ken Dahl's *Monsters*

Artist Ken Dahl (the pen name of Gabby Schulz) is the author of five graphic novels and many more minicomics and web comics. Dahl was a fellow at The Center for Cartoon Studies from 2007-2008. His graphic novel *Monsters* was awarded the Ignatz Award for Outstanding Story and was nominated for an Eisner Award in Best Reality-Based Work.

Ken Dahl's graphic novel *Monsters* (2009) is a semi-autobiographical tale about the author's experience contracting herpes. To contextualise his early attempts to cope with his diagnosis, Dahl visualises popular data, such as what would most likely be found on WebMD or in a pamphlet at a GP's office. He draws from stereotypes of the herpes virus as well as clinical understandings of the disease in his illustrations. In some parts of the book, he literally *becomes* the herpes virus, a strange, revolting, cellular mass. The chaos involved in his initial attempts at reconciling having an STD with his personal identity is apparent in the structure of these pages. In one scene, his naked body is suspended in a black void around explanatory text similar to a medical diagram. However, the use of the comic avatar, rather than a medical illustration typically found in educational books, reminds the reader that a living body is the reference for these anxieties.

Dahl utilises hyper-visualisation to combine the somatic and psychological experience of being diagnosed with an STD. Dahl's commentary around these stereotypical depictions of herpes tackles the social stigma of the virus, which can be used as a model for other fields of study and practice (Czerwiec et al. 2015, p. 53). Visual storytelling is used to show how data can enforce a socially stigmatized identity onto the newly traumatising diagnosed. Including the psychological experience of diagnosis lends a sense of active agency to his visualised parody of illness. He challenges and plays with the social horror connected to his diagnosis in order to humanise the traumatic experience of re-identification.

Toward the end of the memoir he confesses to a new lover that he has herpes. During his confession, he depicts himself as a personified herpes virus, and only finds acceptance when she responds with nonchalance. As she explains that most people have it, he is transformed back into a human – he becomes himself. The data-driven stigma that oppressed him throughout the narrative dissolves away as a human connection is made. *Monsters* provides insight into the struggle of unbecoming and becoming that trauma and illness instils in a person's sense of self. Most importantly, it shows how data often plays a central role in this process.

By Alexandra Alberda

→ Dahl, K. (2009). *Monsters*. Jackson Heights, NY: Secret Acres.

→ Czerwiec, M., Williams, I., Squier, S. M., Green, M. J., Myers, K. R., & Smith, S. T. (2015). *Graphic Medicine Manifesto*. University Park, PA: The Pennsylvania State University Press.

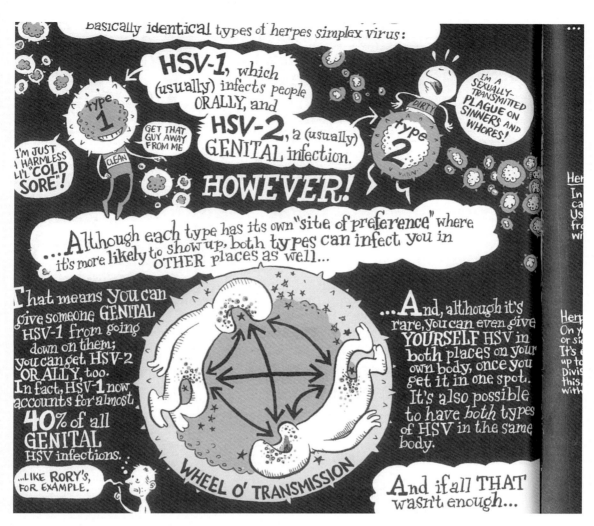

↳ Ken Dahl, excerpt from *Monsters*, 2009. Courtesy of the artist.

Spotlight:
Argumentative mapmaking

Yasuhito Abe is trained as a media and communication studies scholar and is currently teaching at Komazawa University, Japan. He examined the role of citizens in producing alternative data on radioactive contamination after the Fukushima Daiichi Nuclear Disaster of 2011.

The Tohoku earthquake and tsunami of 2011 and the resulting Fukushima Daiichi nuclear disaster created an alternative communication space for digital mapmaking practices. In the wake of this 'triple disaster,' a wide variety of people, from experts to laypeople, tactically engaged to measure radiation for ensuring their health and safety and circulated the collected data by using digital technologies. Taking each datum as a fundamental component of digital data storytelling, they created their own visual representations of radiation contamination in a map form as a rhetorical resource for making an argument.

Just as Rosenberg (2013) suggests, data are essentially rhetorical resources for making a claim. In other words, we collect data for making persuasive claims. From suggestions on how to avoid specific spots where the level of radiation is higher than neighbouring areas ("hotspots") to requests for the decontamination practices from local government, people measure radiation and make maps to persuade others into taking action. Accordingly, the triple disaster witnessed the rise in argumentative mapmaking practices of environmental networks (Abe 2015).

The question then is, to what extent are their media-making practices rhetorically sound? How do people produce data and make maps to tell trustworthy stories? Following in the footstep of Toulmin's (2003) model on argument, argumentative mapmaking as a distinctive form of data storytelling can be seen as the process of making data, warrants, and claims that would persuade people into taking action. Distinct from more general data storytelling, argumentative mapmaking involves an explicit articulation of data collection and representation method as a warrant of an argument, making a clear connection between data and claim in the process of making maps.

For example, take the case of the Minna no Data Site (MDS) or the Combined Database of Independent Radioactivity Measurement Labs. MDS is a grassroots database of citizen-generated data—it records measurement readings of citizens, by citizens and for citizens. Born in 2013, MDS embodies a key theme of argumentative mapping practice as data storytelling in compelling ways: it maps the past and imagines the future to make an argument about the present. From October 2014 to September 2017, more than four thousand MDS volunteers measured soil contamination in seventeen prefectures in East Japan, mapping the collected inputs as a rhetorical resource for making an argument. What is noteworthy is that MDS makes its data collection method available online for a wider audience. Sharing the details of data collection methods is a key storytelling component of argumentative mapping practice for validating the accuracy of each datum, at least rhetorically (Abe 2016).

With the resulting data, MDS visualized its data on soil contamination in light of the past and the future. For example, in order to present the evidence of the scale of the disaster to a wider audience, MDS used collective inputs taken from October 2014 to September 2017 in order to estimate the level of radiation immediately after the disaster and create a projected visualisation. Furthermore, MDS made reference to post-Chernobyl Ukrainian and Belarusian evacuation zones to colour individual datum, engaging with the argumentative mapping practice against the state's authoritative views of the consequences of the triple disaster (Abe 2017).

Telling a data story of the future, MDS produced vis-

ualisations of the residual level of radiation over a hundred years, from 2011 to 2111. This projection allows audiences to imagine what the effects of the disaster will look like in the future. These visualisation practices involve the explicit articulation of representation methods as a rhetorical resource for making a convincing claim—that the disaster isn't over yet.

To reach a wider audience, MDS published a print version of their visualisations as a map-book, embodying their argumentative mapmaking practice. At the moment of writing, the Japanese mass media, and the *Tokyo Shimbun* in particular, widely reported the map-book for a wider audience. It remains to be seen to what extent MDS will make an impact through their argumentative mapping practices. That said, their practice of argumentative mapmaking opens up a new horizon for data storytelling in Japan and elsewhere.

Minna no data site: en.minnanods.net

By Yasuhito Abe

→ Abe, Y., 2015. *Measuring for what: Networked citizen science movements after the Fukushima nuclear accident*. Doctoral dissertation, University of Southern California.

→ Abe, Y., 2016. Redefining post-Fukushima Japanese society with data. In T. Suzuki, T. Kato, A. Kubota, & S. Murai (Eds.). *Proceedings of the 5th Tokyo conference on argumentation*. (pp.9-15), Tokyo, Japan.

→ Abe, Y., 2017. "Mina no Data Site (MDS) and the culture of measurement after Fukushima." *Unmediated: Politics and Communication* (1), pp.68-72.

→ Rosenberg, D., 2013. Data before the fact. In L. Gitelman. (Eds.), *"Raw Data" is an Oxymoron* (pp.15-37). Cambridge, MA: The MIT Press.

→ Toulmin, S. E., 2003. *The Uses of Argument*. Cambridge University Press.

Spotlight:
Photovoice

Pablo Bose is an urban geographer and migration studies scholar based at the University of Vermont. Over the past decade he has been studying forced migration across the globe and in particular looked at refugee resettlement in numerous locations across the world. He is especially interested in the movement of migrants to non-traditional destinations, especially outside of the major metropolitan areas that have long been the most attractive for immigrants.

I employ primarily qualitative methods to ask why migrants are moving to new locations, what happens to them in these places, and what happens to those communities that receive them. This spotlight focuses on the exploration of that last topic through the use of photovoice and other visual methods.

This project to understand the movement of refugees to new places—especially in North America and Western Europe—began in 2008, before the exponential increase in forced migrants and in the resulting xenophobic backlash against them became so great. It was originally more than just about documenting landscape change and perceptions of community within a resettlement site. Using photovoice was a way of identifying places of importance and areas in need of improvement for refugee populations.

Photovoice is a method that has been utilised within diverse fields including urban planning, public health, and critical race and ethnic studies as a way of putting the perspective in the hands of the 'subjects' of research. Participants and collaborators are given prompts and asked to identify what is of most (or least) value to them, based on the parameters of the project. Doing so allows us to view a particular topic from the perspectives of those most closely related to it, rather than from the position of dispassionate observer or outsider.

Our effort to use photovoice was meant to map and document such spaces by the research team and to critique and redefine such meaning-making with our community collaborators, all with the goal of intervening in urban planning decisions and investments by the city and state in specific neighborhoods. But in an era of heightened scrutiny and tension within and among immigrant communities, what does it mean to make oneself and one's significant places so visible—to outsiders of all kinds?

Our project team worked with resettlement agencies in our various study sites to identify such spaces—neighborhoods and areas of cities with relatively high populations of newcomers—and we began to identify some of the landscape changes that were visible to us as outsiders in the research team. In Vermont, for example, we began our project by focusing on two neighborhoods: the Old North End in Burlington, and Main Street in Winooski, a town across the river within the metropolitan region. Both of these have a long history of immigrant settlement (though primarily of French Canadian and European immigrants) and have for the past forty years been the main hub of initial settlement for refugees. In each of these towns we were able to identify new businesses, community gathering spaces, social services, religious institutions, grocery stores, public resources, public space, and food and drink amongst other important spaces. Yet our understanding of all of these was only ever going to be partial given our lack of embeddedness within the communities.

Photovoice for us thus became a method for uncovering what refugee residents saw in terms of changes

↳ An image representing community. Courtesy of the author.

to their local neighborhood. At its best, photovoice is a method that can be used to reveal the narratives, logics, ideologies, and contested visions that lie hidden within and beneath places, processes and people. Our intent at the start of this project had been to use photovoice to identify changes that refugees and their neighbors wished to see in their communities in Vermont—what were the things they valued and how might they advocate for needs that they might articulate?

Our goal was to have the information gleaned from this process make its way into urban development and planning via neighborhood planning assemblies, city departments, municipal councils, and other local actors with whom we might share our data. We recruited a number of newly arrived refugees in each of these two communities, and set them the following four prompts:

1. Take 3 pictures of things you want to see changed in your neighborhood
2. Take 3 pictures of things you want to see stay the same in your neighborhood
3. Take 3 pictures of things that represent USA/Vermont to you in your neighborhood
4. Take 3 pictures of things that represent home/community to you in your neighborhood

Participants then sent these pictures to our researchers along with a description of why they had chosen each image (interpreters were provided where necessary). A follow-up session was to be held consisting of each group collectively meeting to discuss a selection of photos curated by the research team with particularly interesting and compelling photos, especially those that might reveal contested or multi-faceted uses or understandings of particular spaces.

The results of this work have been both fascinating and challenging. Participants spoke openly and often about their own embodied unease at being visible as photographer while brown or black in a predominantly white community. We found that images of outside locations were most often blurred or taken from cars, while those of home and community were often sharp, vivid, and carefully composed. Part of this is not surprising—as valuable a tool as photovoice can be, its potential has always been balanced by ethical concerns regarding representation, voice, the permanency of the images taken, and their ultimate use.

In this project, as immigration became an increasingly controversial topic and refugees had an unflattering spotlight shone on them, it became harder and harder to recruit participants. There were many reasons for this. More than a few people expressed discomfort at being seen in public taking pictures—would this make them appear suspicious, they asked? And while we explicitly asked participants NOT to take pictures of any individual, they still asked about the safety of their data and the anonymity of their responses. But the part most refugees worried about, was in having the conversation with neighbors who were not refugees.

What if they espoused the views heard on cable news or in political rallies they asked? How might life in an otherwise occasionally tense but generally stable neighborhood change? Our use of photovoice in this project thus contributed to a much broader and more substantial questions, not just about the mundane and everyday concerns regarding potholes, graffiti and beautification of neighborhoods, but much deeper issues regarding citizenship, belonging and the right to the city.

By Pablo Bose

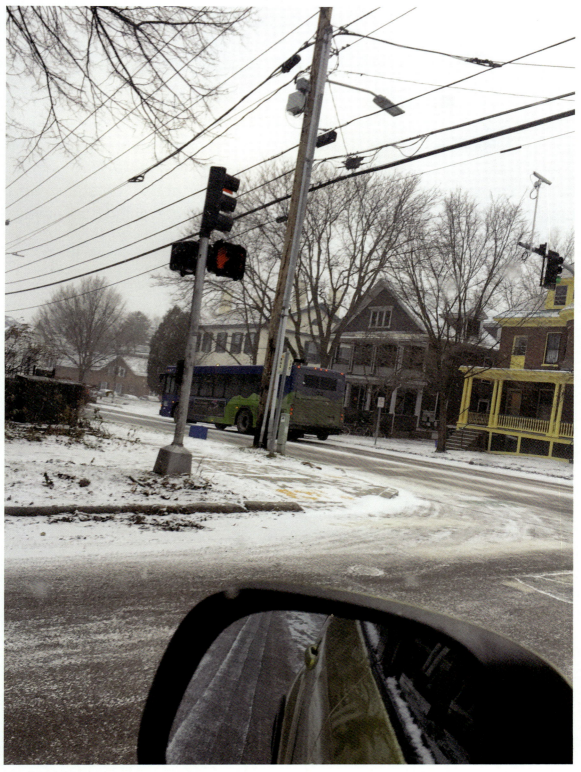

↳ Snow-covered streets, representing something needing to change.
Courtesy of the author.

Spotlight:
Ellen Forney

Ellen Forney is a comics artist who creates graphic memoirs and self-help guides that borrow from traditional forms of data visualisation. She uses bar charts and line graphs in order to develop visual metaphors about mental health. These techniques are incorporated in her deeply personal narratives to remind readers about the human experiences behind data points.

Ellen Forney's most recent book *Rock Steady: Brilliant Advice From My Bipolar Life* (2018) departs from the memoir genre in order to offer concrete coping strategies for readers struggling with anxiety, depression, bipolar disorder, and other mental health issues. Using her own life experiences as an example, each chapter takes the reader through medical data and different treatments, including acupuncture, cognitive behavioural therapy, and even electroconvulsive therapy. In each of these, readers learn about different types of approaches to treatment and are invited to see themselves amidst data, like in the graphs here. As in her earlier work *Marbles: Mania, Depression, Michelangelo, and Me: A Graphic Memoir* (2012), she combines pseudo-data charts with personal narrative to create emotive data visualisations.

"Data visualization was really what *Rock Steady* was all about," she said. "It was one of the things … that is big [in designing the work]. I'm an educator and I love doing that in my comics" (personal interview, September 9, 2019).

Forney's work asks not only what we can know from data, but how people come to know and give meaning to data in their own lives. *Rock Steady* goes beyond presenting data as a way of illustrating her own lived experience to exploring how data visualisations might be used to engage and educate readers on coping and healing practices. Receiving a diagnosis often involves a deep entanglement with statistics and numbers for personal decision-making. Revealing this layer of experience through the integration of statistics with internal monologues from the genre of graphic narrative allows for a depiction of complex personhood, but also a more personal and individualised

way of interacting with health data that doesn't isolate the reader. It considers context, highlighting embodiment and affect (D'Ignazio and Klein, 2016) in the sick person's reckoning with their identity.

Her work prompts the question: How can we present data in a way that reflects upon and perceives the individuals encountering it? Forney's reaction to this question, which is seen in many graphic pathographies and illness narratives that explore the moment of diagnosis, is to communicate the psychological experience of encountering data tied to their new illness identity. The inclusion of these perspectives allows for multiplicity in health and illness experiences. By breaking away from a binaristic view of 'normal' versus 'abnormal' health, Forney creates data visualisations that are more authentic, making for richer and more fluid visualisations (D'Ignazio & Klein, 2016).

By Alexandra Alberda

→ D'Ignazio, C. & Klein, L. (2016). Feminist data visualization. Presented at and published in the workshop proceedings from the *Workshop on Visualization for the Digital Humanities* at IEEE VIS Conference.

→ Forney, E. (2012). *Marbles: Mania, Depression, Michelangelo, and Me: A Graphic Memoir*. New York, NY: Gotham Books.

→ Forney, E. (2018). *Rock Steady: Brilliant Advice from My Bipolar Life*. Seattle: Fantagraphics Books.

ANOTHER ASPECT OF MOOD DISORDERS IS THAT WE **CYCLE** THROUGH OUR MOOD STATES. BECAUSE WE HAVE A RANGE OF MOODS, IT MEANS WE NEED TO HANDLE UPS, DOWNS, MIDDLES, & THE SWINGS BETWEEN THEM. FOR EXAMPLE, THIS IS A COMMON BIPOLAR I PATTERN:

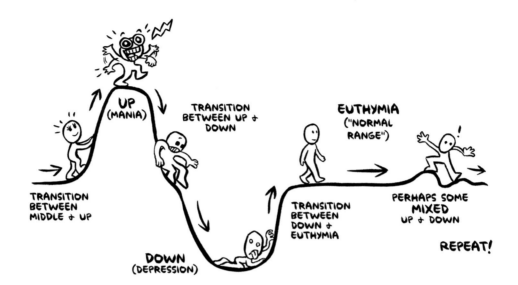

THE PATTERNS ARE DIFFERENT FOR DIFFERENT PEOPLE & AT DIFFERENT TIMES — HOW HIGH, HOW LOW, HOW FREQUENT, ETC.

THIS IS MY APPROXIMATE PATTERN THROUGH MY 20s:

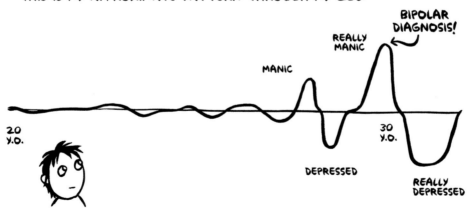

SOMETIMES I'M ASKED IF I WISH I'D BEEN DIAGNOSED IN MY TEENS OR EARLY 20s. BUT I DON'T THINK I REALLY HAD A *DISORDER* THEN. INCREASING STRETCHES OF HIGHER OR LOWER MOOD, BUT WITHIN NORMAL RANGE — NOT ACUTE ENOUGH TO DISORDER THINGS UNTIL MY LATE 20s.

↳ Ellen Forney, *Rock Steady: Brilliant Advice from My Bipolar Life* (29), 2018. Courtesy of the author and Fantagraphics Books.

Activity:
An Introduction to Power Mapping

 Author

Name
Anna Feigenbaum

Affiliation
Bournemouth University

Biography
Dr. Anna Feigenbaum is the founder of BU Civic Media Hub.

Twitter
@drfigtree

 Materials

→ A3 or poster sized paper
→ Pencils
→ Erasers
→ Different coloured markers or pencils

 Space Needed

Groups should work around tables or desks pulled together to create drawing space and make the power map visual to everyone in the group as you work.

 Aim

This activity will introduce you to social network research and link analysis. Participants will learn how to create nodes and links, evaluate connections and lay them out in a network graph.

 Go Digital / Go Analogue

Go Digital – Record your entities and links on a spreadsheet template and upload it onto a network mapping software platform to work digitally. We recommend Little Sister's Oligrapher, Kumu and Graph Commons.

 Group Size

This activity can be scaled. If participants are making a collaborative power map, groups should be comprised of 4–5 people. The activity can also be done individually.

 Duration

1–2 hours for research and recording connections (this can be independent or as a group) and 1–2 hours for creating the power map.

Top Tips or Additional Notes?

You can find business connections using these resources, among other, online: Little Sister, Open Corporates, Companies House, Bloomberg Business Profiles, LinkedIn

If every member of a group is assigned a single starting person, when you go to put the map together, the tables can be combined before mapping to create even more connections.

Task

Begin your power mapping by selecting a powerful person or organisation. (In our Media, Journalism & Society class we start with a media owner, for example, Rupert Murdoch).

Use websites and resources from the list below to find connections (links/edges) between your powerful person or organisation (nodes/entities) and other key people or organisations. Try to find the following:
→ A minimum of 3 entities your powerful person or organisation is connected to
→ A minimum of 2 more entities connected to those nodes.
This should give you a total of at least 9 entities linked to your starting point.

Give a ranking to your connections. The connections you find between entities will be different. In many power maps, connections are divided into different types and strengths. As you do your research, create a key of the different types and strengths of connections you would like to record.

When you are thinking about types and strengths of connections, look for:
→ Influence – How might the businesses or people your media owner is connected to have influence? Could it create media opportunities? Bias politics? Be partial to special interest lobbying?
→ Intimacy – How close are the relationships between people or companies? Are some people more connected than others? Are there relatives? Old classmates?
→ Intensity – Are some people connected to each other more than once? This can show stronger connections and help you see where concentrations of influence might exist.

Sample Activity Plan

Based on a workshop or seminar class divided into a few groups of 4-5.

15 min:	Introduce the activity by showing an example of a power map and its elements (entities, links, etc.). Perhaps have students read our section from this workbook on Narrative Networks as prep for the activity.
15 min:	Introduce participants to the web resources they can use to search for connections.
1–2 hour:	Independent or small group research to identify connections and record this on a spreadsheet or table template.
30 min:	Sketch out the connections in pencil and finalise your key to identify types and strengths of connections.
15 min:	Add colour to your power map. Create a colour-coded key to let the audience know what the colours (patterns, icons, textures, etc.) on your power map represent. Follow our principles in the 4 Pillars to help with your use of symbol, colour, caption and editorial layout.

Activity:
Deconstruct/Reconstruct an Icon

 Author

Name
Anna Feigenbaum

Affiliation
Bournemouth University

Biography
Dr. Anna Feigenbaum is the founder of BU Civic Media Hub

Twitter
@drfigtree

 Materials

→ Sketching materials or access to image editing software

 Space Needed

Any classroom or meeting space.

 Aim

The aim of this activity is to apply Barthes, concepts of semiotics to better understand how iconography makes and shapes visual meanings.

 Go Digital / Go Analogue

You can use online photo editing software rather than sketching materials to reconstruct your icons. Or you can mix it up, creating the new icons digitally and mocking them up onto a print-out of the data visualisation.

 Group Size

This activity can be scaled; it was original designed as a class assignment for a group of 20-30.

 Top Tips or Additional Notes?

This assignment was designed to be done over the course of a week or two, outside the classroom. I've found that the presentations create lots of engagement and discussion around the nuances of iconography and the difficulty of creating icons for sensitive issues. Depending on class size and time allotted, the style and length of the presentation can be adapted.

To make this assignment a formal assessment, you can add a further written component asking participants to write-up their deconstruction and reconstruction process, along with a reflection.

 Duration

1-2 weeks prep, 2-3 hours for presentations.

Task

Select a piece of data visualisation that uses iconography to discuss a sensitive, complex or controversial issue. It will work best to select a data visualisation that you think could be improved.

De-construct the icons

Using Barthes' method of semiotics (denotation, connotation and myth) explain how the icons function in your selected data visualisation. Describe how the icon generates meaning on the level of denotation (basic description of shapes, colours, etc.) and connotation (values, emotions). Is there a broader ideology that gives meaning to the icon? Is myth operating and if so, how? What kinds of assumptions does the icon make about target audiences? Are captions used for anchorage to limit the interpretation of what the icon might mean?

Re-construct the icons

Construct an alternative set of icons that you think better express the data or humanise the data in the visualisation. Create a new mock up for the data visualisation that uses your icons and in your written report and presentation, explain the choices you made in terms of their denotation, connotation and myth.

Present the icons

Prepare a 5 minute oral presentation to accompany your work. This will be shared with other participants.

 Sample Activity Plan

Based on a 20-person seminar or workshop

1–2 weeks:	Preparation time
3 hour:	Showcase and feedback on work

Activity:
Creating a 6-Panel Data Comic

 Author

Name
Alexandra Alberda

Affiliation
Bournemouth University

Biography
Alexandra Alberda is a PhD researcher in Graphic Medicine & Curatorial Practice at Bournemouth University, a member of the BU Civic Media Hub, and a comics artist.

Twitter
@ZandraAlberda

 Aim

This exercise is designed to teach participants the basic components of creating a data comic.

 Group Size

This activity works best in a workshop group of 5–20.

 Duration

1–2 hours. Time can be scaled depending on what kind of introductory masterclass and how much drawing time you want to give participants.)

 Materials

→ Paper
→ Pencils
→ Erasers
→ Black ink pens
→ Rulers

 Space Needed

Tables large enough for drawing.

 Go Digital / Go Analogue

Go Digital – Use a free online tool to generate your comic such as Canva or Comic Touch.

≡ **Top Tips or Additional Notes?**

You can provide participants with a 6-panel template to help guide their comic creation. We use a simple A3/legal size document made in word with 6 empty text boxes.

Task

Create a 6-panel comic that tells a story arising from or incorporating your data. Try to include the following elements in your comic:

→ at least 1 caption box
→ 2-3 characters
→ 8 communication bubbles
→ illustrate 1 speech or thought bubble
→ communicate tone and voice in the text

Sample Activity Plan

Based on a 2-hour workshop.

30 min:	Introduction to task and key elements of data comics
45–60 min:	Sketching your data comic
30 min:	Showcase of participants' comics and feedback
15 min:	Debrief on what we learnt about creating our own comics

Activity:
Creating a JS Timeline

 Author

Name
Anna Feigenbaum

Affiliation
Bournemouth University

Biography
Dr. Anna Feigenbaum is the founder of BU Civic Media Hub.

Twitter
@drfigtree

 Materials

→ Laptop
→ Google Docs account
→ Internet access

 Space Needed

Any space with a stable wi-fi connection.

 Aim

The purpose of this activity is to learn how to select, edit, and present information for a digital, multi-media timeline.

 Go Digital / Go Analogue

Go Analogue – Instead of using JS Timeline, this activity can be done with craft materials. Bring a range of craft materials to a room with large tables and let participants choose how to translate their entries into a visual form.

 Group Size

This activity can be done individually or in groups.

 Top Tips or Additional Notes?

If you want to cut down the time this activity takes, you can cut out the research phase by preparing the 10 timeline entries in advance and have participants work from these entries to create their multimedia timelines.

Likewise, if you want to extend the activity into an assignment or portfolio project, increase the number or length of entries and have students submit their preparatory material, works cited and reflections, along with the final product.

 Duration

Duration should be scaled to the number and depth of entries on the timeline. For a 10 entry timeline, allocate 1–2 days for research and at least 3 hours for creating the timeline with 50–100 word entries.

Task

Select a topic that you can tell a chronological narrative history about. Conduct research on this topic and select at least 10 key events, moments or other influences that you would like to include on your timeline. For each of these timeline entries:

1. Come up with a headline
2. Write a 50-100 word description of why this is a key date
3. Source an online image, audio or video clip that can accompany your entry. Make sure to note down the source to credit and check permissions.

Input your entries onto the JS Timeline template. Instructions for how to download and use the template can be found on the JS Timeline website: http://timeline.knightlab.com/

Publish your timeline to the web. Check for any mistakes or content that is not working. Go back into your spreadsheet to correct these, refresh your timeline and check again until you are happy with the final outcome.

Now your timeline is ready to share! Grab the embed code for your timeline if you'd like to post it in a blog or website.

Sample Activity Plan

30 min:	Begin with a discussion of timelines and their roles in society. What can timelines capture? Why are they useful storytelling devices? What are their limitations? This can be paired with the section from this workbook on Tinkering with Timelines.
30 min:	Introduce participants to JS Timeline. Use the examples in the gallery to show how others have constructed a timeline using this storytelling tool.
1–2 days:	Research your selected timeline topic and create at least 10 entries for your timeline.
2 hours:	JS Timeline creation lab. Have participants bring their work and laptops to a workshop or 'lab' space. Have someone on hand to help troubleshoot any technical problems.
1 hour:	Showcase the results! Have participants pull their timelines up on computers. Have half the participants circle around the room, interacting with others' timelines and asking questions. After 30 minutes, swap around and have the presenters switch to viewers.
Reflection:	Schedule time to debrief or have participants write-up a diary-style reflection on the process of creating their timeline.

Data Storytelling with Maps

Making Maps that Matter

If a picture was once worth 1,000 words, today a beautiful map is worth 10,000. By spatially visualising data, maps represent not just data points, but also a particular geographical imagination of the world. In the past decade geospatial technologies have transformed from solely a tool for experts to software packages that can be freely available and offered as open source products. In recent years maps have flourished across the web. From cultural guides on where to buy the best ice cream to time lapses of melting icecaps, people make maps to tell stories, to answer questions, and to create connections. This rise in mapping is due in large part to digital technologies like Google Maps that have transformed the ways people relate to visual representations of geographic space in their everyday lives. Through zoom functionality on street view and reviews of local spots, platforms like Google Maps make us reimagine relationships between people and places.

Through Google Maps, as well as specialised platforms like ArcGIS StoryMaps, people can produce their own visual representations of the spaces that matter to them by linking multimedia content to mapped locations. Drawing on more sophisticated technology, RSS feeds and APIs allow for information to be drawn from data sources to create real-time maps. Such interactive maps are often populated with user-generated or crowd-sourced content, engaging the activity of amateurs from citizen scientists to citizen journalists.

The mapping platform and civic engagement initiative Ushahidi innovated digital mapping practices by linking social media and smart phone technologies to visual representations of space. Often referred to as crowd mapping, Ushahidi allowed users anywhere in the world with internet access to send mappable information to its platform, allowing for real-time views of what was going on around the world. Governmental aid agencies as well as local activists and campaigners have used Ushahidi's dynamic software. Now partnered with large foundations including Rockefeller, Ford, and MacArthur, as well as collaborating with Google, Ushahidi has been deployed over 90,000 times for everything from traffic management to disaster relief.

These collaborative mapping practices open up new opportunities for civic engagement and challenge traditional notions of cartography. Jeremy Crampton (2008) discussed these changes as 'maps 2.0.' Just as the term Web 2.0 is used to describe how social media platforms and the lower entry cost to content production has made it easier for people to make and share their own creative work, digital mapping technologies have done the same for cartography. As geographers Dodge and Kitchin (2013) put it, by making mapping tools available to everyday people and not just experts, these new technologies can help counter the fixed, objective, and authoritative aspects of traditional cartography.

Yet while digital technologies have led to a surge in computer-assisted map-making, maps have long accompanied our storytelling, from colonial tales of travel to 'new' lands to the counter-mapping practices of environmental groups. The power of maps and their authority are importantly bound up in histories of colonisation that remain embedded in the software programmes and symbolising techniques used in cartography today. This chapter begins by asking: What can we learn from mapping pasts? Here we introduce and critically reflect on key debates in mapping related to power, representation, and symbolising. Exploring practices of participatory mapping, counter-mapping, and even mapping without maps, the chapter offers insight into visualisation strategies for telling place and space-based data stories.

Storytelling with Maps

with Jason Pearl

Europeans mapped the world beyond Europe long before they explored it. Many of these maps were based on religious and scientific paradigms, but some were more imaginative. For instance, consider the engraved maps that accompanied Thomas More's *Utopia* (1516) and Jonathan Swift's *Gulliver's Travels* (1726). More's fictional island, dug from a peninsula to maintain its separateness, was imagined by the artist Ambrosius Holbein in a woodcut map that arrayed the state's political organization visually. The various lands described by Swift were depicted by the map-maker Herman Moll, who slyly emplaced his images in what were then acknowledged gaps in geographic knowledge.

More subtly, though, all geography at least partially relies on storytelling in the sense that the scale of human experience usually restricts us to the perception of relatively small units of space. We imagine our nations with maps, and with many other forms, according to Benedict Anderson, because we never actually experience them in their extensive and disparate wholes. We understand other places—foreign nations, distant continents—still more imperfectly, often generalizing from politically charged biases embedded in tales of travel, as Edward Said's (1978) book *Orientalism* has shown.

→ First published in 1978, Edward Said explored how the West's perceptions of the East were made through storytelling. These colonial stories often pitted the civilised West, in particular the UK and France, against the 'barbaric' East. This system of representation helped justify the violence of colonialsim.

Storytelling with maps always imposes an imaginary order, privileging one set of details—or one specific agenda—often to the exclusion of others. Think, for instance, of the relatively benign symbolism of weather maps. Now think of political maps that portray immigration patterns. In some cases, the bold lines of a map bisect what are, in fact, culturally continuous landscapes. Or nationalistic maps that assign ownership for one or another contested territory: Kashmir, for instance. The solid colours within the lines often cover over a real diversity on the ground.

Deciding what and how to map is always a matter of making decisions about audience and character, tension and conflict, the presence and absence of details. Understanding that maps and cartography have a long history is crucial for becoming better mapmakers. One of the most significant concepts for considering present days maps and their long history is the notion of the cartographic gaze.

The Cartographic Gaze

with Doug Specht

The cartographic gaze bridges the gap between cartography and social theory by revealing the power that is embedded within maps through their elevated projection of space. The gaze emphasizes the relational dynamics between the mapper and the mapped, how this translates into the production of space, and how it reproduces the status quo.

→ In social theory and psychoanalysis 'the gaze' refers to the act of seeing and being seen.

The cartographic gaze found dominance with the printing revolution, new instruments of measurement, and newly 'discovered' lands, which led to a prolific expansion of mapping activities in the 16th century, producing increasingly detailed bird's-eye views of the world. These views from above worked to serve as tools of possession. The explorer and cartographer's elevated position and the commanding view provided by the maps mirrored the divine gaze of God, positioning the commissioner of the map in a seemingly omniscient position.

In this way the cartographic gaze was the precursor to the surveillant gaze, epitomized by Jeremy Bentham's Panopticon and the work of French philosopher Michel Foucault. These new maps of the 16th century allowed for increased control, and far-reaching power on behalf of the monarchs and landowners. Ownership over space became defined in robust terms, and alongside the process of enclosure, the positions of the peasantry, landowners, and the Monarchy became ever solidified, changing the perception and understanding of space itself.

→ The Panopticon was an idea for an architectural surveillance system thought up by English social theorist Jeremy Bentham in the late 1700s. A single, central tower would allow guards to watch over all prisoners in their cells. But because the tower looked out, and the prisoners couldn't look in, they would never know if someone was actually watching. This gave the guards an "invisible omnipresence." The aim was to discipline and control prisoners who would act as if they were always being watched. While at the time Bentham's work was conceptual, in the years that followed many prisons were built in this fashion.

→ Jeremy Bentham's vision for the Panopticon.

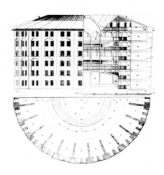

→ In social theory 'The Other' stands in for the individual or group that is perceived as not belonging.

This becomes particularly prevalent in the use of maps as colonial objects where God-like views of the world were used to carve up new territories, and define peoples, resources, and power across newly 'discovered' territories. These maps were instrumental in the forming of 'the Other,' and with that the domination and control of the Other. Following from this, the cartographic gaze turns the Other into an object on the map. Much like the gaze of Medusa that turned the onlooker to stone, so too can the map solidify relations and immobilize those who are mapped.

The cartographic gaze then is not a way of looking at the world, but is a medium for spreading domination through the models of power at the heart of colonialism, positioning the map-maker in a divine position and causing the mapped to lose its self-determination, limiting insurrection. Becoming familiar with this idea of the gaze in the history of colonial cartography can help mapmakers navigate decision-making in creating their own maps and engaging our geographical imaginations, while understanding the problems of representation.

The Problem with Maps as Representations

with Doug Specht

Keeping the cartographic gaze in mind, today we might say that all maps have a fundamental problem: they can only ever be a partial representation of the world. As Branston and Stafford (2010), among others, have noted, "no representation can contain more than a fraction of its real-world subject" (p. 129). No map can be a perfect depiction of territory; in fact, for a map to be a truly faithful representation of space, it would need to be at a scale of 1:1, including every feature of the landscape.

In reality, making a map is about making choices as to what will and will not be included. While great efforts are often made to make maps more representational of the landscape and the people they reference, particular sets of ideas, values, attitudes and identities are embedded in these choices, and get reproduced in the map. Priority for what to include on a map is often given to the kinds of representations that already conform to what Matthew H. Edney (2019) calls the "ideal of cartography"—reinforcing the creation of what we might think of as normative maps.

This happens most frequently when normative representations of locations, geographical features, and people get reproduced by mapmakers. Like falling back on stereotypes in films, maps can reproduce dominant narratives inherited from history, further erasing different perspectives and marginal voices.

However, these erasures can also happen when cartography makes an explicit effort to represent different perspectives. The story that the map maker wishes to tell, and the one that is later interpreted by the map reader, can be very different.

Case Study: John Snow's Cholera Map

Even John Snow's famous cholera map, claimed by *The Guardian* to have "changed the world," was interpreted differently by readers.

In the 1800s outbreaks of cholera were common in London. At the time doctors believed that cholera, which causes stomach cramps, vomiting, and diarrhoea, was transmitted through the air. But physician John Snow rejected this theory. After another cholera outbreak in 1854, Snow was able to evidence his alternative ideas.

Using a bespoke London street map designed by a local engraver, Snow plotted the home addresses of people who died from cholera, taking the data off official reports. Representing each death as a small bar, it became clear that the density of the bars were clustered around a popular water pump on Broad street.

With this map, alongside a broader statistical analysis and case studies, Snow was able to show that cholera was not an air-borne disease, but in fact, travelled through water.

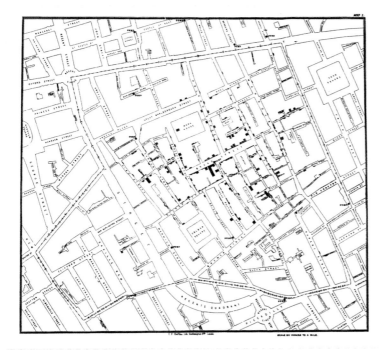

→ Original map made by John Snow in 1854. Cholera cases are highlighted in black.

However, as different readers can interpret maps in different ways, not everyone was convinced that this is what the map—or Snow's other data—represented. Physicians such as E.A. Parkes, who had long been promoting an air-borne thesis, argued that there was simply not enough evidence to support Snow's conclusions. In an 1855 *British and Foreign Medical Review* article on John Snow's *Mode of Communication of Cholera* that contained a reprint of the cholera map, Parkes wrote:

> "This certainly looks more like the effect of an atmospheric cause than any other; if it were owing to the water, why should not the cholera have prevailed equally everywhere where the water was drunk?"

As this example of John Snow's cholera maps demonstrates, our own background, prejudices, and previous knowledge changes the way we read a map, and furthermore, as Stuart Hall (1997) reminds us, no person, location, or object ever has a single, fixed, and unchanging meaning.

Learn more about John Snow's Cholera Maps

→ John Snow Archive and Research Companion
https://johnsnow.matrix.msu.edu/index.php

→ Simon Rogers (2013) John Snow's data journalism: the cholera map that changed the world
https://www.theguardian.com/news/datablog/2013/mar/15/john-snow-cholera-map

→ Koch, T., & Denike, K. (2010). Essential, illustrative, or... just propaganda? Rethinking John Snow's Broad Street map. *Cartographica: The International Journal for Geographic Information and Geovisualization, 45*(1), 19-31.

Mini Exercise: Reflection Questions on John Snow's Cholera Map

After reading the case study on the Cholera Map, answer these reflection questions.

1. One objection people had to Snow's map was that it did not take account of population density. Why would this matter? What might have been Snow's reasons for leaving this out of the map?
2. Use Yasuhito Abe's spotlight to think about John Snow's cholera map. How can the concept of argumentative map-making in Abe's spotlight help us understand the data story Snow was trying to tell?
3. Can you think of a time when you and another person both looked at a map and interpreted it in different ways? What were your different perspectives and are there any past experiences or prejudices that might have informed them?

While it is possible to take a great deal of care over the production of a map to ensure different voices and perspectives are represented, two things remain important to reflect upon about maps. First, as with all representations, some meanings will be encoded into the map and others won't make it. As it is not possible to represent everything, cartographers always have to make decisions about what to include and leave out. Second, both the meanings put into the map and those the map reader takes away will be influenced by the 'ideal of cartography.' The way people make and read maps is deeply embedded in the history that gave rise to cartography.

As with a painting or a movie, this can make it difficult for more experimental forms of representation to be understood by map readers. Similar to the challenges faced by artists and filmmakers, cartographers that seek to explore new practices of representation have to confront the norms that already exist for makers and viewers. This is why it is essential to approach the production and reading of any map as a representation and to always ask, who or what is missing—and why?

Participatory Maps

Often in an attempt to gain more perspectives and shift the gaze, in participatory mapping people work together to build maps that represent their struggles, experiences, and perspectives. For example, instead of a government map that draws neighbourhood lines based on official records, a participatory map might create unfixed and wobbly borders that mark the lived experience of residents in that city. In many participatory mapping projects, amateur mapmakers work directly with people who live in the places that are being mapped. Through dialogue and exchange, participatory mapping can allow the mapped to become the mapmakers.

Many digital participatory maps begin with markers and paper and a group of people sitting around a table. Other community maps never move from the analogue to the digital, remaining hand drawn and print-based. One such map, *Reclaim Brixton*, was made by the anti-gentrification neighbourhood group BAGAGE (Brixton Action Group Against Gentrification and Evictions).

"The Reclaim Brixton map is both visual and textual," BAGAGE explains. "On the front is a simplified, colour drawing of Brixton, broken hearts representing all the places either threatened with eviction or in some way or other under attack. On the back, interviews with the people who are directly at risk: shopkeepers, café owners, housing estate residents." BAGAGE used excerpts from their interviews on the map in efforts to give local people "a platform to express their anger and sadness at what is happening to their livelihoods." BAGAGE's common goal for the project was to contribute to a wider public understanding of the harms of gentrification and its emotional consequences.

For BAGAGE, in addition to circulating a PDF version of their map online and across social media, it was important to distribute the maps in print. They brought thousands of copies to demonstrations, country shows, and traders' stalls that ran along Atlantic Road. By distributing these maps of people's livelihoods and records of their emotional responses to the threat of being shut down, BAGAGE hoped "to be helping people to recognise common ground and a common plight, a recognition which will lead to dialogue." This bringing together, through the active involvement of the people being mapped, is an excellent example of participatory mapping. It bridged hand-drawn map-making with digital resources for distribution, offering extra information through web links.

→ Reclaim Brixton Map. Images courtesy of BAGAGE.

Counter-Mapping

→ See Spotlight: Counter-Cartographies Collective for more.

As more and more people are able to engage with map-making, we also see a rise in 'counter-mapping.' Counter-mapping is the process of creating geographical representations that challenge the status quo. Distinct from more general uses of digital mapping, counter-mapping involves an explicit engagement with the ethics and risks that arise in the process of making maps together. This often involves critical analysis of how people, and the places they inhabit, become represented.

The Counter Cartography Collective (2012) argues that this kind of counter-mapping "opens up possibilities for new forms of knowledge production and political change" (p.461). Some mapping projects serve both as a participatory mapping platform and as counter-mapping practice that seeks to challenge authoritative visions of the world. For example, Voz is a participatory platform that enables users to map human rights abuses on a global scale.

→ See Spotlight: Voz for more.

Story Mapping

Story Mapping refers to the practice of integrating narratives into cartographic practice. In the past decade, there has been growing scholarly and artistic interest in the relationship between mapping and storytelling. As Sébastien Caquard notes (2013), "The history of cartography cannot be dissociated from narratives" (136). Not only have mapmakers historically relied on first-hand testimony to construct their maps, people used completed maps to locate and legitimize their storytelling practices. In recent years, critical cartographers have called attention to the more subtle ways that narratives are embedded in maps; for example, how the nation state uses maps to represent a coherent territory to itself and outsiders (Dodge, M., Kitchin, R., & Perkins, C, 2011).

Robert MacFarlane (2018) distinguishes between "the grid map" and "the story map." The grid map "places an abstract geometric meshwork upon a space," creating an abstract representation of any given location in which any individual can locate themselves. Grid maps, exemplified by the road map, are primarily functional. Story maps, on the other hand, "represent a place as it is perceived by an individual or by a culture moving through it." It is a way of representing the world through a specific journey. Story maps are subjective and inefficient because they are born from an unauthoritative account of a single person. By zooming in, story maps offer us a more detailed and subjective accounting of space.

This productive tension is best exemplified by story maps that take migrant journeys as their subject. Conventional data-driven maps of migration and migrant journeys, while more technologically sophisticated than ever before, often advance traditional notions of scientific objectivity—they can be thought of as 'grid maps'—that elide more complex narratives. In contrast, recent mapping projects work directly with migrants to solicit their first-hand experience of the spaces and places they've travelled between.

In 2013, the charity Group 484 invited Đorđe Balmazović from the artist collective Škart to collaborate with asylum seekers in Serbia to generate new data about the experience of migrants' journeys. The resulting project, *Migration Maps* (2013-2015), illustrates the long and fraught journeys of the asylum seekers from their homes to Serbia. Group 484 sought to engage with alternative research methods, specifically participatory models of storytelling. These maps point to the fragmentary nature of the migrants' knowledge, even about their own experiences: some of the maps lack detail because the migrants didn't know where they were; at other stages, they were unclear or didn't want to disclose details of a particular stage of their journey. Balmazović writes that they "wanted to avoid pathos and the illustration of their sufferings. We wanted to show them their routes factually" (2017).

→ See Spotlight: Migration Maps for more.

Like the kinds of illustrations found in graphic social science work, these maps use a hand-drawn aesthetic. This kind of mark-making highlights the immediacy of first-hand testimony. It is also indexical, which in semiotics is a sign that directly points back to its referent—in this case, the human body.

Federica Fragapane's *The Stories Behind a Line* (2017) is an interesting counterexample because it uses the same general concept as *Migrant Maps*—incorporating first-person narratives into a mapping format—but uses radically different formal elements. These maps are digital, rather than hand-drawn. Unlike the formal chaos of *Migrant Maps, Stories* brings a visual simplicity to the migrants' narratives. Fragapane writes, "I really wanted to provide a clean, rational and simple narrative of these stories. And this point for me is a focal one. I think that such a complex topic deserves rationality and also a simple clearness, to be communicated properly and—especially—understood" (2018). The form of the line becomes a way of understanding both the migrants' journeys and also as a metaphor for life itself.

→ *The Stories Behind a Line*, 2017. Concept, interviews and design by Federica Fragapane, created in collaboration with Alex Piacentini.

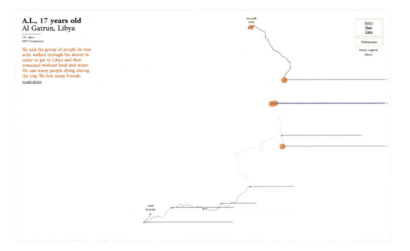

The project's formal simplicity is in clear response to the "specularization" of the media that, according to Fragapane, "undermines a rational approach and a clear narrative." These maps have an interactive interface, which helps create a relationship between the viewer and the data as they 'travel' through each story. Overlaid on each line are clickable red dots, which open a sidebar containing further information about that segment of the journey. The interface also offers different view modes, which give more or less detail depending on where the viewer clicks on the screen and how much information they want to know.

Too often, the migrant story is overwhelmed with partisan debate and numerical data. In contrast, these maps bring the human narrative to the fore. As the 'migrant crisis' continues, remembering the humans behind the data becomes more important than ever.

Seeing Cartographically

with Phillipa Gillingham

Just as you make choices with bar charts and data comics on what colours, fonts, and shapes to use, the same is true for maps. In cartography the visual elements of maps are called symbolism. Inspired by the emergent field of semiotics, French cartographer Jacques Bertin is credited with being the first to describe the visual variables that can be varied to encode information on maps and related information visualisations. In other words, they are the basic building blocks for data storytelling with maps. In 2017, Robert Roth built on Bertin's original list, adapting the work of MacEachren et al., 2012, to offer a visual taxonomy of 12 visual variables.

1. **Location** – position of a map symbol in relation to its coordinate system (pin drop on)

2. **Size** – manipulate proportions and show value-by-area

3. **Shape** – used as reference, can be either abstract or iconic

4. **Orientation** – how map symbols are positioned

5. **Colour Hue** – use of colour spectrums on a map

6. **Colour Value** – how light or dark a colour is

7. **Colour Saturation** – intensity of a colour

8. **Texture** – use of fill patterns within a map symbol

9. **Arrangement** – layout of graphic marks of a map symbol

10. **Crispness** – use of clear or fuzzy boundary on a map symbol, can depict uncertainty

11. **Resolution** – level of abstraction in display of a map symbol

12. **Transparency** – how opaque a map symbol is in relation to the background or map symbols below it

Like all visual representations, maps capture, construct, and communicate meaning. Questions of how best to use map symbols to visually represent places, quantities, topical issues, experiences, or anything else that you have decided to map will always be fraught with debate. The next sessions explore some of these challenges.

No Symbol is Neutral

Imagine you are mapping changes in climate in winter to show where they are most significant. You choose a heat map that represents intensity. But you are talking about winter—so do you make your heat map in the traditional shades of red or instead choose shades of blue? One might be easier for audiences to recognise right away, while the other makes more visual sense for the narrative or data story you want to tell.

Now let's say in addition to mapping winter temperatures, you are looking at the cost of heating compared to the average income in those areas. How do you represent the profit of energy companies? Or the number of people at risk of freezing? Do you use the category label 'fuel poverty' or is that an analysis rather than a description for when people cannot afford to heat their homes?

No matter how many maps you make, there will never be one right answer to these questions. This is because, to adapt a famous line from the poet Adrienne Rich, "No coding is neutral." Assigning category labels and visual representations to data, what cartographers call coding and symbolising, throws up questions around how categories, colours, logos are chosen.

Mapmakers code items so that you can immediately see what an issue is and begin to analyse how different events and actions fit together. This brings up issues in terms of who decides those categories, colours, and logos. Even if this power to label is turned over to participants, one person's deforestation issue can be another person's indigenous rights issue.

This is because categories themselves have politics. For example, does a code for 'anti-austerity' make assumptions about the root of a problem? Does it put forward a European critique as a global classification? Other kinds of categories such as 'electoral fraud' and 'unlawful killing,' carry with them assumptions about legal and human rights. While it may not be possible to remove these problems from coding, as a mapmaker you can make users aware of the issues by being transparent about your methods and decision-making when you circulate your maps.

Contested Coordinates

with Doug Specht

Contested coordinates come in two forms: first, those that occur through technological accidents and mistranslations of data between projections and base maps; and second, those that are sociological in basis, formed through epistemological understandings of space.

In terms of the first group of contested coordinates, these most frequently appear when data sets are added to base maps which have been constructed using different projections. Numerous projections—the process of turning a spherical planet into a flat map—exist. The most frequently used is the Mercator projection, but even this projection has differences between software and publishers. Thus, it becomes imperative to examine the co-ordinate system and apply the necessary transformation to each data set to ensure an accurate representation. These kinds of contested coordinates have also become increasingly prevalent in the age of digital geographies, where lay persons are increasingly encouraged to help map the world through projects such as Open Street Map. In these cases, coordinates become contested through either the misunderstanding of tools or poor cartographic practice. As with projects such as Wikipedia, these contested moments are dealt with for the most part by the public and continuous edits and updates by the mapping community.

This in itself can lead to the second type of contested coordinates, those that arise from epistemological and ontological differences. In these cases, the arguments over the coordinates are based more firmly in beliefs about where boundaries should be drawn or how coordinates should be labelled. These often come in the form of disputes around international boundaries. For example, all coordinates in Kosovo return an 'unknown' location through Google's API. There are numerous disputes over coordinates in the Himalayas as the topographical and geopolitical landscapes move borders on a regular basis. There are contested spaces such as Bi'r Tawīl between Egypt and Sudan, in which a 2,060 km2 parcel of land is rejected by both countries, or around mining projects in Colombia, where the extractive sector and protestors disagree on coordinate systems and land access.

These contested coordinates, whether data/projection-driven or driven by land disputes, have potentially far-reaching geopolitical implications and will not be easily resolved. The debate over who has a definitive say on coordinates remains problematic for the inclusion of occluded knowledges and geographic epistemologies.

No Platform is Neutral

with Doug Specht

Following new media scholars, platforms can be considered as computational software that offers affordances and limitations to users' participation and interactions. The 'politics' of a platform refers to how power gets embedded into computational layers, as well as how relations play out through user engagement with the platform (Gillespie, 2010; Helmond, 2015; Langlois and Elmer, 2013). Mapping platforms are sites at which decisions around programming, often hidden from users, are deeply embroiled in politics. As mapping platforms often pre-determine places and their meanings, they shape users' spatial imaginations and limit what is possible to map.

As noted above, the rise of digital mapping platforms was born first from the colonial roots of the cartographic gaze of the Enlightenment era, through the military development of geographic information systems (GIS), computing, and satellite technologies, and then on to participatory platforms. Whether elite or lay produced, all mapping, even that which aims to counter the status quo, is based upon classification and codification of real-world objects into taxonomies and terminology. The slots into which data might fit are defined by those who make the software, not those who create the knowledge (Brown et al., 2013). For a long time, the knowledge of local peoples has been translated through tools and language suited to the needs of the coloniser (Kitchin and Thrift, 2009), resulting in mapping platforms that resemble or make programmable the coloniser's renderings of place and space.

In this way colonial histories can become embedded in mapping platforms. Zoom into the disputed areas between Palestine and Israel on OpenStreetMap and you will find the city of Jerusalem, named in Hebrew. A few years back, zooming in on the area could yield results in Arabic or Hebrew, depending on which of the community's mapping warriors—a term used to describe those who engage in such online mapping conflicts—had most recently updated their wiki style database. The OpenStreetMap team, in order to stop the constant changing of the city's name, locked the database, deciding to follow a policy of naming in favour of what they call the 'dominant controlling power' in a region. The open platform, designed for participation and for countering the dominant structures in global mapping, becomes compromised by its coding and by the pervasive nature of global politics.

This kind of platform politics can be found across other similar incidents. In Crimea, as the Russian government renames cities and streets, OpenStreetMap must decide who is the dominant power. Related occurrences have appeared on Google Maps, which allows for public participation in naming places and updating data. In 2011, as rebels advanced on Muammar Gaddafi in Libya, Green Square was returned to its pre-Gaddafi era name of Martyrs Square. Maps don't just reflect conflicts on the ground; their power can shape territorial disputes. In 2010, Nicaragua accidentally invaded Costa Rica because of a Google Maps error that placed the border in accordance with an outdated 1858 treaty. (What the Nicaraguan army were doing relying solely on Google Maps is another question.) Even when making counter-maps, it is not possible to escape these platform politics. As Sean Cubitt (1998) reminds us, while computers will talk to anyone, it is the privileged and historically powerful that teach them to speak.

Case Study: Anna Feigenbaum explains 'how not to make an online map'

When I first set out to map tear gas use around the world it was a one-person-with-a-laptop operation. Bored of traditional content analysis in my field of Media Studies, and taken by the toys of geographers, I began my very first research map.

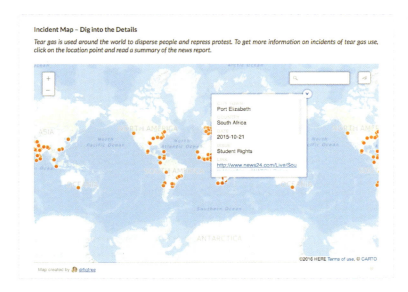

Incident Map – Dig into the Details

Tear gas is used around the world to disperse people and repress protest. To get more information on incidents of tear gas use, click on the location point and read a summary of the news report.

→ This interactive map allowed users to point and click on a location where tear gas was used to discover the place, date and protest issue. It also provided a link to the news story where the incident data came from.

To begin I applied the basic skills that I learnt from mapping the bar crawl route for a friend's bachelorette party. The method was simple: read a news article delivered through a Google News alert (key word: tear gas), Google Map the incident location, drop a pin, cut-and-paste key information. There was no plotting, no coding, and no symbolising.

Yet even though this first map failed in methodological terms, it succeeded as a visualisation. With over 25,000 views and copied onto news articles and blogs around the world, this map told a different story about my research and the world we live in, one that I could never capture in linear prose. It opened up new audiences to the issue of tear gas misuse, and in an instant revealed insights into conflicts and communities—and the ways the media covers them. Click deeper and you got a global sample of news coverage from around the world to explore as you wish, offering features no written article alone could provide.

But alas, it wasn't very pretty and the data was in no shape to share. So I went in search of real mapmakers. In 2014 I presented a ragtag version of the Tear Gas Map at the American Association of Geographers, arriving with a plea for help. And as luck would have it, help sat in the audience. Matt Ellis, then an undergraduate geography student from Texas Christian University, came on board, teaching me about 'coordinates' and CSV files. Matt created a series of maps, designed and hosted for free at CartoDB.

The second time around, in 2015, I learnt from these early mistakes. Committed to failing better, the 2015 tear gas mapping project started with a clear structure, a wonderful research assistant named Laura McKinna, and a Google spreadsheet. While it was tempting to point and click and plot pretty coloured pins, rather than stare at never-ending numeric rows, working from a basic spreadsheet (or database) ultimately gave us much more control over the data and allowed us to tell better data stories. While we continued to use a Google alert to gather tear gas incidents, now they were thinking like mapmakers. We recorded more precise locations, taken from the news articles and recorded by city/town and country.

Once the whole year of alerts was mapped into the spreadsheet, we were able to turn the location names from text into coordinates for mapping in a matter of minutes. BU Civic Media Hub team member Dr. Phillipa Gillingham introduced them to the free, open source tool QGIS and its batch geocoding plugin—a huge time saver.

Using the CartoDB skills Matt Ellis bestowed, we made our own set of maps for 2015. These included a time lapse map to show the use of tear gas over the year, a heat map drawing attention to places where lots of tear gas is used, and an incident map that archived all of the summaries of tear gas use in the dataset.

For the 2015 project we also coded their recorded incidents for the type of location where tear gas was used (i.e. in a street or in a home), as well as for the kind of incident that took place (a protest over electoral issues or a sporting event).

By adding this extra step of coding to the spatial or place-based data we were able to tell more data stories, going beyond 'who are the top tear gas users' to look at everything from the tear gassing of young people, to the safety protocols that surround the misuse of tear gas in confined spaces. By adding these simple details, the data became particularly useful for human rights and governmental organisations like Amnesty International and the Council of Europe.

For more visit:

→ 2015 Tear Gas Maps
http://www.civicmedia.io/projects/tear-gas-maps-2015/

→ Report on Misuse of Tear Gas for Council of Europe
http://www.civicmedia.io/bu-civic-media-hub-the-omega-research-
foundation-publish-report-on-the-misuse-of-tear-gas-in-europe/

While the interactive mapping projects that we encounter online often seem shiny and sophisticated, when many people begin to make maps they have no clue what they are doing. As we have suggested throughout this workbook, it is completely OK to not know what you are doing when you begin. Data storytelling is a new field and like any new visual form that is in its infancy, it is full of good and bad experiments. As the old adage from Samuel Beckett goes, "Try Again. Fail again. Fail better."

Mapping without Maps

"Is there any motif so malleable, so ripe for appropriation, as maps?" So asks Katharine Harmon in her introduction to *The Map As Art: Contemporary Artists Explore Cartography* (Harmon & Clemans, 2009, p. 10). In all kinds of ways, contemporary artists play with, upend, subvert, and transform mapping conventions in their practice. Although these examples are not straightforward data visualisations, they offer important examples of how designers and researchers can push disciplinary boundaries to see the world in a new way. By using the phrase "Mapping Without Maps" we refer to mapping practices that so radically depart from convention, they seem to create a whole new visual genre altogether. Mapping without maps is a way to chart space and our relationship to it outside of conventional cartographic practices.

Artist Alban Biaussat's *The Green(er) Side of the Line* (2005) invokes the two-dimensional map in three-dimensional space via the Israel-Palestine conflict. During negotiations in 1949, an Israeli military commander famously used a green pencil to demarcate the armistice lines between the West Bank and Israel on a map. According to Harmon, "The Green Line looms large in the region's psyche" (p. 23). Biaussat brings the pencilled line to life in his documentary project, a collection of stunning photographs that show the green line as a green ribbon and green painted balls placed delicately across the Palestinian landscape.

→ The Israeli occupation of Palestine has been generative for artists using counter-cartographic strategies, not only because of its political salience but because the situation vividly highlights the instability and violence of borders, and the way that maps are used as tools for colonisation and occupation.

The project is both gentle and visually beautiful, yet the historical brutality that resulted from the commander's gesture sits as an ever-present backdrop to the work. But if the project allegorises the very real geopolitical mechanism of the Israeli border, it does so by emphasising the border's contingency, as fluctuating as a soft green ribbon blowing in the wind.

Taken together, Biaussat's photographs form a kind of 'map,' but it is one that challenges the two-dimensional authority inscribed on paper by literalising it in space.

→ Alban Biaussat, *The Green(er) Side of the Line*, 2005. Made with the support of the Al-Ma'mal Foundation for Contemporary Art in Jerusalem. Photo courtesy of the artist.

According to Catherine D'Ignazio (2009), one of the main drivers of the cartographic turn in contemporary art is globalisation. 'Globalisation' is a slippery term, but generally speaking it refers to the economic, political, and social expansion and circulation of goods, capital, and people. The changes brought about by globalisation were greatly accelerated by contemporaneous technological developments, particularly in communications technologies such as the Internet and social media, as well as online shopping and global distribution networks. These developments effectively created an immaterial layer of reality, a 'virtual landscape' by which the material world is increasingly mediated. Many recent projects have attempted to map this invisible terrain, in much the same way that early cartographers tried to map the New World.

→ Heath Bunting, detail from *A Terrorist – The Status Project*, 2008.

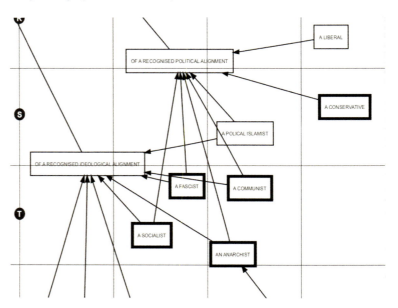

One example is Heath Bunting's *The Status Project—A Terrorist* (2008), an ambitious diagram of what's required to purchase goods over the Internet following the UK government's 2006 Terrorism Act. The work highlights the complexity of the security state in relation to global commerce, where personal information provided during digital transactions (such as our name and credit cards details) is used to surveil private citizens in the name of anti-terrorism. Bunting (2008) calls this work "a map of terrorism," which reveals "the borderline between 'the everyday', embodied by 'the high street' and the global terror fantastic." That anti-terrorism efforts are situated alongside global commerce transactions is not a coincidence. By placing them alongside each other, Bunting highlights the paradoxical nature of 'freedom' in a globalized society, wherein goods and commerce flow unimpeded, while humans are more restricted by border control than ever before.

Bunting's work maps the invisible: each node on the map is connected by arrows to indicate their relationship to each other, but these have no bearing in actual physical space. He invokes cartographic language in order to visualise new 'territories' of power and control. Other projects map the invisible by revealing the material infrastructure that supports it. Along with a dozen of his colleagues, University of Wisconsin computer science professor Paul Barford created a map of the 542 long-haul fibre-optic cables that transport Internet data 113,000 miles across the continental United States. Although the map looks like a fairly standard map of the United States, similar to a highway map, it took approximately four years to produce and is the first time this information has been made publicly available. The researchers pulled information from a variety of sources to piece together the exact location of the cables: maps from cable providers and ISPs such as Comcast and Verizon, as well as publicly available permit records to lay the cables held by county clerks and other state organisations.

→ From "InterTubes: A study of the US long-haul fiber-optic infrastructure," by R. Durairajan, P. Barford, J. Sommers, and W. Willinger, 2015, in *Proceedings of the 2015 ACM Conference on Special Interest Group on Data Communication* (SIGCOMM '15). ACM, New York, NY, USA, 565-578. Reprinted with permission.

The fibre-optic infrastructure map also raises important questions about ownership. The Internet is now so deeply embedded in social life that many argue it should be considered a public good, like water, and the fibre-optic cables public infrastructure. Yet it is privately owned networks that operate the cables and that have kept their locations out of public knowledge.

This and other counter-mapping efforts challenge the prevailing assumptions of cartography: that maps must remain exclusively in the realm of physical space. They show not only that other types of spaces (digital, infrastructural, juridical) can be mapped, but that mapping is more crucial than ever to understanding our globalized world.

Works Cited and Further Reading

→ Ash, J., Kitchin, R., & Leszczynski, A. (2016). Digital turn, digital geographies? *Progress in Human Geography*. Retrieved from https://journals.sagepub.com/doi/10.1177/0309132516664800.

→ Balmazović, D. (2017, March 9). *Škart Maps*. Retrieved from: https://www.internationaleonline.org/research/real_democracy/87_kart_maps.

→ Branston, G., & Stafford, R. (2010). *The Media Student's Book* (5th ed.). New York, NY: Routledge.

→ Brown, M., Sharples, S., Harding, J., Parker, C.J., Bearman, N., Maguire, M., Forrest, D., Haklay, M., & Jackson, M. (2013). Usability of geographic information: current challenges and future directions. *Applied Ergonomics, 44*(6), 855-865.

→ Bunting, H. (2008, April 15). *A Map of Terrorism*. Retrieved from http://status.irational.org/map_of_terrorism/.

→ Caquard, S. (2013). Cartography I: Mapping narrative cartography. *Progress in Human Geography*, 37(1), 135-144.

→ Chambers, R. (2006). Participatory mapping and geographic information systems: whose map? Who is empowered and who disempowered? Who gains and who loses? *The Electronic Journal of Information Systems in Developing Countries*, 25(2), 1-11.

→ Counter Cartography Collective, Dalton, C., & Mason-Deese, L. (2012). Counter (mapping) actions: mapping as militant research. *ACME: An International E-Journal for Critical Geographies*, 11(3), 439-466.

→ Crampton, J.W. (2001). Maps as social constructions: power, communication and visualization. *Progress in Human Geography*, 25(2), 235-252.

→ Crampton, J. W. (2008). "Cartography: maps 2.0." *Progress in Human Geography*, 33(1), 91-100.

→ Crampton, J. W. (2010). *Mapping: A Critical Introduction to Cartography and GIS* (Vol. 11). Oxford, UK: John Wiley & Sons.

→ Crampton, J.W. and Krygier, J. (2005). An introduction to critical cartography. *ACME: An International e-Journal for Critical Geographies*, 4(1), 11-33.

→ Cubitt, S. (1998). *Digital Aesthetics*. London, UK: Sage.

→ D'Ignazio, C. (2009). Art and cartography. In R. Kitchin & N. Thrift (Eds.), *The International Encyclopedia of Human Geography* (pp. 190-206). Amsterdam: Elsevier.

→ Dodge, M. & Kitchin, R. (2013). Crowdsourced cartography: mapping experience and knowledge. *Environment and Planning A*, 45(1), 19-36.

→ Dunn, C.E. (2007). Participatory GIS—a people's GIS? *Progress in Human Geography*, 31(5), 616-637.

→ Edney, M. (2019). *Cartography: The Ideal and its History*. Chicago, IL: University of Chicago Press.

→ Elwood, S. (2008). Volunteered geographic information: Future research directions motivated by critical, participatory, and feminist GIS. *GeoJournal*, 72(3-4), 173-183.

→ Elwood, S. (2011). Geographic information science: Visualization, visual methods, and the geoweb. *Progress in Human Geography*, 35(3): 401-408.

→ Foucault, M. (1977). *Discipline and Punish: The Birth of the Prison*. New York, NY: Vintage Books.

→ Fragapane, F. (2018, November 28). The stories behind a line: How—and why—I designed a visual narrative of six asylum seekers' routes. Retrieved from https://medium.com/@frcfr/the-stories-behind-a-line-73a1bb247978.

→ Gillespie, T. (2010). The politics of 'platforms'. *New Media & Society*, 12(3), 347-364.

→ Goodchild, M. (2007). Citizens as sensors: the world of volunteered geography. *GeoJournal*, 69(4), 211-221.

→ Gordon, E., Elwood, S., & Mitchell, K. (2016). Critical spatial learning: Participatory mapping, spatial histories, and youth civic engagement. *Children's Geographies*, 1-15.

→ Hall, S. (1997). The work of representation. *Representation: Cultural Representations and Signifying Practices*, 2, 13-74.

→ Harmon, K.A., & Clemans, G. (2009). *The Map as Art: Contemporary Artists Explore Cartography*. New York, NY: Princeton Architectural Press.

→ Helmond, A. (2015). The platformization of the web: Making web data platform ready. *Social Media+ Society*, 1(2), 1-11.

→ Kitchin, R., & Thrift, N. (2009). *International Encyclopedia of Human Geography*. London: Elsevier.

→ Kitchin, R., & Dodge, M. (2011). *Code/Space: Software and Everyday Life*. Cambridge, MA: The MIT Press.

→ Dodge, M., Kitchin, R., & Perkins, C. (Eds.). (2011). *The map reader: theories of mapping practice and cartographic representation*. John Wiley & Sons.

→ Langlois, G., & Elmer, G. (2013). The research politics of social media platforms. *Culture Machine*, 14.

→ Macfarlane, R. (2018, September 22). Wizards, Moomins and pirates: The magic and mystery of literary maps. The Guardian. Retrieved from https://www.theguardian.com/books/2018/sep/22/wizards-moomins-and-gold-the-magic-and-mysteries-of-maps.

→ MacEachren, A.M., Roth, R.E., O'Brien, J., Li, B., Swingley, D., & Gahegan, M. (2012). Visual semiotics & uncertainty visualization: An empirical study. *IEEE Transactions on Visualization and Computer Graphics, 18*(12), 2496-2505.

→ More, T., Logan, G.M., & Adams, R.M. (2002). *Thomas More: Utopia*. Cambridge, UK: Cambridge University Press.

→ Peluso, N.L. (1995). Whose woods are these? Counter-mapping forest territories in Kalimantan, Indonesia. *Antipode*, 27(4), 383-406.

→ Roth, R. (2017). Visual variables. In D. Richardson, N. Castree, M.F. Goodchild, A. Kobayashki, W. Liu, & R.A. Marston (Eds.), *The International Encyclopedia of Geography* (pp. 1-11). Chichester, UK: John Wiley & Sons.

→ Said, E.W. (1978). *Orientalism*. New York, NY: Pantheon Books.

→ Simonite, T. (2015, September 15). First detailed public map of U.S. internet backbone could make it stronger. *MIT Technology Review*. Retrieved from https://www.technologyreview.com/s/540721/first-detailed-public-map-of-us-internet-backbone-could-make-it-stronger/.

→ Swift, J., & Rivero, A.J. (2002). *Gulliver's Travels: Based on the 1726 Text: Contexts, Criticism*. New York, NY: Norton.

Spotlight:
Anatomy of AI

Kate Crawford is a Distinguished Research Professor at New York University and the co-founder and co-director of the AI Now Institute at New York University. Vladan Joler is a Professor in the New Media department at the University of Novi Sad in Serbia and the co-founder of SHARE Foundation. You can view Anatomy of AI at: www.anatomyof.ai.

Over the past two decades, technology has increasingly made the physical shopping store obsolete; now, many people purchase goods via the Internet and online marketplaces such as Amazon or AliExpress. On these websites, one simply scrolls, clicks, and waits for the object to arrive. But set against this seamless process are the myriad systems of production that make it possible—the labour involved in conceiving of the object, the engineering required to produce it, and the transportation logistics involved in getting it to the consumer. There is no other economic system that hides the human labour involved in these processes as effectively as capitalism, where companies such as Amazon or Apple rely on diffuse production networks scattered around the world. Commodities may be developed in America, manufactured in China (using material resources mined in Africa), and finally distribution in chains back in the United States. The consumer only sees the end product, while the story of how it arrived at her doorstep is kept out of sight and out of mind.

In their project *Anatomy of AI* (2018), Kate Crawford and Vladan Joler set out to visualise these hidden systems of production. The work, which they refer to as an "anatomical map of human labor, data and planetary resources," uses the Amazon Echo as a case study in order to demonstrate the material stakes of technological developments. The Echo is a particularly fascinating case study because it is part of a new generation of home technologies that use artificial intelligence. Everything about its interface and design is made to feel like magic: the AI helper, Alexa, can perform any number of duties related to home automation, including providing real-time weather reports

and playing music, and in conjunction with other devices, turning on and off lights or controlling room temperature. Yet Crawford and Joler remind the viewer that "each small moment of convenience...requires a vast planetary network" that far exceeds the energy outputs required to flip a light switch or turn on indoor heating. As Alexa is only able to receive voice-based commands, physical interaction with the object is entirely removed from the equation.

The work is composed of two parts: a large diagram (or map), which stands two meters high and five meters across, and a long-form essay. The map is divided into three parts, each visualising a particular extractive process required to produce and run a single Amazon Echo. On the left, there is the material resources; a tree diagram reveals the path travelled by a single metal—in this case, the chemical element lithium—from mining to smelting, then manufacture and assembly. The middle section examines how an Echo organises and extracts data, both from the natural world and from the domestic environment. Notably, this section designates the human operator as a source of raw data for the Echo to extract. The final section illustrates the afterlife of an Echo, once it is discarded as waste.

At the top left of the diagram they include a small diagram of Karl Marx's dialectic between subject and object. In addition to the dialectic, the project strongly recalls Marx's concept of commodity fetishism. Commodity fetishism refers to the ways in which labour processes are naturalised as economic—rather than social—relationships. *Anatomy of AI* can be read as visualising Marx's critique: the commodity, the

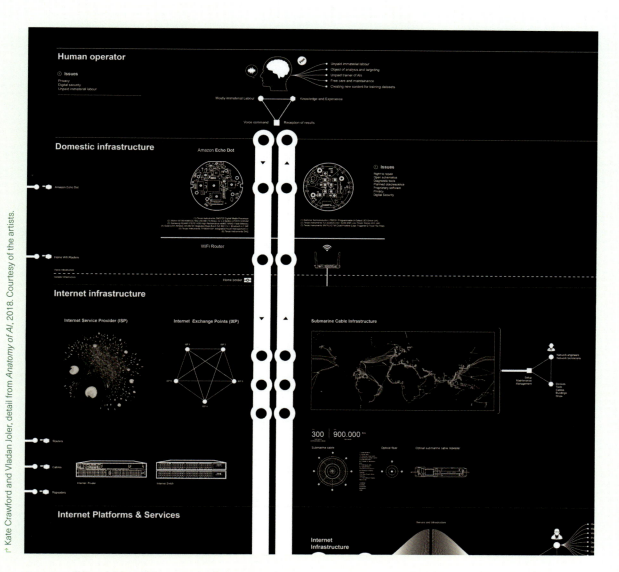

↑ Kate Crawford and Vladan Joler, detail from *Anatomy of AI*, 2018. Courtesy of the artists.

Amazon Echo, is mystifying precisely because it obscures the social realities that bring it to life.

One function of commodity fetishism is that it naturalises the subjective value of an object. A commodity's value is seen as objective, natural, and intrinsic to the object, rather than related to the human labour required to make it. In the case of the Echo, which requires a global system of production almost too large to see clearly, its value is almost wholly disconnected from this vast quantity of labor. In this sense, the Echo is extractive. Crawford and Joler reference Sandro Mezzadra and Brett Neilson's concept of extractivism to describe the relation between different extractive operations in global capitalism. What distinguishes technology such as the Echo from other extractive

commodities, however, is that the extraction does not end once the object has been purchased; rather, end users continue to provide unpaid labour to Amazon in the form of product training, and consumer preferences and habits become profiles that can then be sold to advertisers.

As their map aptly illustrates, behind even the most magical of objects is the human: the muscles that dig, the hands that build, the mind that composes. *Anatomy of AI* is a trenchant reminder of this basic reality.

→ Mezzadra, S., & Neilson, B. (2017). On the multiple frontiers of extraction: excavating contemporary capitalism. *Cultural Studies*, 31(2-3), pp. 185-204.

Spotlight:
The Detroit Geographical Expedition and Institute

The Detroit Geographical Expedition and Institute was formed by Dr. William Bunge and Gwendolyn Warren in 1968 as a radical experiment in spatial geography. The expedition explored racial inequality in Detroit by training community members in geographic techniques and publishing research on the spatiality of racism.

The Detroit Geographical Expedition and Institute (DGEI) was a radical experiment in geographic methods and data collection that has had a lasting legacy in the field. The project was part of a larger movement within higher education in the 1960s to radically de-hierarchise knowledge and to bridge the wide chasm between academic knowledge production and community-led knowledge. Rather than viewing the university as a space to train experts, who would then be sent into a community to solve problems, the Detroit Geographic Expedition and Institute understood the community members to already be experts, who just needed further training in specific academic methods. This ethos is reflected in the expedition's leadership: Dr. William Bunge of Wayne State University served as Research Director, and Gwendolyn Warren, a local community leader who was only eighteen-years old at the project's commencement, led the project as its Administrative Director.

The expedition had two primary arms: education and research. The education arm facilitated free university classes for college-credit to people in inner-city Detroit, primarily in the fields of geography and urban planning (Knudson, 2). Students who completed a year's worth of college credits could enroll as a sophomore in any Michigan university. The programme was taught by volunteer faculty and took place in regular university facilities.

The research arm undertook expeditions – three in total – and published the results in the form of discussion papers called "Field Notes." Detroit was a potent location for the project. Just a year prior to the expedition's founding, the city experienced five-day-long riots catalysed primarily by conflicts between Black residents and the Detroit City Police. The expeditions sought to explore the kinds of inequalities that sparked the riots: segregation, unequal access to education, and relations with law enforcement. "Field Notes II: A Report to the Parents of Detroit on School Decentralization," focused on the impact of school zoning on education quality. It was produced in part by the work of students in two of the courses offered in the free university programme, 'Cartography' and 'Geographical Aspects of Urban Planning.' According to Ronald J. Horvath, until the decentralisation study was introduced, the courses struggled with morale and focus; the material "just did not seem terribly important to the students... some came hungry, others couldn't afford bus fare, one student had been living in a car for five weeks" (77). The study offered a concrete exercise in applying geography and statistical methods to everyday life.

"Field Notes II" was a response to the proposed redistricting plans put forward by the Detroit Board of Education in 1970. According to the Expedition's report, the Board's plans "preclude[d] local ethnic expression, local citizen participation, and local political control" (8). Researchers ran statistical analyses to show how four of the eight plans proposed by the Board were actually illegal. Their work forced a response from the Board and helped shape the zoning decisions in the city. The report aptly illustrated how districting – at its most literal, simply drawn lines on a map – influences levels of inequality between racial groups.

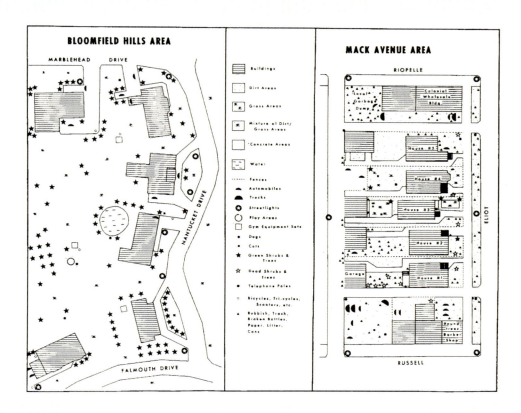

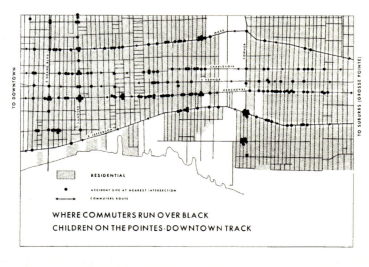

↳ Detroit Geographical Expedition and Institute, map comparing the Bloomfield Hills Area with the Mack Avenue Area, 1971. Courtesy of Bob Colenutt.

→ Detroit Geographical Expedition and Institute, *Where Commuters Run Over Black Children on the Pointes-Downtown Track*, 1971. Courtesy of Bob Colenutt.

The next report, "Field Notes III: The Geography of Children," used qualitative data from interviews and observations to estimate the quality of life and achievement opportunities granted to children in racially segregated neighbourhoods. One section, "Mack Avenue and Bloomfield Hills – From a Child's Point of View," cites interviews with children from different neighbourhoods and compares their responses on a range of social and economic indicators. Mack Avenue, a majority Black neighbourhood, is described as "filthy and cluttered with rubbish, debris and broken glass"; in contrast, Bloomfield Hills is a "spacious and beautifully landscaped" (20) white-majority area composed of large homes and clean playgrounds. Data such as number of television sets per household, number of bottles of whiskey or beer per household, and amount of educational material in the home were used to compare the two neighbourhoods and to draw larger conclusions about life outcomes for Black children.

Perhaps the most shocking graph in "Field Notes III" is "Where Commuters Run Over Black Children on the Pointes-Downtown Track." Warren used data on commuter traffic to demonstrate how Detroit's Black children are the most susceptible to automobile deaths. The map establishes clear clusters, proving what the local residents knew to be true: Black children were at a greater risk of automobile-caused death based on where they lived. Like most other American cities, Detroit was subject to 'white flight' in the middle of the twentieth century. Black inner-city neighbourhoods were not simply residential districts but commuter zones, used by white people travelling in from the suburbs to their jobs downtown. The risk of automobile death was compounded by the lack of play spaces in Black neighbourhoods, which were primarily composed of high-rise buildings.

The DGEI deepened our collective understanding of spatial injustice and the concept of 'counter-mapping' by making visible the relationships between people, objects, and space. The Expedition strove to not only include local people but to work side-by-side with them, in a democratic, rather than hierarchical, pursuit of knowledge. The Detroit Expedition closed in 1971, in part due to declining relations between the DGEI and Michigan State University, its main sponsor. Although the project was short-lived, it still has much to teach us about the radical possibilities that emerge when theory and practice come together.

→ Bunge, W. (1969). The first years of the Detroit Geographical Expedition: A personal report. In R.J. Horvath and E.J. Vander Velde (Eds.), *Field Notes, The Detroit Geographic Expedition, A Series Dedicated to the Human Exploration of Our Planet, Discussion Paper No. 1, The Detroit Geographical Expedition Institute* (pp. 1-30). East Lansing, MI: Michigan State University.

→ Horvath, R.J. (1971). The 'Detroit Geographical Expedition and Institute' experience. *Antipode*, 3, 73-85. doi:10.1111/j.1467-8330.1971.tb00544.x

→ Knudson, C. (2017). Detroit Geographical Expedition Institute: Unpacking the history and structure of the DGEI. In *The Detroit Geographical Expedition and Institute Then and Now...: Commentaries on Field Notes No.4: The Trumbull Community*. Antipode Foundation. Retrieved from URL: https://radicalantipode.files.wordpress.com/2017/02/dgei-field-notes_chris-knudson.pdf

→ Colvard, Y. and Cozzens, S. (Eds.). (1970). *Field Notes No.2: School Decentralization*. Detroit: Detroit Geographical Expedition and Institute. Retrieved from URL: https://radicalantipode.files.wordpress.com/2017/01/dgei_fieldnotes-ii.pdf (last accessed 13 January 2017)

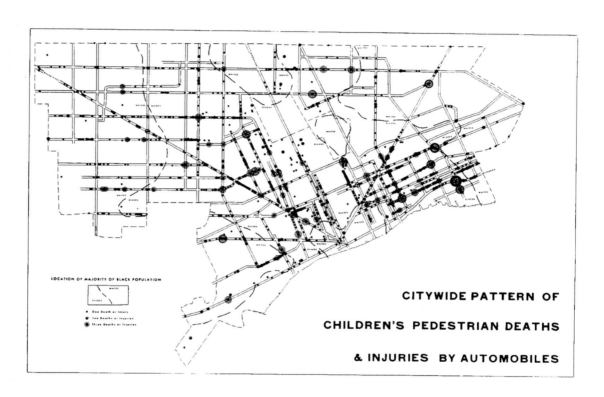

CITYWIDE PATTERN OF

CHILDREN'S PEDESTRIAN DEATHS

& INJURIES BY AUTOMOBILES

↳ Detroit Geographical Expedition and Institute, *Citywide Pattern of Children's Deaths & Injuries by Automobiles*, 1971. Courtesy of Bob Colenutt.

Spotlight:
Migrant Maps

Đorđe Balmazović is a member of Škart collective, which was founded in Belgrade, Yugoslavia in 1990. Since 2013, Škart has conducted workshops with asylum seekers based in Serbia.

In 2013, the Serbian organisation Group 484 invited the artist collective Škart to collaborate with asylum seekers in a village near Valjevo, Serbia. Together, they conceived of *Migrant Maps* as a way for the migrants to share stories of their journeys. The maps are roughly sketched in a tangle of black and red lines; the red lines represent the borders of countries while the black lines track the migrant's route. The maps are scattered with small cartoonish drawings as well as supplementary text, appearing in cramped handwriting, describing portions of the trek. In the upper-left corner they are labelled with the name of the narrator and the date of the journey. On one map, *ABDUL RAHMAN, 24, APRIL 2014*, there is a small sketch of a crowd above the handwritten text, "10 DAYS IN ATHENS, 180 € TO GET FAKE ID CARD (YOU HAVE TO FIND SOMEONE LOOKING LIKE YOU)." Another map, *SULEJMAN HUGENI SHIRZAD, 27.5.2007*, depicts a speckle of figures aboard a boat travelling from İzmir, Turkey to Mytilene, Greece. The corresponding text reads "28 PEOPLE IN 2M BOAT. PLASTIC, COUSIN DIED IN THE SAME BOAT BEFORE."

These maps do not conform to cartographic conventions. Country borders do not resemble geographical reality; they are not drawn to scale, nor do their shapes correspond to the physical land masses they are meant to represent. Đorđe Balmazović, one of the artists working on the project, stated, "I realized that crossing all these borders of unknown countries is a bit chaotic for [the migrants]. I decided to subvert geographical borders and country sizes to the events that happened to them. Therefore, the borders drawn as red are just provisional, just to show how many of them they had to go over" (email interview, December 18, 2017). If this unrealistic representation makes the maps harder to read, it only parallels the confusing, dizzying experience of the migrants themselves, who leave the familiarity of their homelands to cross into the unknown.

In some ways, the maps abandon cartography altogether. Sulejman's journey, which starts in Afghanistan and ends in Croatia, should be depicted cartographically from right to left, according to the geographic location of each country; but instead, it is drawn in a narrative format from left to right. This makes the project more comprehensible as a story, but less comprehensible as a map. This is only reinforced by the textual portions, which were lifted directly from interviews with migrants. There is an immediacy to their testimony, both because they are hand-written but also because they stay true to the fragmented English in which they were spoken.

According to Balmazović, the maps were drafted in collaboration with the migrants, to ensure that they approved of his presentation of the events. Beyond the collaboration between artist and researcher, there was a sense of community throughout the production process. Balmazović states, "Map making was a point to people to [sic] gather and talk" (2017). Speaking together, sharing stories, and listening is at the heart of the project. For Balmazović, 'data' are the "testimonies of people who are invisible to mainstream politics" (2017). Moving beyond numbers, the project places first-hand testimonies front and centre, as valuable map-making tools in their own right.

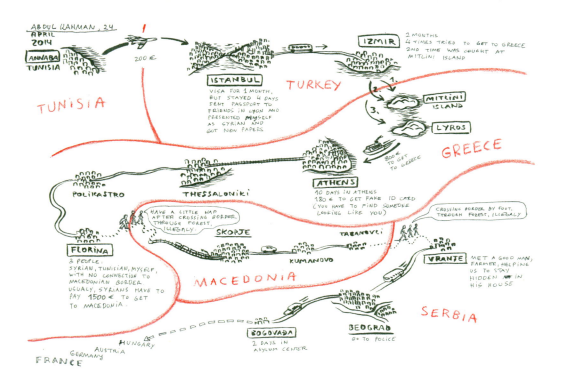

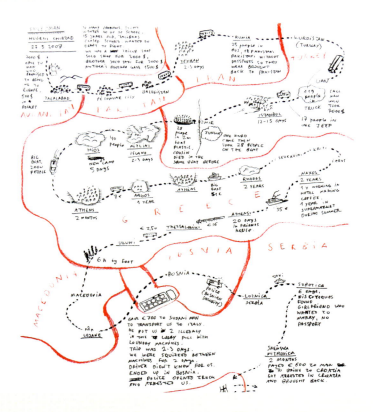

↳ Đorđe Balmazović (Škart collective) in collaboration with asylum seekers in Banja Koviljača camp in Serbia, *Abdul Rahman, 24, April 2014*. Edition 1/4. Courtesy of the artist.

→ Đorđe Balmazović (Škart collective) in collaboration with asylum seekers in Banja Koviljača camp in Serbia, *Sulejman Hugeni Shirzad, 27/5/2007*. Edition 1/4. Courtesy of the artist.

Spotlight:
Voz

Doug Specht was trained as a geography teacher and taught in Latin America. He started Voz while working in Toronto at a university that was sponsored by big mining corporations. In efforts to make visible some of the harms of the mining industry, Doug embarked on a project to map human rights abuses at Canadian-owned gold mines in Latin America. This initiative eventually led to the creation of something much bigger.

My project took off after the mining map was featured by the Environmental Network for Central America. Although well received, the information kept going out of date as human rights abuses were piling up faster than any one person could map.

On top of that, there was a clunky API that required knowledge of numerous short-codes and Keyhole Markup Language, all run through an ugly interface that hardly inspired anyone but the most hardened geek. This meant that even though the map was open for participation, few were willing or able to contribute.

Many map-making software options are still either too simple for most data tasks (such as Datawrapper), too complex or expensive for non-programmers (ArcGIS) or too clunky for participatory collaboration (Google Maps). Even the most user-friendly mapping tools, like CartoDB and Zeemaps, require a great deal of time to master, beyond their click and point wizards.

For Voz, the need to build a whole new platform, with high levels of encryption, meant looking beyond the GIS community for a web developer and coder. Fortunately the search ended quickly, after a phone call to my brother Todd, owner of *CreateElement*. Todd initially signed up to build a quick and cheap mapping tool for use in Colombia. Three years and no pay cheques later, he continues to dedicate huge amounts of time to developing Voz on a global scale, paid in compliments to find technical solutions to the challenges that mapping social justice throws in our paths.

Today the Voz platform supports local campaign groups to upload reports of human rights abuses that they categorise and locate. As users around the world do the same, connections can be made across campaigns. This allows media organisations and NGOs around the world to pick up stories, while local organisations can make global links around human rights abuses.

Explore Voz at: 1voz.org. For more on the origins of Voz, read Jen Wilton's article for New International magazine, *Mapping human rights from Colombia to Congo*: www.newint.org/features/web-exclusive/2015/06/26/mapping-human-rights.

By Doug Specht

The Voz platform. Courtesy of Doug Specht.

Spotlight:
Counter-Cartographies Collective

The Counter-Cartographies Collective (or '3Cs') "is born out of our enthusiasm with the power of maps." They draw inspiration from all kinds of different social movements, theorists and creative practices, while embracing the struggles of collaboration and the joys of play. Explore 3Cs at: www.countercartographies.org.

We work on mapping in order to:

→ render new images and practices of economies and social relations.

→ destabilize centered and exclusionary representations of the social and economic.

→ construct new imaginaries of collective struggle and alternative worlds.

We seek to create collaborations for engaged research and cartography — transforming the conditions of how we think, write and map and the conditions about which we think, write and map.

We work in a variety of media and have engaged in a variety of projects, from drifts to dis-orientation guides, from community-led convergences to hosting major academic cartographers, as well as participating in direct actions and publishing in activist and scholarly publications and conferences.

Our affiliations cross disciplinary, institutional and national boundaries. We work with artists, independent scholars, grassroots communities and university folks, in a range of settings including: cartographic collaborations, exchange of material, hosting and visiting, conference and publication participation, convergences, direct action organizing, and as much as our imagination and own capacities can deal with... we are open to improvisation.

By the Counter-Cartographies Collective

DISORIENTATION²

(y)our guide to the University of North Carolina at Chapel Hill

Crisis... at school?!?

The news is full of stories about the economic crisis... How did it start? Who feels the pinch? Is it over yet? What does the crisis mean for the university? Will UNC's budget be cut by 7%? 10%? More?! What about next year? Who will lose their jobs? How much will tuition increase? Which classes will be canceled? Will we be able to graduate? Though the crisis may feel new, these changes are part of a long-underway transformation in the university: the casualization of teaching labor, the defunding of the humanities, the decline of faculty governance, and the rise of administrative power. *So much for the "ivory tower"...*

Welcome to the university = Welcome to the real world.

In this guidemap: UNC is a space of multiple and unseen kinds of labor made precarious under the pressures of the economic crisis; UNC is a site where borders and migration policy are put into effect; UNC is a site of historical struggles; UNC is competing in administrative ranking games unrelated to the actual teaching that benefits students and faculty; UNC is an increasingly bureaucratic machine, making it more difficult to democratically participate in important university decisions; finally, UNC is part of a growing, worldwide wave of social mobilizations fighting for other, better universities.

The Counter Cartographies Collective (3Cs) is an autonomous mapping working group based at the University of North Carolina at Chapel Hill. In our first disOrientation Guide (2006), we mapped out some of the multiple realities of our university: UNC, as a factory and body, shapes the way we inhabit the world. Learn more about us and get a copy of our first guide-map to UNC in glossy color at *www.countercartographies.org*.

PRECARITY ON CAMPUS

Precarity is about not being able to afford health-care; about being on a visa that won't allow you to change jobs or not having papers at all. It is about not being able to pay your rent or mortgage; about graduating with so much debt you have to work for years just to pay it off. Precarity is about not being part of a collective organization to improve your working conditions. Look at the icons on this map to find the laborers on campus - the people who teach classes, lead labs and sections, serve food in Lenoir, students, and... ...perhaps even you?

longer shifts
get more work done!
furloughs (paycuts)
unemployed summers
more vacation
ORGANIZE!
layoffs get a hobby!
higher tuition
healthcare cuts take aspirin!
student debt go to grad school!

NAVIGATING BORDERS AT UNC...

News reports may focus on the US-Mexico border or raids by federal agents, but universities like UNC are important nodes for generating visas and policing the movements of international migrants. Since 2001, international students and their work have faced intensifying scrutiny and Homeland Security's bureaucracy. A star region for R&D, the Research Triangle and its universities attract people from all over the world. International students, scholars, technical workers, service workers and domestic staff help make UNC, IBM, and other local institutions more competitive and profitable.

...AND THE MIGRANT RESEARCH TRIANGLE

UNC-Chapel Hill
Chapel Hill
Durham
Synergy Solutions
IBM
Cisco
GSK
Research Triangle Park
SAS
Informerica
Cary
NC State University
Raleigh

Number of visas by employer:
2000
1000
300

Visa category:
H1-B F-1 J-1

H1-B = Total applications since 2001
F-1 = Total visa-holders employed, 2008
J-1 = Total visa-holders employed, 2008
J-1 data from NCSU not available

funding, if you work (legal or illegal) t have to drop out

U.S. Border

Have enough funding?

F-1 J-1

Keep academic interests?

Transfer to another program

If your visa is rejected, quitting your program might be the only choice you can make. And it can take many months before you find out if your visa is approved or not..

Go abroad for fieldwork... can you get back into the country?

After graduation

Librarian
Student
Research Assistant
Teaching Assistant
Technician
Chef
House-keeper
Nurse
Construction labor
Farm-worker
Artist
Teacher

H2-B
H1-B
H1-C H2-A

Non-immigrant visas

SK-3 SK-1 EB-3
EB-2 EB-1

Immigrant visas

Find a job?

Stay or

Green

Not every foreigner who comes to the United States to study even wants to have a job there. Many return to their home country after graduation...

Visa. n. ˈvē-zə: a document that dictates what a foreigner legally can or cannot do within a country's borders. A visa is one mechanism for controlling and governing a border. Whether the visa-holder is a student or a technician, visas function as devices for monitoring individuals and channeling their daily lives. However, things are not as clean-cut as

officially speaking...

"...the **J visa** is for educational and cultural exchange programs designated by the Dept. of State, Bureau of Consular Affairs..."

"...the **F visa** is reserved for non-immigrants wishing to pursue

↳ Counter-Cartographies Collective, detail from disOrientation², 2009.
Courtesy of Counter-Cartographies Collective.

Spotlight:
Photodrive

Photographic methodologies have been demonstrated to help elucidate different forms of knowledge in urban spaces, but less work has been demonstrated in rural geographic studies. In this pilot study, geographer John Paul Henry explores hidden experiences of slow violence in rural, western Kentucky using a photodrive.

I was sitting in a fast-food restaurant with a retired pipe fitter and a pastor when the pipe fitter pulled up his sleeve to show me a mark of discoloration on his arm. "Is it cancerous?" I asked with a wince. "Not yet," he replied. "But it turns into cancer. That was over at Goodrich...."

Goodrich, now owned by Westlake Vinyls, is one of sixteen industrial facilities comprising the Calvert City Industrial Complex (CCIC) on the southern bank of the Tennessee River in Marshall County, Kentucky, thirteen miles from the confluence of the Ohio River. Westlake Vinyls discharged the highest levels of dioxins in the country in 2010 (Sturgis 2012). Dioxins, cancer-causing and genome-altering industrial by-products, are created through waste incineration and PVC production, both of which the CCIC is known for (White and Birnbaum 2009).

The pipe fitter had worked in these facilities since 1973. He built such a familiarity with the facilities that he drew a mental map on the diner table with his index finger. "If you go in the construction entrance, you go to the first street, make a left, go down one street, make a right and you go down and there's barriers, and right there to the right there's an EPA well," he said. The well had gotten plugged, but he said EPA officials hadn't bled the pressure off. That's where the accident happened.

Photowalks have been demonstrated as valuable for negotiating a shared perspective and revealing hidden places in urban spaces (Cannuscio et al. 2009). Applying this methodology to rural geographies though, proves difficult given the impracticalities of

navigating rural, industrial highways on foot. To better understand the nuanced and obscured experiences of slow violence (Nixon 2011; O'Lear 2021) we set off in his car. The pipe fitter drove his own car while the pastor and I accompanied him, my audio recorder and camera in tow. This mobile interview gave rise to a completely new perspective of places I had visited myself just days prior. My attention turned from the emission stacks with pilot flames perched on top, to more everyday experiences.

As we accelerated away from the diner it was obvious the nature of the interview was changing dramatically. Details about this typical Kentucky town surfaced through the pastor's narration: 'The police hide here... Those horseback riders are from so-and-so family... Almost every house in that subdivision has someone who has cancer....' During the traditional, semi-structured interview in the fast-food booth, the pipe fitter focused on his history laboring at the chemical facilities, the incidents of danger befallen on him and his contemporaries. 'The Pit,' where an explosion killed a friend. The metallurgical factory where another friend was crushed. We passed these places on our photodrive, those narratives resurfacing each time. But as we sat outside the construction gate of Westlake Vinyls, the hidden nature of his toxic exposure crystalized. He pointed me in the direction of the hidden EPA well. It became obvious that his toxic experience was now safely hidden behind a clean corporate facade. But the other experiences coming to light were more revealing about the everyday, incremental experiences of those lives lived bordering the fences of industrial facilities.

↳ A corporate facade obscures the place where a retired pipe fitter said he was contaminated with toxic well water. The image was created during a photodrive in western Kentucky. Courtesy of the author.

We pull into a typical neighborhood generally deemed safe and stopped outside of a brick ranch style house. "From my mother's front porch right there, you could see that flame in the sky and hear the roar of the jet engine. It sounds like a jet engine when that goes off," the pastor said. These types of experiences are routinized through years of exposure through living near chemical facilities (Davies 2018). "It's kind of terrifying when you look up into the sky and there's a big black cloud of smoke. We had to leave. They had some kind of emergency at the plant, and we had to leave our house because of the way the air was blowing." Homes closer to the chemical facilities are deemed less desirable.

We arrived at the trailer park adjacent to the chemical plants, a fence-lined community. "This is what he's talking about living on this side of the tracks. No one wants to live on this side of the tracks in Calvert City," the pastor said. The town's racial makeup, with 99% of the population identifying as white, surfaced by some unknown signifier. "But if you was black I definitely wouldn't come down here. Because I can take you to where they got the flag usually, and it's a confederate flag. It's Ku Klux Klan headquarters of western Kentucky," the pipe fitter said. Other visible details sparked conversation in the photodrive. "Another thing about living in Calvert, everything corrodes really fast. Like the outside brass on our house. And we live five miles from the plants," the pastor said. Like a flip of a light switch, I suddenly began to see the corrosion everywhere. A stop sign's paint was flaked and peeling on the side facing the chemical facilities; the opposite side, pristine. Furthermore, co-navigating places drew on collaborators' emotions, drawing out statements of place meaning (Adams 2017). "People used to live here because of the plants. But now it's just a big, sad area," the pastor told me. "I have a parishioner that lives down here and she was embarrassed for me to come to her house."

This case study demonstrates the value of collaborative photographic methodologies in rural geographic research by showing how different information surfaces while co-navigating toxic places, compared to stationary interviews. Photodrives mimic photo elicitation interviews by evoking richer, "at times encyclopedic" descriptions (Rose 2016, 305), but are applicable in contexts where no photo documentation exists. The reflexive coding process of photodrive images (Rose 2016, 304; Suchar 1997) brings forth the complexity of how places are deemed safe even though industrial encroachment in 'safe' places has become normalized.

John Paul Henry is a PhD aspirant studying political geography, slow violence, and critical geopolitics at the University of Kansas. He uses collaborative and photographic methodologies to elicit forms of agency, embodied experience, and resistance in relation to slow violence and discourse.

By John Paul Henry

→   Adams, P.C. (2017). Epilogue: Methodologies of place attachment research, *Explorations in Place Attachment*. London: Routledge.

→   Cannuscio, C.C., Weiss, E.E., Fruchtman, H., Schroeder, J., Weiner, J. and Asch, D.A. (2009). Visual epidemiology: Photographs as tools for probing street-level etiologies, *Social Science & Medicine*. 69, 553-564.

→   Davies, T. (2018). Toxic space and time: Slow violence, necropolitics, and petrochemical pollution, *Annals of the American Association of Geographers*. DOI: 10.1080/24694452.2018.1470924

→   Nixon, R. (2011). *Slow Violence and the Environmentalism of the Poor*. Cambridge, MA: Harvard University Press.

→   O'Lear, S. (2021). *Geographies of Slow Violence: A Research Agenda*. Edward Eigar Publishing. In Press.

→   Rose, G. (2016). *Research Methodologies: An Introduction to Researching with Visual Materials*. London: Sage.

→   Schwartz, P.M. et al (1983). Lake Michigan fish consumption as a source of polychlorinated biphenyls in human cord serum, maternal serum, and milk. *American Journal of Public Health*. 73:3, 293-295.

→   Sturgis, S. (2012). Dumping dioxin on Dixie, facing south. *The Institute for Southern Studies*. Website accessed March 7, 2019. https://www.facingsouth.org/2012/01/dumping-dioxin-on-dixie.html

→   Suchar, S.C. (1997). Grounding visual sociology research in shooting scripts, *Qualitative Sociology*. 20:1.

→   White, S.S., & Birnbaum, L.S. (2009). An overview of the effects of dioxins and dioxin-like compounds on vertebrates, as documented in human and ecological epidemiology, *Journal of Environmental Science and Health. Part C, Environmental Carcinogenesis & Ecotoxicology Reviews*, 27:4, 197–211. http://doi.org/10.1080/10590500903310047

↳ During the photodrive, the retired pipefitter notices details I otherwise would have overlooked of underground effluent surfacing from a manhole adjacent the Tennessee River. "They could be pumping water back into the river. Now look at that water, now. You see the bubbles on it? Does water normally bubble that way?" Courtesy of the author.

Future-Proof Principles

The Four Cs

with Alexandra Alberda

While software can become out-dated, websites no longer available, and online tools get discontinued, the principles covered in this book are designed to work across these changes. In the past five years we have seen some of our favourite platforms for training people in data storytelling go defunct. Others got turned from free tools into prohibitively expensive pay-for packages. And others pivoted in a new direction, moving away from the collaborative ethos that was part of its foundation. As teachers and facilitators we have to adapt, modifying our lessons to fit new—and often less optimal—tools for data storytelling. But whatever products we use as part of technological chains for creating data stories, the foundational concepts found in this book serve as a guide. Their lessons are not bound to the latest digital trend, design aesthetic, or venture capitalist imitative. They are, for the most part, future-proof. In our ever-changing working and technological environments, we believe that the foundations for becoming a data storyteller should be able to move with the times.

→ Technological chains refers to the selection of software and platforms, as well as the ways in which they are ordered to function most productively together.

Resources, workflows, departmental structures, job descriptions and—of course—data continually change. With these changes we are forced to not only renew and re-evaluate the way we work, but also to maintain our working relationships with others. As so many data storytelling projects require expertise and input from others, collaboration is at the heart of much of what we do. In this last section of our workbook we offer a final set of concepts. We call them our "Four Cs for Collaboration." These final principles reflect our ethos for collaboration: Curiosity, Clarity, Coordination, and Care.

Principle 1: Curiosity

Fundamental to all of our collaborative projects is a shared sense of the project's goal. While our interest in working toward that goal may be motivated by our different roles and expertise, it is crucial that we are driven intrinsically by a shared curiosity. Ideally that curiosity is linked to the subject we are investigating. As a primary motivator, curiosity drives engagement. Research has found that curiosity can help navigate uncertainty, lead to more creative problem-solving and help reduce group conflict (Gino, 2018).

To help foster curiosity throughout our teams, we involve designers from the early stages of the research or analysis process. This allows everyone better access to each other's perspectives, as we map out the problems before us from research perspectives, as well as design and storytelling perspectives. It helps our researchers think like designers, our data analysts think like storytellers, and our designers dive into the world of research and problems of analysis. Together we ask questions about our data's backstory, bringing the potential biases, complexities, and absences we are likely to encounter to the forefront of our conversations. It is this collaborative approach to storytelling with data that allows us to share in the process and not just the final product.

Principle 2: Clarity

While you often may not know what data stories you want to tell at the beginning of a project, it is important to be clear about your expectations throughout the process of any project. This means having clearly defined roles, a solid overview of available resources, and establishing open channels of communication between collaborators. With these things in place, when ideas, resources, or available funding changes, it is much easier to make updates to tasks and timeframes.

In particular, clarity—and transparency—is important around budgets and pay rates. While some of us may work for companies with large design budgets, others may be scraping together funding from a variety of sources. Always let your designers or artists know if the budget can be stretched or not. Have a clear arrangement in advance of the workflow, times for edits or check-ins, and how much, if any, budget is available to make amends later in a project. Likewise, artists and designers need to be clear with researchers and analysts what they need to be able to do their jobs. As data storytelling collaborations often involve working with people that use completely different terminologies and backgrounds, the more we can translate our expectations and visions to each other clearly, the easier it will be to navigate the process of a project. We often make jargon-busting a key conversation in early planning meetings to make sure that everyone is on the same page.

Principle 3: Coordination

Once project goals and expectations are laid out, coordination becomes a key concern. It is useful to establish what software and communication platforms you will use to carry out your project, particularly if face-to-face meetings will be limited or not an option at all. We often use collaborative tools for our data storytelling projects that allow for live editing, such as Google Sheets and Google Docs. Slack channels, Whatsapp groups and Skype (or other video conferencing providers), work well in place of face-to-face meetings as they allow for easily and quickly sharing links, photos, and other work-in-progress materials. Make sure you select software and communication systems that can accommodate everyone in your collaboration and that everyone on board knows how to use these tools.

It is also a good idea to set up shared repository or archive of your data storytelling work in advance. If you are using Google Drive tools, you will automatically be saving old versions. Likewise, you can record video conference calls and make sure your chat platforms are set to save and archive conversations. However, in addition to this functionality, we find it useful to also make a copy of work in regular intervals and save old versions in a specified, shared folder. Make sure you are using a standard labelling system for any shared folders and files, ideally that include the data or version number. This will save you lots of time when going back through old material. More importantly, repositories of project work give participants a sense of shared ownership and allow you to map progress—or lack of progress!—together.

Principle 4: Care

The most important component of our ethos for collaboration is the principle of care. When we work together with others we try to take care to map out fair and equitable working processes from the beginning. This is embodied in our principles of Clarity and Coordination. In addition, care means recognising each other as whole people. During the lifespan of a project collaborators may have child, parental, partner, or other care responsibilities that shape how available they can be for your shared project. In addition to any disclosed disabilities or illnesses, people on your project may have invisible disabilities, chronic conditions, or other issues and challenges that you cannot anticipate and may be unfamiliar with. This is particularly significant on projects that involve working with sensitive data, may cause vicarious trauma, or may trigger past traumas.

→ Vicarious trauma refers to the indirect exposure to trauma. In data storytelling this often comes from working with testimony, images and other mediated forms that document trauma.

Sam Dubberley & Michele Grant's (2017) Journalism and *Vicarious Trauma: A Guide for Journalists, Editor and News Organisations* offers an excellent introductory resource for anyone working with traumatic materials. It is available to freely download online at www.firstdraftnews.org/wp-content/uploads/2017/04/vicarioustrauma.pdf.

Care means putting each other's wellbeing before the successful completion of a project. Care means giving each other the benefit of the doubt. Care means holding on to our complex personhood when under pressure—and recognising when we fail to do so. Care means acknowledging that individual vulnerabilities are tethered to larger structures of inequality. That people's backgrounds are not always visible, but will always shape the ways we interact.

Practically speaking, care can be as simple as rescheduling a meeting. It can be making cups of tea. It can be paying for a taxi or swapping a task list. Care can be saying don't come to work. Care is how we communicate, how we problem-solve, and how we engage with each other on a day-to-day basis. Care challenges us to "collectivise vulnerability." As Claire English (2017) argues, we can nurture our ability to see individual vulnerabilities as shared in order to negotiate responses together. Like all the other aspects of becoming a data storyteller, care is a capacity that grows with reflection and practice.

Act like the Data Storyteller You Want to Be

Working to tell data stories together is a daunting task. In addition to all of the technical and collaborative aspects of data storytelling, writing nonfiction requires a diligent commitment to gathering evidence and documenting information. This is serious stuff. But at the same time as we work to maintain rigorous data practices, it is also important that we foster playful, experimental spaces to stretch and grow our storytelling muscles. However, in most data and evidence-based environments like universities, think tanks, research centres, and statistics offices, there is little room to make an inventive mess. When limited by the conventions of one's workplace or job role, the question becomes: Where else can I be messy, creative, and playful?

Some of you reading this workbook may be in the same boat. Perhaps your boss doesn't want you experimenting, or there is no room in your current industry to pitch a hero's journey of health statistics. The trick is to find other outlets to develop your creativity. To become a data story-teller, you must learn to carve out spaces, find collaborators, and make connections that allow our less disciplined selves and voices to speak.

Once we tune into our creative energy, we realise these spaces for ex-perimentation with storytelling exist all around us. And while we might not immediately get credit in the form of promotions or by-lines, there will always be people who notice, though they may be 'friends in low places.' But as anyone who has delved into the outskirts of their industry can tell you, it is often our friends in low places that are the most crucial part of our networks. They are the ones who support your outlandish ideas, who bring you with them as their careers progress, who offer guidance when it feels like no one else can see what you're on about. It is in these carved out spaces for creative expression and imaginative experimentation that real professional development and emotional support occur. While many of us think we should only invest in networking up, it is equally, if not more important, to be networking across, and mentoring those coming up behind us. Our boldness to be creative is what allows for the next generation to break the moulds.

With the proliferation of web-based tools and platforms, we are able to showcase and narrate our own creative ethos. We can curate project portfolios that tell our stories, working beyond the confines of journal article image guidelines and staff profile templates that constrict our ability to express our imaginations. Harnessed well, this self-showcas-ing of your budding data storyteller persona can establish consistency between your projects and help you build bridges between the research, community, and industry spaces you want to reach.

As you establish networks and showcase work on your own terms, you also begin to create your own archives. You can find new ways to generate collaborative databases that 'count' professionally, as well as to find communities who 'count' these projects based on their own value systems. This is how many data storytellers got started—as well as how graphic medicine, graphic social science and related visual communication fields emerged. Groups of people found each other in their desire to bridge the worlds of evidence and experience. They made knowledge matter through their art and their empathy. They insisted that stories and 'facts' could be beautiful across the full palette of human emotions.

A metaphor we use to make sense of this approach to creative work involves the symbol of a thyrsus. A thyrsus is a staff used by the Maenads of the Dionysus cult. It is a mythical object for self-defence against male aggressors that spurts out springs of wine when it strikes the ground. On the end of the staff there is a pinecone. The pinecone's scales are overlapping; when they open up they drop their seeds. Through wind and the movements of the forest, these seeds scatter, but only some grow into trees.

→ We channel the fury of this maenad, who holds a thyrsus in her right hand and a leopard in her left.

We never know exactly which of our innovative ideas, failed experiments, or friends in low places are going to click and stick and make a difference. All we can do is have the courage to push ourselves—and our collaborators—beyond the confines of established practice. Harnessing curiosity, clarity, coordination, and care, we can foster creative communities for telling data stories together.

Works Cited and Further Reading

→ English, C.L. (2017). *Safe Cracking: From Safe (r) Spaces to Collectivising Vulnerability in Migrant Solidarity Organising.* (Doctoral dissertation, School of Management).

→ Gino, F. (2018). The business case for curiosity. *Harvard Business Review.* Retrieved from https://hbr.org/2018/09/curiosity.

Index

A

accountability → 68, 80, 93, 105–107, 111
AI → 70, 223–224
Alberda, Alexandra → 21, 33, 36, 51–52, 138, 160, 163, 183, 191, 197
algorithms → 75, 80, 84, 99, 101, 103, 150, 175
Amnesty International → 99–102, 107, 113, 217
audience → 2, 4, 13, 20–27, 29–30, 32, 35–36, 38, 40, 42, 47, 56–59, 61, 63–66, 75, 114, 116, 118, 122, 126, 128, 130, 134–138, 142, 160, 165, 173, 185–186, 194, 196, 204, 213, 216–217

B

backstory → 22, 35–36, 41–42, 65, 116–117, 123, 144, 240
BAGAGE → 208–209
Balmazović, Đorđe → 210, 221, 229–230
Barthes, Roland → 124–125, 135, 170, 195–196
bias → 8, 69–70, 80, 116–118, 123, 155, 194, 203, 240
big data → 2, 7, 26, 32, 39, 54, 56, 69, 74–77, 84–86, 91, 116, 120, 126
Bournemouth University → 2–3, 12, 15, 33, 61, 63, 65, 105, 109, 152, 171, 193, 195, 197, 199

C

Cambridge Analytica → 77
caption → 116, 122, 126, 134–135, 137–138, 154, 156, 162, 194, 196, 198
cartographic gaze → 204–205, 208, 215
Centre for Investigative Journalism → 5, 9, 90, 105
characters → 13, 15, 28, 30, 34–36, 38, 59, 65, 73, 103, 131, 144, 155, 161–162, 175, 198, 204
chartjunk → 140–142, 171
cities → 2, 43, 49, 77, 121, 167–168, 181, 187–189, 208, 215, 217, 225–227, 235–237
citizen-generated data → 54, 79, 86, 119, 185
Civic Media Hub → 2–3, 6, 8–9, 11, 21, 36, 61, 63, 65, 105, 109,

117–118, 142, 160, 193, 195, 197, 199, 217–218
climate change → 59, 69, 103, 121, 163, 181, 213, 241
colour → 20, 54, 56, 61, 63–64, 76, 87, 116, 120, 122, 124–126, 130–133, 136, 141–143, 145, 150, 152, 154, 175, 185, 193–194, 196, 203, 208, 212, 217
complex personhood → 120, 163, 190, 242
Concrete Action → 105
conflict → 37–42, 137, 155, 204, 216, 218, 225
counter-mapping → 203, 209, 221, 227
cytoscape → 154
Czerwiec, M.K. → 59, 160, 164, 170, 183

D

D'Ignazio, Catherine → 118–120, 170, 177, 191, 219, 221
D3 → 116, 120
data cleaning → 116, 124
data comics → 3, 160, 162–163, 170, 198, 212
data discrimination → 8, 69–70, 73, 84, 93
data divide → 68–71
data journalism → 5, 54, 89, 103, 207
Data Justice Lab → 93–94
data mining → 26, 154
data validation → 114, 124
database → 72, 101, 105, 107, 109, 153, 185, 215, 217
dataified → 68, 84
death → 35, 75–76, 149, 164, 206, 227
dirty data → 78
Demirkol, Ozlem → 5

E

editorial → 41, 59, 122, 126, 136–137, 140, 154, 156, 194
emotional communication → 4, 20–21, 23, 25, 30, 32, 38, 45, 47, 56, 59, 119–120, 124–125, 134–135, 173, 196, 208–209, 237, 243
empathy → 36, 56, 120, 161, 168, 173, 243
environmental data → 6, 68, 84, 87, 95, 105, 111, 125, 135–136, 166–168, 181, 185, 203, 223, 231, 237

E (cont.)

ethics → 5, 51, 189, 209
Evans, Kate → 59–60, 156
evidenced-based storytelling → 3–5, 13, 37, 41–42, 70, 80, 82, 95–97, 99–101, 105, 121–122, 138, 141–142, 158, 185, 206–207, 242–243
Excel → 5, 105, 144

F

feminist data visualisation → 117–120, 131
financial data → 70, 111–112, 144, 150, 153
Forensic Architecture → 95–98
Forney, Ellen → 59, 191–192
Freedom of Information → 42, 49, 72, 93, 105

G

gender → 68, 81, 117–119, 131, 141, 159, 175
Gephi → 116, 154
Google Maps → 202, 215–216, 231
Google Sheets → 105, 124, 241
graphic medicine → 7, 59, 142, 163–165, 183, 197, 243
graphic social science → 165–166, 211, 243
graphical plots → 108, 141, 143, 167, 206, 216–217
Gray, Jonathan → 53–54, 72, 79, 103–104
Gyori, Brad → 34

H

Hall, Stuart → 129, 207
hero's journey → 33–35, 51
health → 2–3, 6, 21, 24, 33–36, 51, 68, 78, 84, 129, 132–134, 156, 158, 160–161, 163–165, 185, 187, 191, 237, 243
housing → 49–50, 78, 105–108, 121, 132, 150, 173, 208
human rights → 6, 45, 57, 78, 95–97, 99, 107, 113–114, 209, 213, 217, 231

I

icon → 117, 125–127, 133, 145, 164, 195–196
infographics → 2–3, 38–39, 45–46,

75, 87, 117, 126, 132, 134, 136, 149, 155–157

J

justice → 11, 45, 50, 83, 93–95, 105–107, 231

K

Kanngieser, AM → 166–167
Kennedy, Helen → 55–56, 116, 120
Kirk, Andy → 45, 55–56, 122, 133, 143–145, 147–148, 159

L

Life Course Narrative → 158

M

machine learning → 84, 101
MacFarlane, Robert → 210
migration → 55, 59, 64, 69–70, 79, 91, 95, 97, 103, 121, 132, 173, 187, 189, 203, 210–211, 229
Minute Works → 11, 24, 136, 149–150, 153, 155
multisensory data visualisation → 7, 166–168

N

narrative → 2–4, 6, 15, 17, 22, 27–34, 39–40, 59, 68, 73, 87, 135, 137, 151, 154, 160, 166, 183, 191, 194, 200, 213, 229
narrative visualisation → 138, 151,
narrative plots → 13, 31–34, 51, 137
narrative structure → 15, 27–29, 33, 51, 87
network analysis → 3, 116, 152–154
Nightingale, Florence → 75–76, 116
no data → 77–79

O

Omega Research Foundation → 149, 218
open data → 2, 71–73, 77–78, 113–114, 144, 193
open source → 116, 124, 154, 202, 214–215, 217, 231

P

participatory data infrastructures → 72, 105–107
participatory design → 132, 134, 210
participatory mapping → 203, 208
pictograms → 129–130, 143, 145
police → 41–42, 49, 78–82, 95, 118, 131, 152–153, 175, 225, 235
power mapping → 152, 193–194
ProPublica → 84
public health → 24, 51, 156, 187, 237
Public Health Dorset → 21, 33, 36

R

racial data → 80, 82, 118–119, 159, 175, 179, 187, 225–227
RiotID → 23–24, 149–150, 155–156

S

Seeing Data project → 55, 147
semiotics → 122, 124–127, 134–135, 195–196, 211–212
sensitive subjects → 3, 69–70, 114, 117, 125, 159–160, 166, 173, 195–196, 242
sequential art → 87, 137, 160, 161
sexual assault and rape data → 69, 114, 118
sexuality → 117–119
smell maps → 166–168
Snow, John → 116, 206–207
socio-economic data → 32, 78, 84, 118, 132, 142, 158, 179, 213
social media listening → 26, 64–65
Specht, Doug → 204–205, 214–215, 231–232
spreadsheets → 2, 7, 19, 118, 122–123, 124, 157, 193–194, 200, 217
standpoints → 7, 59, 82–83, 117, 119–120, 125–126, 135, 155
story maps → 210
structured data → 19, 99–101, 122–124
symbol → 35, 116–117, 122, 126–130, 132–133, 136–138, 142–143, 145, 149, 181, 194, 212–213

T

Tableau → 5, 116, 137
tanglegram → 121
Think, Feel, Do → 20–21, 23–26, 65, 135–137

timelines → 32, 95, 107, 154–157, 199–200
transparency → 2, 5, 8, 37, 54, 68, 71, 93, 105, 134, 153, 212–213, 241
trauma → 183–184, 242
treemaps → 150–151
Tufte, Edward → 140–142

U

universal design principles → 126

V

variables → 18, 107, 123, 124, 131–132, 141, 144–145, 154, 157, 168, 212

W

Weissmann, Daniel → 21, 33, 118, 131
Wilkinson, Phil → 32, 74, 76

Y

Yau, Nathan → 20, 36